I0813040

POSTCARD HISTORY SERIES

Glendale

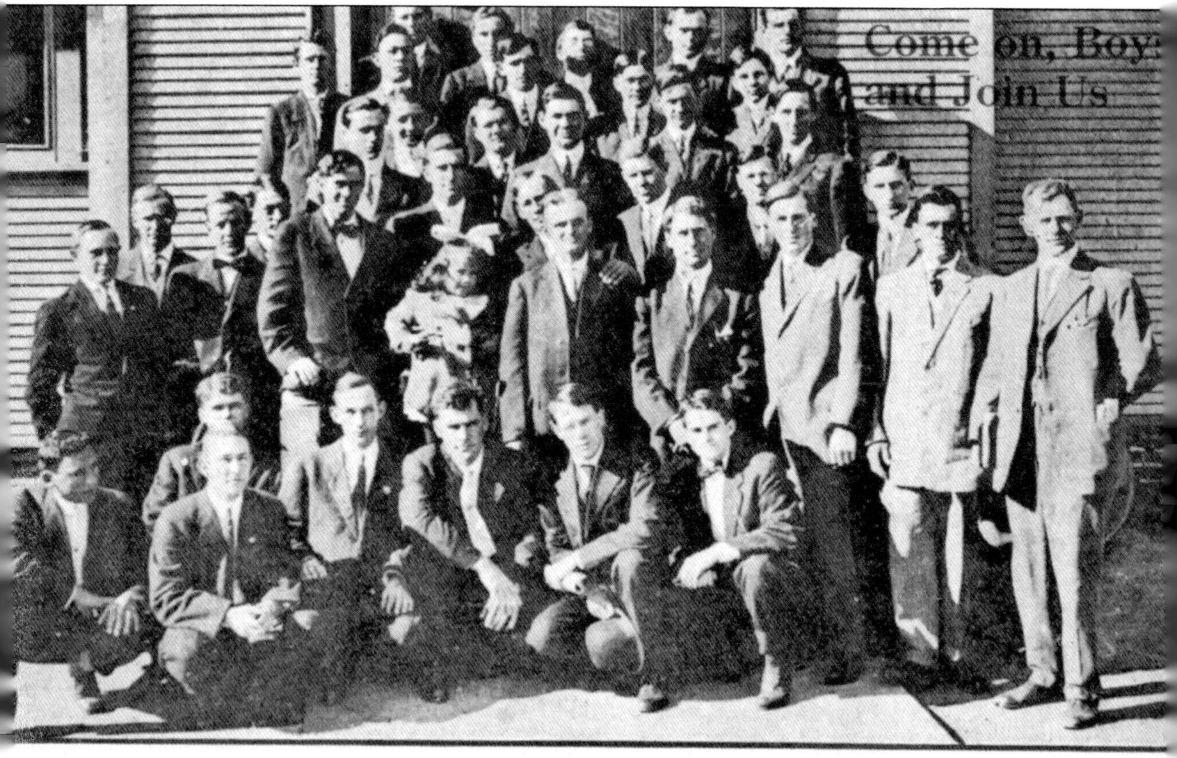

BARACA CLASS, FIRST M. E. CHURCH, GLENDALE, CAL.

Sunday morning religion classes were a very important part of Glendale's early life. By 1914, the First Methodist Episcopal Church had 500 students in its Sunday school program. Here the Baraca Sunday school class stands in front of the church. (Courtesy of the First United Methodist Church, Glendale.)

On the Cover: Leslie C. Brand, who played a major role in the development of Glendale, built his home, known as El Miradero, in the nearby foothills. He later donated the house and grounds to the city for a library and park.

POSTCARD HISTORY SERIES

Glendale

Juliet M. Arroyo, Katherine Peters Yamada, and George Ellison

ARCADIA PUBLISHING

ISBN 978-0-7385-4765-7

Published by Arcadia Publishing
Charleston, South Carolina

Printed in the United States of America

Library of Congress Catalog Card Number: 2007922173

For all general information contact Arcadia Publishing at:
Telephone 843-853-2070
Fax 843-853-0044
E-mail sales@arcadiapublishing.com
For customer service and orders:
Toll-Free 1-888-313-2665

Visit us on the Internet at www.arcadiapublishing.com

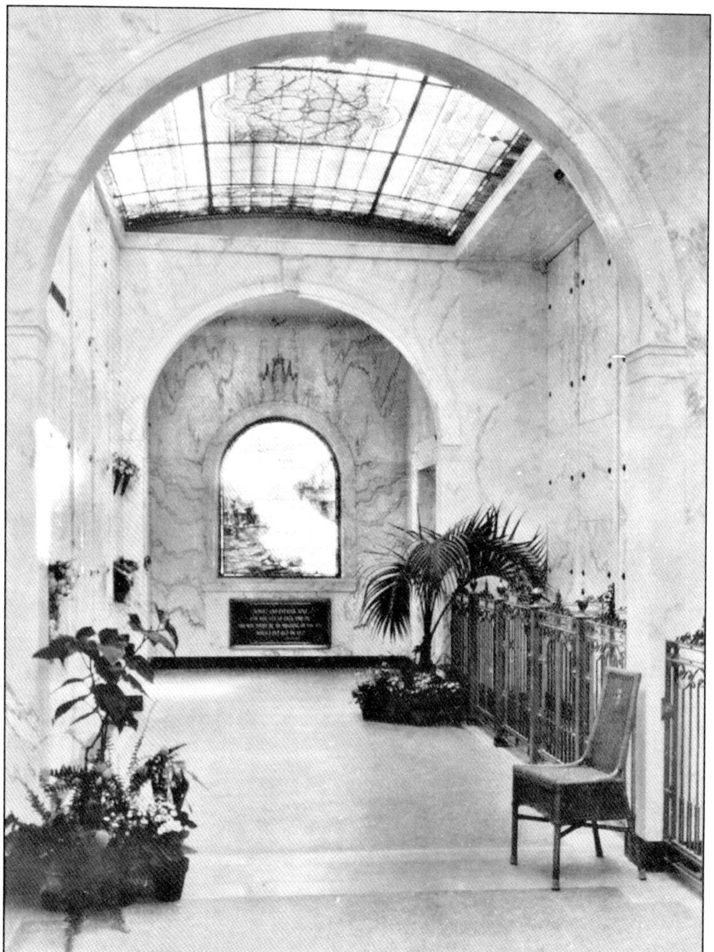

A large stained-glass window at the east end of Coleus Terrace in the Great Mausoleum at Forest Lawn portrays Alfred Tennyson's *Crossing the Bar.* This postcard was printed about 1924. (Courtesy of the Special Collections Room, Glendale Public Library.)

Contents

ACKNOWLEDGMENTS

The authors would like to acknowledge the staff of the Glendale Public Library for its support of this book and for its stewardship of Glendale's historical photographs and documents housed in the Special Collections Room. Special thanks go to key members of the Glendale Historical Society, including Arlene Vidor, who has worked for years advocating for the preservation of Glendale's heritage, and Isabelle Meyer, who has for decades supported the Doctor's House Museum and has stayed actively involved in Glendale events.

The authors would also like to thank Adriene Biondo, chair of the Los Angeles Conservancy Modern Committee; Michael Morgan, a local historian; and John Underwood, the author of two books on Grand Central Air Terminal, for sharing their knowledge of Glendale. We are grateful to Bruce B. Herman, who loaned postcards from his private collection. Finally, we wish to acknowledge the invaluable assistance of Jan Craig, who helped proofread this document.

INTRODUCTION

Despite the tremendous population change that has given Glendale a new face, residents remember the good old days when Glendale was a quiet town with not much going on. Old-style institutions like the YMCA are still very much alive today and have taken on a greater meaning than originally envisioned. Brand Boulevard remains the heart of Glendale entertainment and shopping. City hall is still in the same location it was in 1912. The intersections of Broadway with Brand Boulevard on the west and Glendale Avenue on the east continue to be the activity centers they were 100 years ago. Glendale families take part in school, religious, and civic activities like they have for all of the town's history.

Postcards provide us with a vintage view of places from the past. We are still familiar with many of these locations today. They allow us to imagine what our hometown must have been like in the past. We can see how places have changed and how tranquil life must have been. At one time, postcard collecting was a widely popular American pastime. Thanks to this passion of the past, we have these vignettes of history to enjoy today.

Most of the postcards in this book were obtained from the Special Collections Room of the Glendale Public Library, a wonderful resource for discovering Glendale's past. Other postcards were kindly donated from the private collections of Glendale history fans and organizations. The authors have included postcards from their private collections and new acquisitions from postcard shows and the Internet.

The intention of this book is to stir interest in Glendale's picturesque past among the young and old. There remains much more to discover about Glendale, particularly the small places tucked away throughout the city. Although Glendale was not covered in landmark buildings like other nearby cities, its low profile and pastoral nature have made it popular. Famous across the nation through icons such as Forest Lawn, the Glendale Sanitarium, Casa Verdugo, and Grand Central Air Terminal, Glendale is today a unique place in Southern California with a distinctive past.

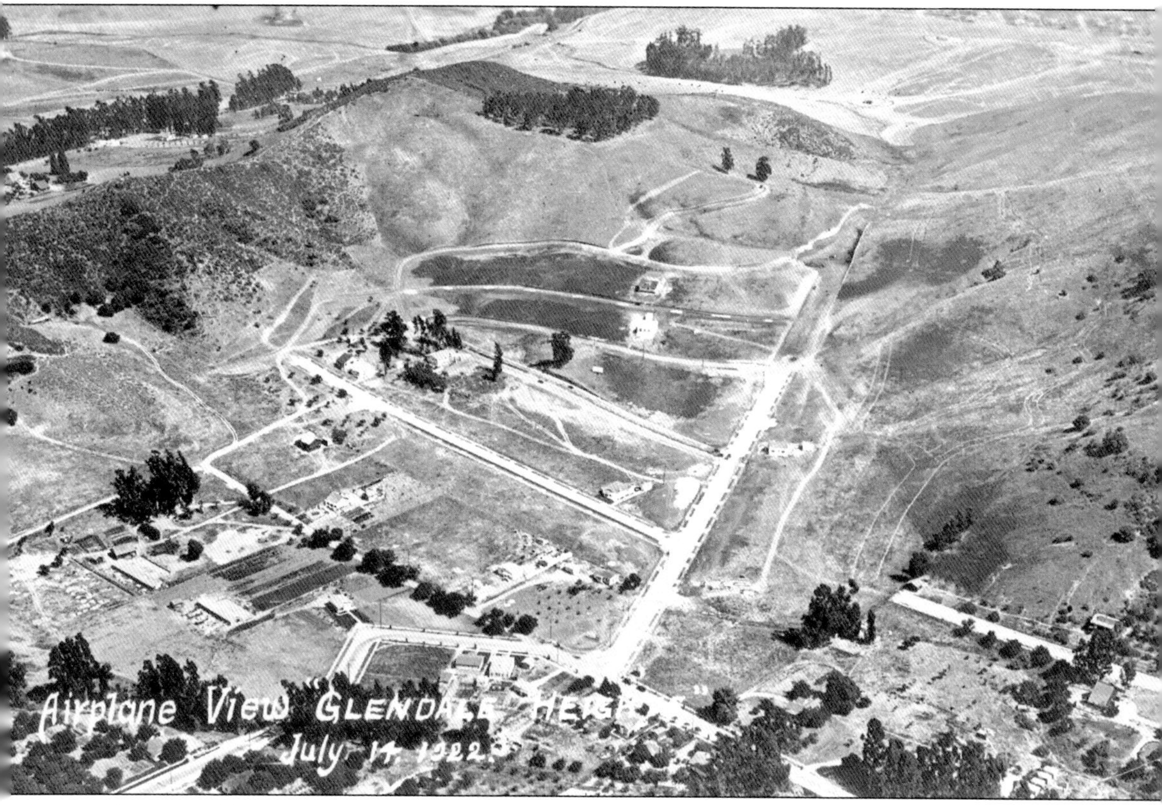

Many of Glendale's early houses were clustered in the flat land around the city's center. By the 1920s, developers began promoting the outlying area. Glendale Heights, seen here, was an early subdivision in the Adams Hill area. (Courtesy of the Bruce B. Herman Collection.)

One

Homes and Neighborhoods

In its early years, Glendale was known as a community of homes and was advertised as such by the chamber of commerce and various business-promoting organizations. The large resident population base helped fuel local and small businesses. Glendale's housing spurt occurred after World War I but had actually begun earlier, when the Pacific Electric streetcar system expanded in the region and offered excellent service between Los Angeles and the large tracts of open space in Glendale's picturesque valley. Prior to 1904, much of Glendale's housing consisted of ranch homes and farmhouses evenly distributed between the flatlands and the foothills that referenced the town of Glendale as a small outpost.

Stately homes were built in the foothill areas on large lots with spectacular views of the valley below. The most famous was the exotic residence built on expansive grounds by Leslie C. Brand. The home, with a castle-like exterior and a domestic interior, served as a showplace, its presence influencing the residential hillside subdivision explosion of the early 1920s. The founding father of modern Glendale, L. C. Brand willed his home and gardens to the city for a park and library for future generations to enjoy.

In the flatlands, many charming homes built in the Craftsman style lined street after street, laid out on perfectly drawn rectangular subdivisions, evenly set back from the sidewalks and streets. The neighborhood around Orange Street and Lexington Drive became the place where notable Glendale families of doctors and other professional men constructed their new homes. Smaller houses radiated from this center.

By the late 1920s, the popular revival-style homes were being built along the foothills, including some excellent examples of the extravagant Spanish Revival design. Apartment houses also became popular and were found spaced between single-family homes.

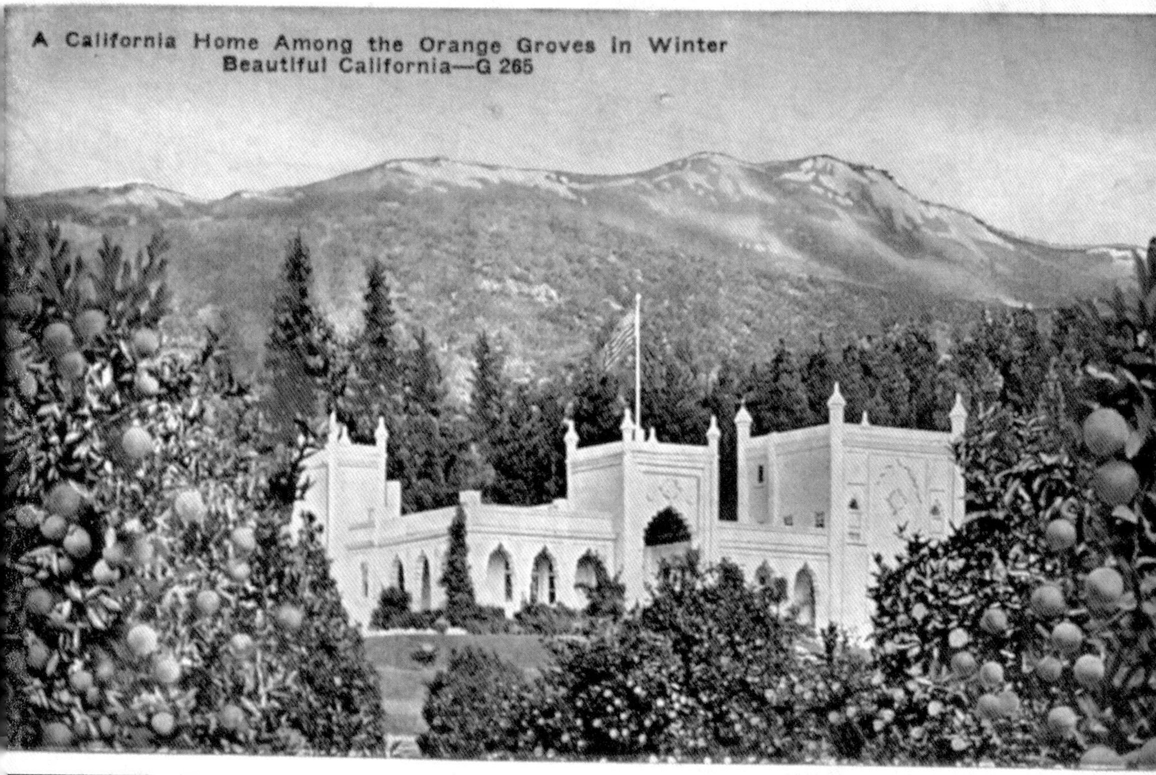

The home of Leslie C. and Mary Louise Brand, located at the base of the Verdugo Mountains, overlooked Glendale and the San Fernando Valley. The architecture of the Brand family home, inspired by a building at the 1893 World's Columbian Exposition in Chicago, featured domes, horseshoe arches, and elaborately decorated surfaces. Craftsmen spent a year on the structure, completing it in 1904 at a cost of $60,000. Brand was an important figure in Glendale's development, bringing the Pacific Electric Railway to the city and playing a major role in establishing a bank, a country club, and the telephone, light, and water companies. This postcard was published by the Pacific Novelty Company of San Francisco about 1917. (Courtesy of the Special Collections Room, Glendale Public Library.)

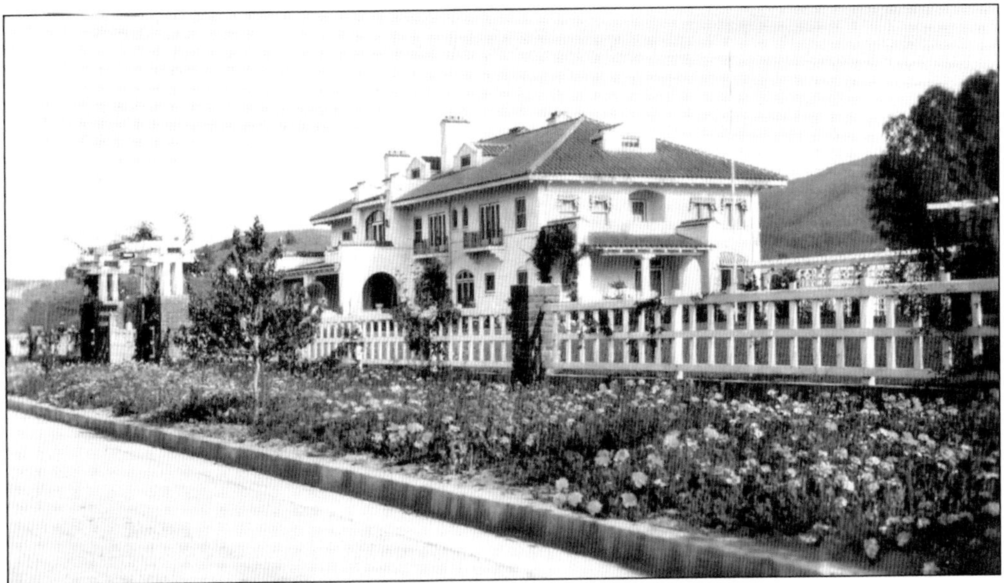

One of the many stately and picturesque homes built in Glendale in the early part of the century was surrounded by gardens. The region was home to a mere dozen families in 1883, but by 1908 it had a population of 3,500 and more than 700 houses. Many new residents were transplants from the Midwest and from the East Coast who brought with them a desire for substantial homes. (Courtesy of the Special Collections Room, Glendale Public Library.)

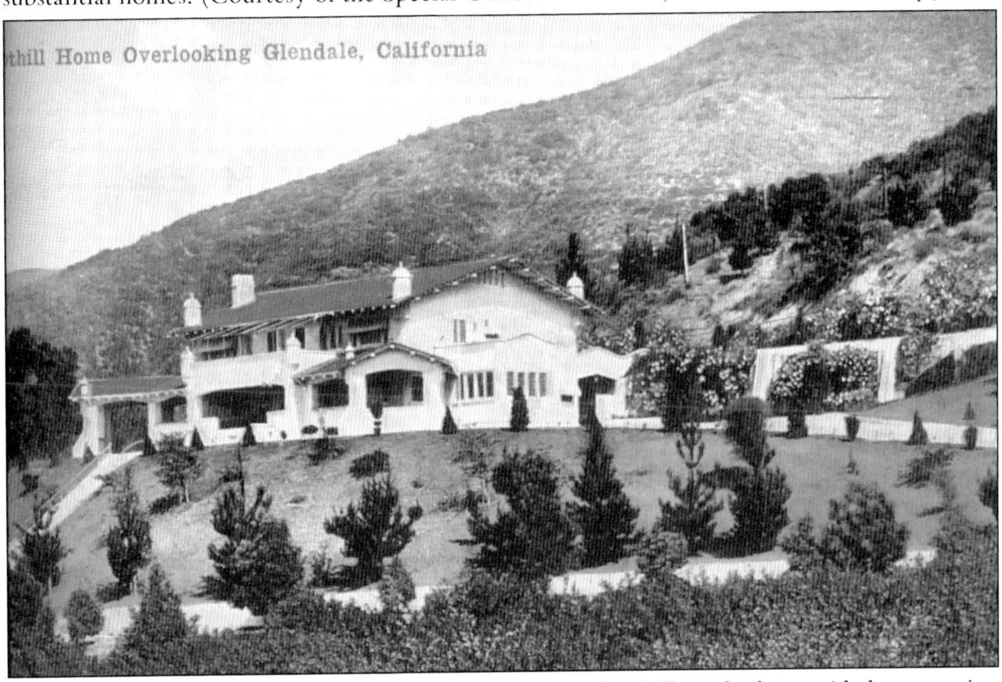

This home overlooking Glendale was nestled in the foothills, which provided a stunning backdrop for the home and for the city. The hills and mountains surrounding Glendale were originally occupied by the Tongva Indians, who were renamed the Gabrielenos by Spanish missionaries. This postcard was published by the Van Ornum Colorprint Company of Los Angeles around 1915. (Courtesy of the Bruce B. Herman Collection.)

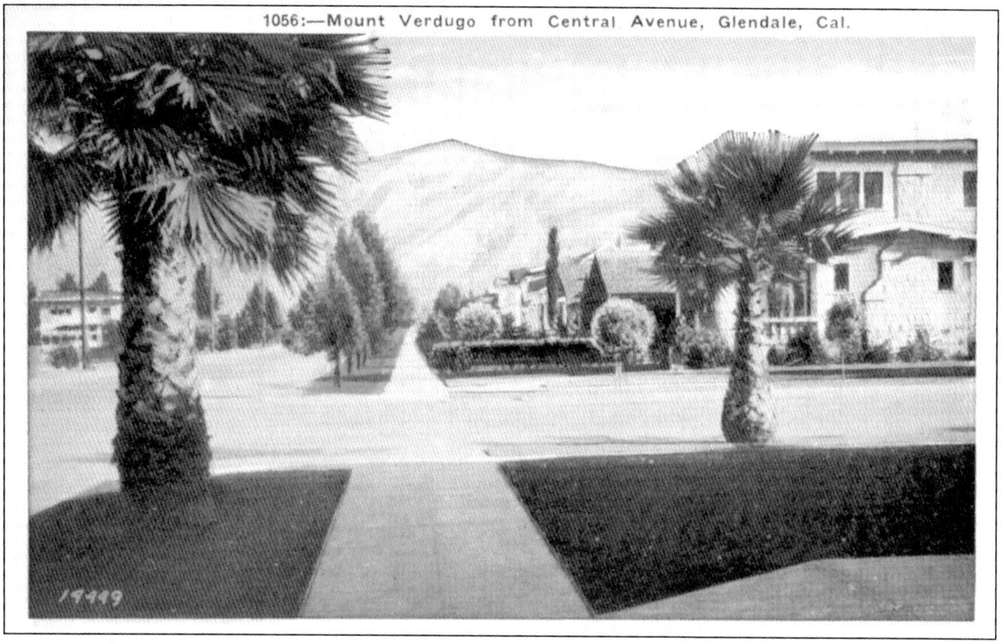

Substantial houses were built on Central Avenue near Lexington Drive. Seen in the background, the Verdugo Mountains were named for Jose Maria Verdugo, who received a huge parcel of land that later included Glendale from the king of Spain in 1784. This postcard was published by the M. Kashower Company of Los Angeles. (Courtesy of the Special Collections Room, Glendale Public Library.)

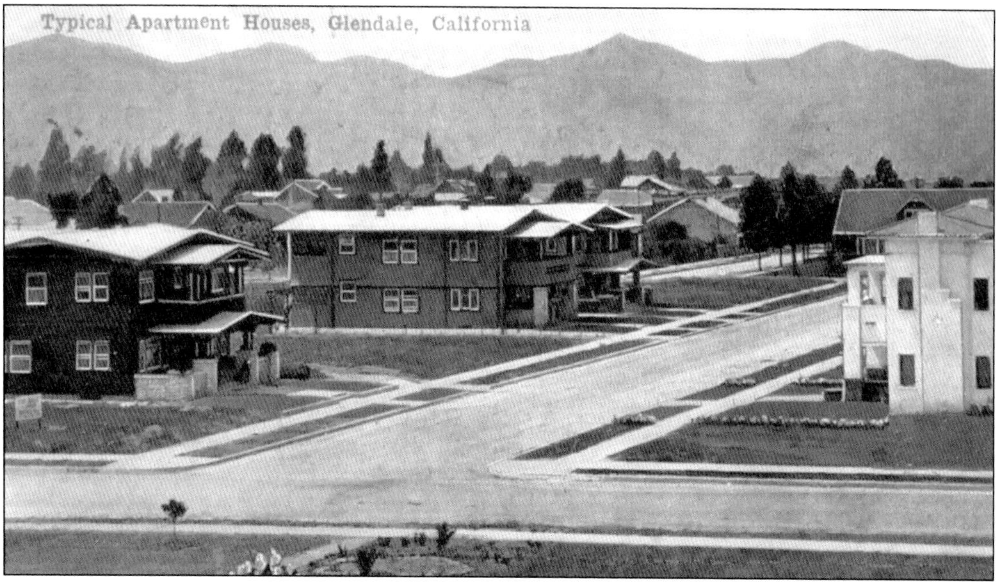

Apartment homes were constructed along with the large homes that lined the new streets. The Pacific Electric cars provided a fast and efficient commute between Los Angeles and Glendale. The advertised time of 23 minutes between the two locations, and departures of more than 30 trains per day, brought many more families to the city. This postcard was published by the Van Ornum Colorprint Company of Los Angeles about 1915. (Courtesy of the George Ellison Collection.)

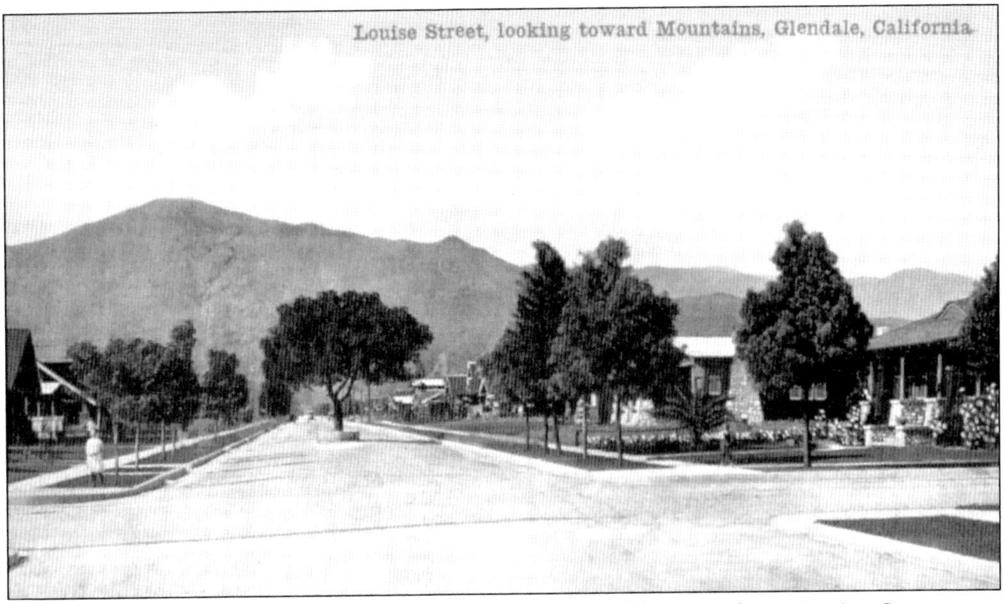

Looking toward the Verdugo Mountains, this view of homes along Louise Street near Lexington Drive shows a residential tract typical of those springing up around the city. These tracts offered large lots at modest prices, achieved with a low down payment. This postcard was published by the Van Ornum Colorprint Company of Los Angeles around 1919. (Courtesy of the Bruce B. Herman Collection.)

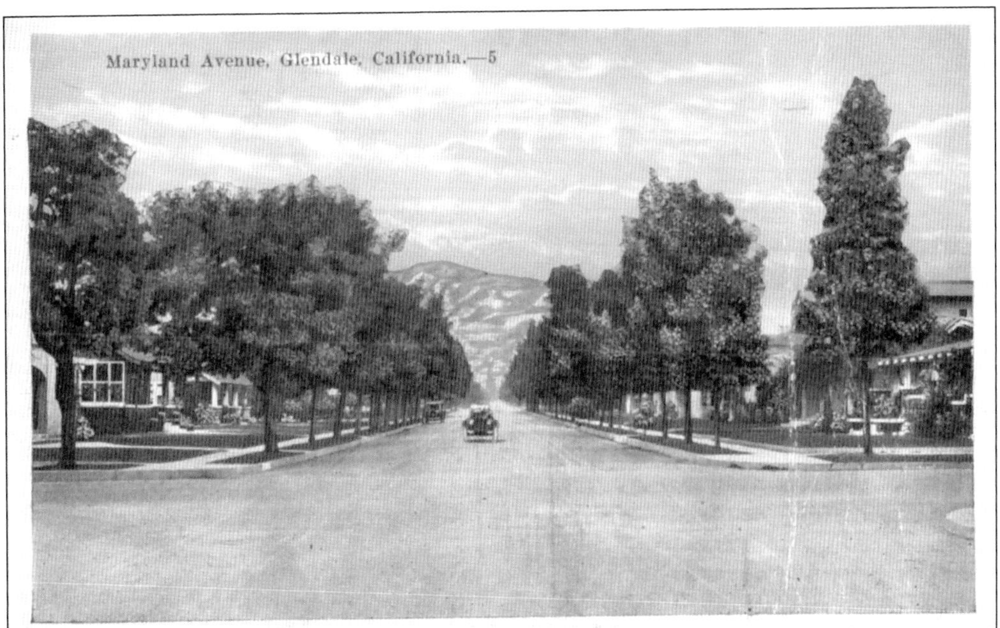

Landowner L. C. Brand named Maryland Avenue for Mary Williams, the daughter of his tract manager, and for her fiancé, who was named Land. This postcard was published by S. H. Kress and Company around 1920. (Courtesy of the Special Collections Room, Glendale Public Library.)

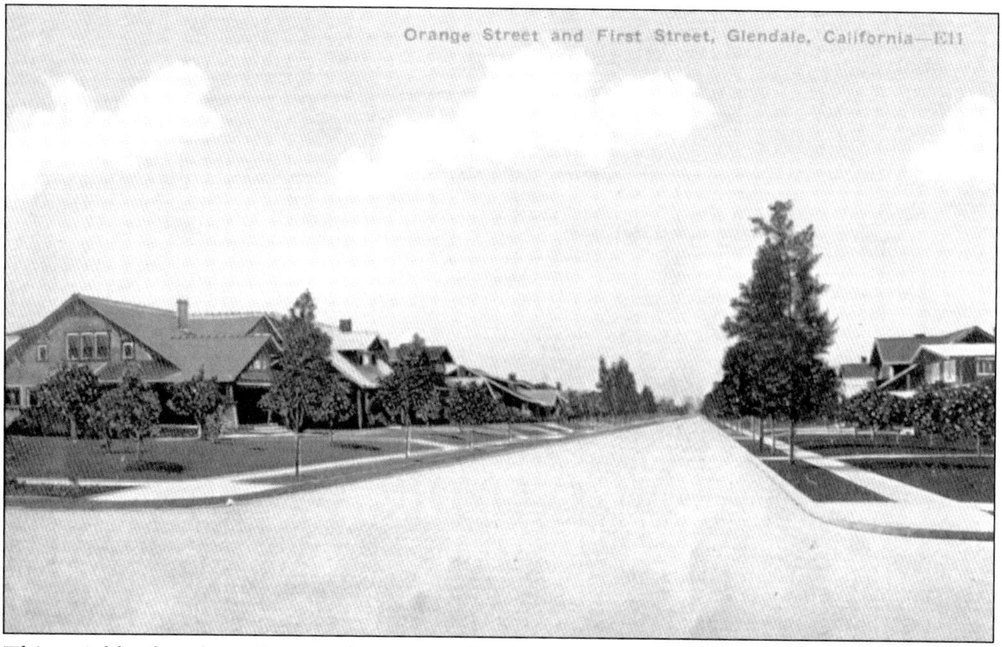

This neighborhood on Orange Street near Lexington Drive had wide streets complete with curbs and sidewalks. The choice of Orange as a street name reflected the many acres of orange groves surrounding the city. This postcard was published by the Pacific Novelty Company of San Francisco about 1915. (Courtesy of the Special Collections Room, Glendale Public Library.)

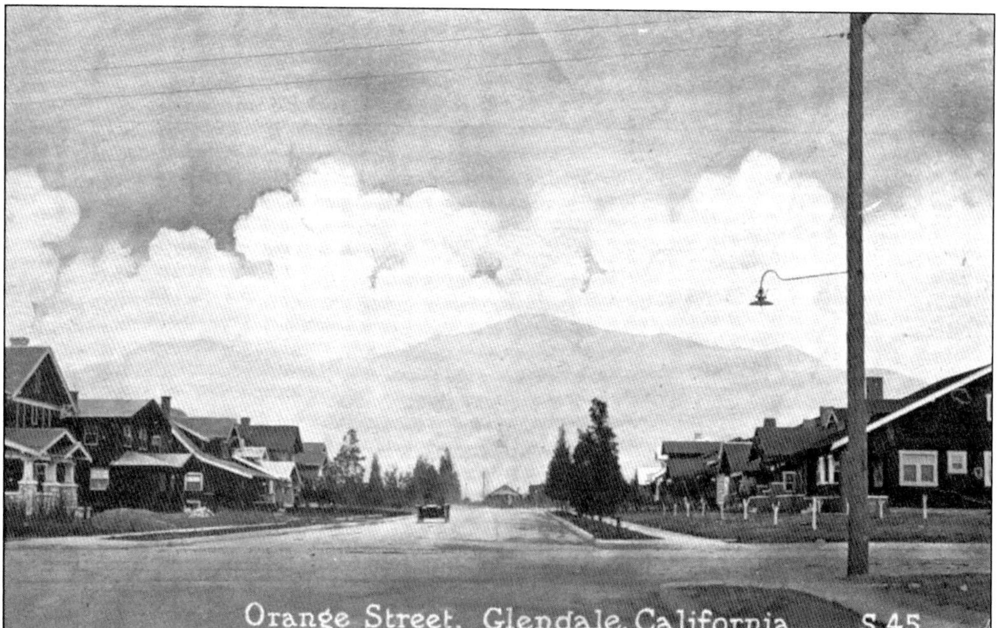

Electricity and streetlights were important additions to the new tracts, as shown in this view looking north along Orange Street. The new homes often came with restrictions, including an anti-liquor clause and a ban on outbuildings on the property. This postcard was published by the Souvenir Publishing Company around 1915. (Courtesy of the Bruce B. Herman Collection.)

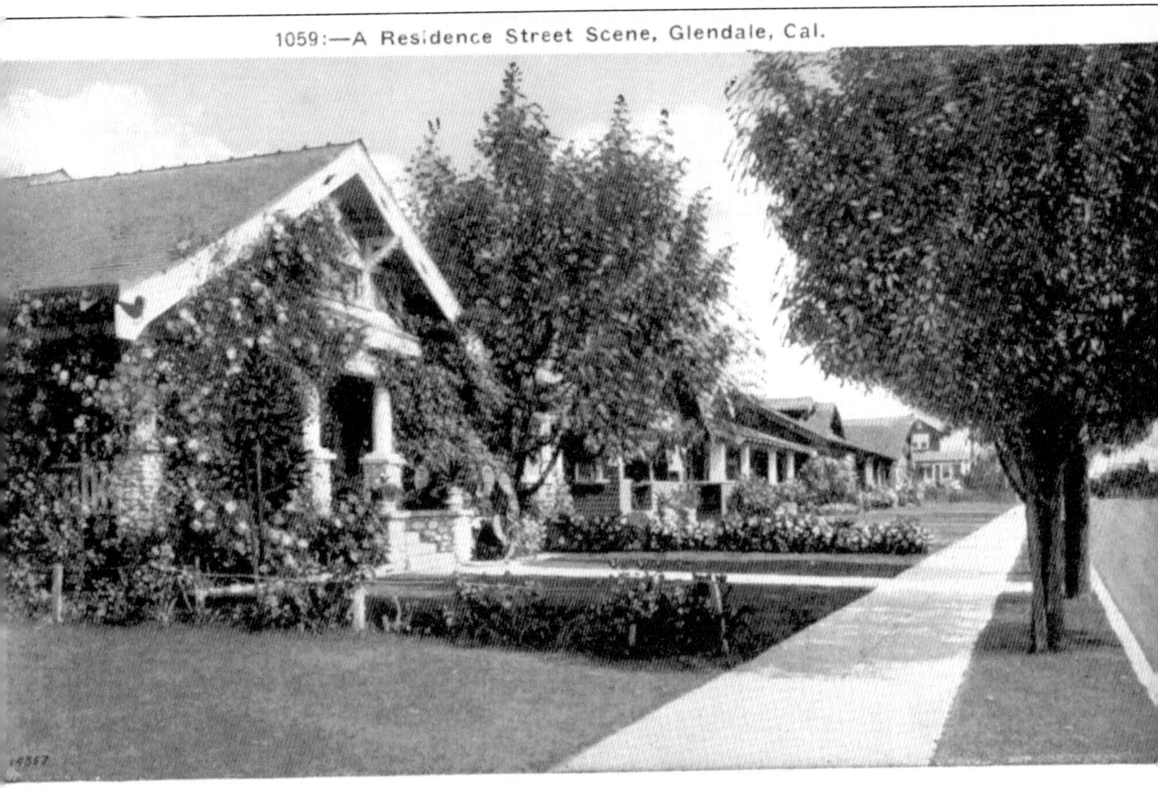

California bungalow-style architecture was very popular during this era. The houses offered five or six rooms, hardwood floors, and beamed ceilings. This postcard was published by the M. Kashower Company of Los Angeles about 1915. (Courtesy of the Special Collections Room, Glendale Public Library.)

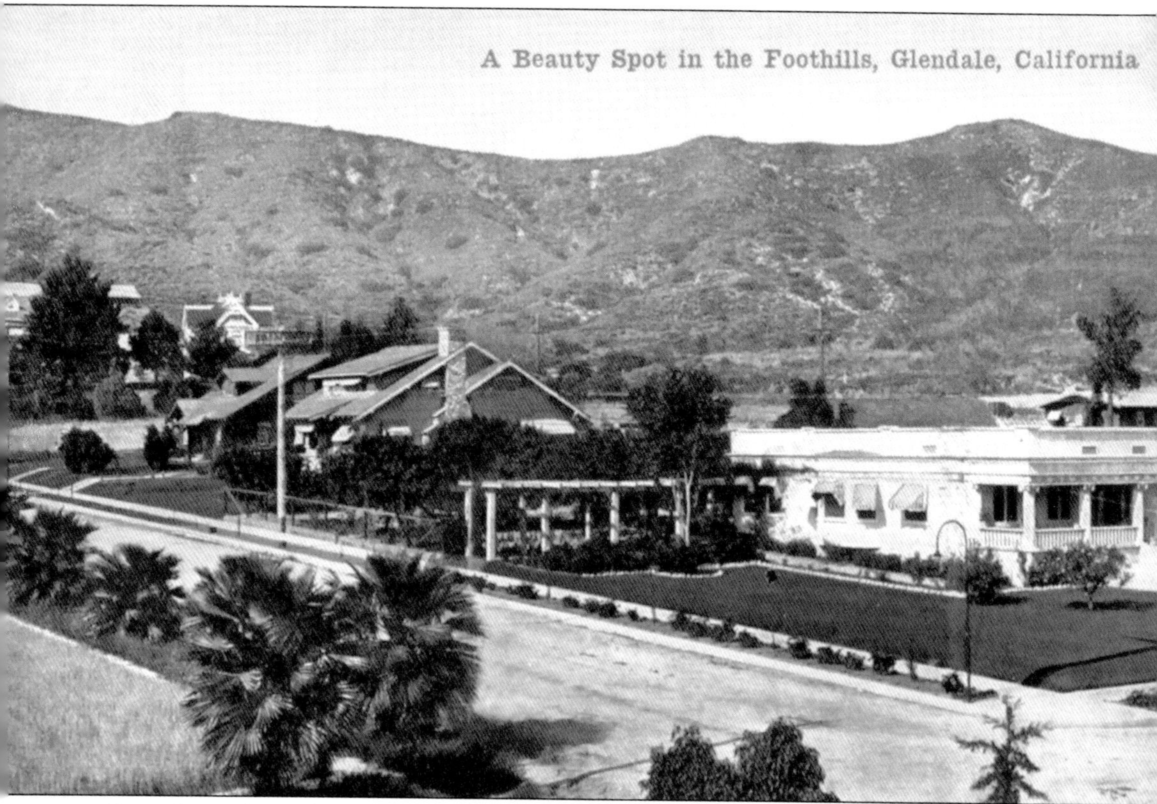

Several popular architectural styles can be found at the intersection of Louise and Randolph Streets in the community of Casa Verdugo. Developer L. C. Brand named Louise Street in honor of his wife and Randolph Street for his brother-in-law. This postcard was published by the Van Ornum Colorprint Company of Los Angeles around 1915. (Courtesy of the Special Collections Room, Glendale Public Library.)

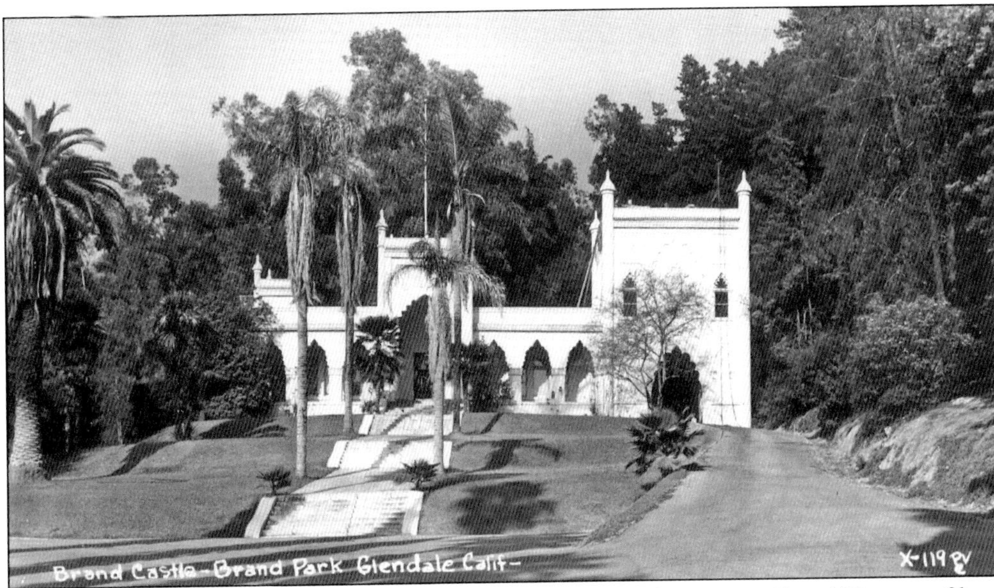

Before his death in 1925, L. C. Brand willed his home and the surrounding 660 acres of land to the City of Glendale to be developed as a park and public library. The grounds opened for picnics and hiking shortly after he died. Mary Louise Brand remained in the residence until her death in 1945. Their home was opened in 1956 as an arts and music library. This postcard was published by the Angeleno Photo Service of Los Angeles around 1950. (Courtesy of the Special Collections Room, Glendale Public Library.)

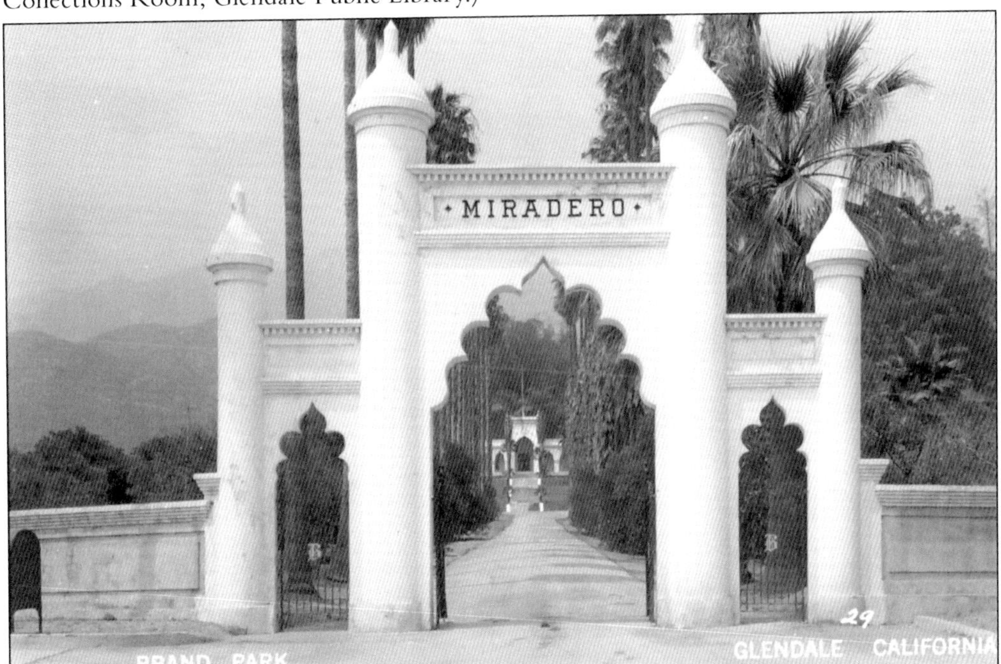

The entrance to Brand Park was marked by an arched gateway reflecting the East Indian style of Brand's home, which he named El Miradero. This postcard was published by the Angeleno Photo Service of Los Angeles about 1950. (Courtesy of the Special Collections Room, Glendale Public Library.)

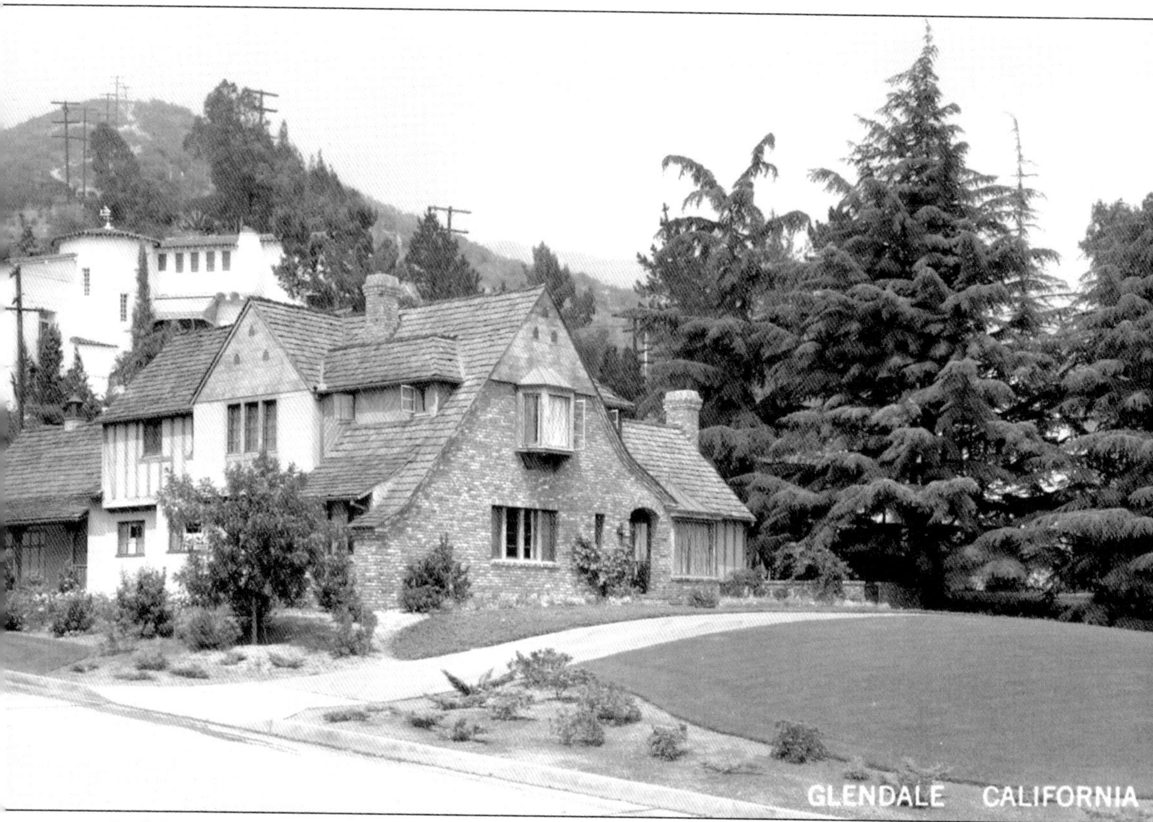

Architect George Postle designed the house in the foreground for Dolliver Webb in 1949. Webb, the proprietor of Glendale Hardware, propagated chrysanthemums in his northwest Glendale home and actively participated in civic affairs. This postcard was published by the Angeleno Photo Service of Los Angeles around 1950. (Courtesy of the Special Collections Room, Glendale Public Library.)

Two

Schools and Churches

Glendale's earliest settlers brought with them a mission to build schools. With the old Sepulveda School System serving much of the old Rancho San Rafael population, it was not until after the town of Glendale was established that a more localized and larger school system was needed. A highly significant event in Glendale's history occurred at the beginning of the 20th century, when town leaders came together to form the Glendale Union High School District. They raised the funds to build the valley's first high school, located in the middle of open space and farmland near today's corner of Brand Boulevard and Broadway. Glendale Union High School served students as far away as Burbank, Eagle Rock, Tropico, and La Crescenta. This event not only helped shape the development of the Glendale School System but also helped form the physical layout of the city to come.

The Long Beach earthquake of 1933 damaged many of Glendale's educational institutions. By the 1950s, most of these schools had been modernized. Glendale High School has been located on four different sites, including its current site on Broadway at Verdugo Road. Hoover is Glendale's second high school, built in the late 1920s to serve a growing student population in the foothills. Glendale College, which began on Glendale High School's campus, was originally known as Glendale Junior College.

Along with schools, early settlers established churches that became centers of sparsely populated settlements throughout the valley. The locations of early churches helped to delineate the communities that were beginning to form. In the early years, social, philanthropic, civic, and patriotic organizations emerged from the various churches. As the population grew, so did the churches; each surge in population meant a new, bigger and grander church would be built. Most churches today are in central Glendale, with a scattering of smaller churches through the neighborhoods.

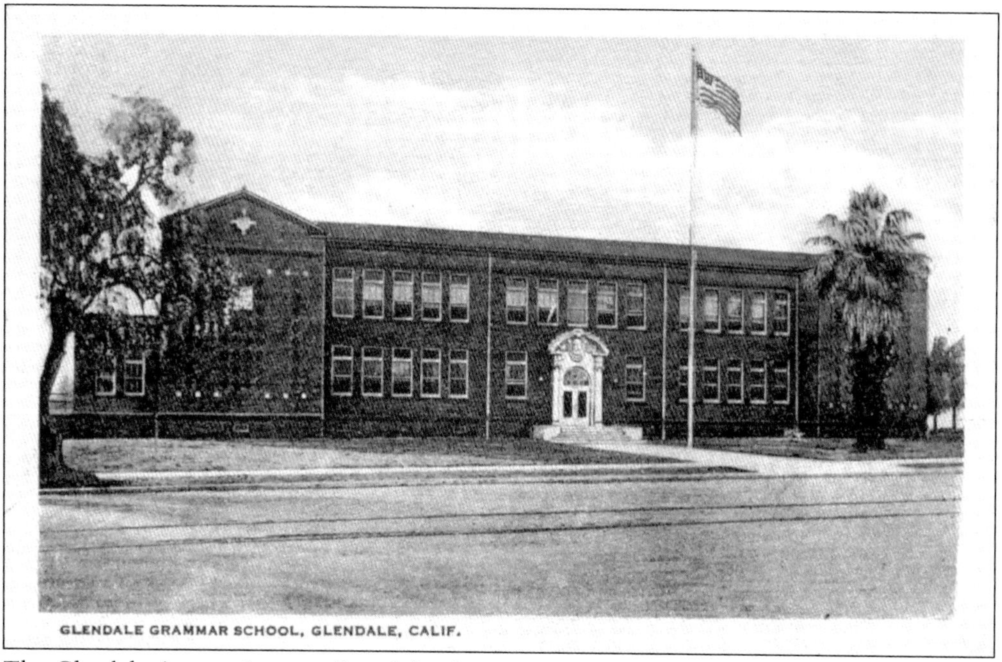

The Glendale Avenue Intermediate School was constructed in 1922 to serve the children in the southern portion of the newly combined Glendale and Tropico School Districts. It was later renamed for Pres. Theodore Roosevelt. This postcard was published by the Artochrom Lithograph Company of Los Angeles around 1922. (Courtesy of the Special Collections Room, Glendale Public Library.)

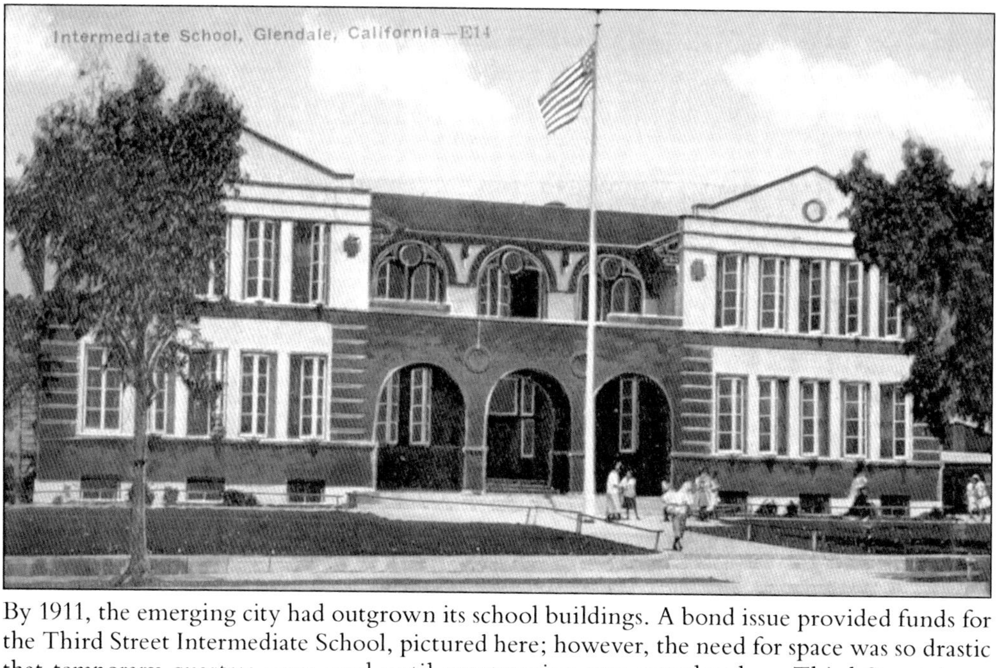

By 1911, the emerging city had outgrown its school buildings. A bond issue provided funds for the Third Street Intermediate School, pictured here; however, the need for space was so drastic that temporary quarters were used until construction was completed on Third Street (now Wilson Avenue) between Jackson and Kenwood Streets. This postcard was published by the Pacific Novelty Company of Los Angeles. (Courtesy of the George Ellison Collection.)

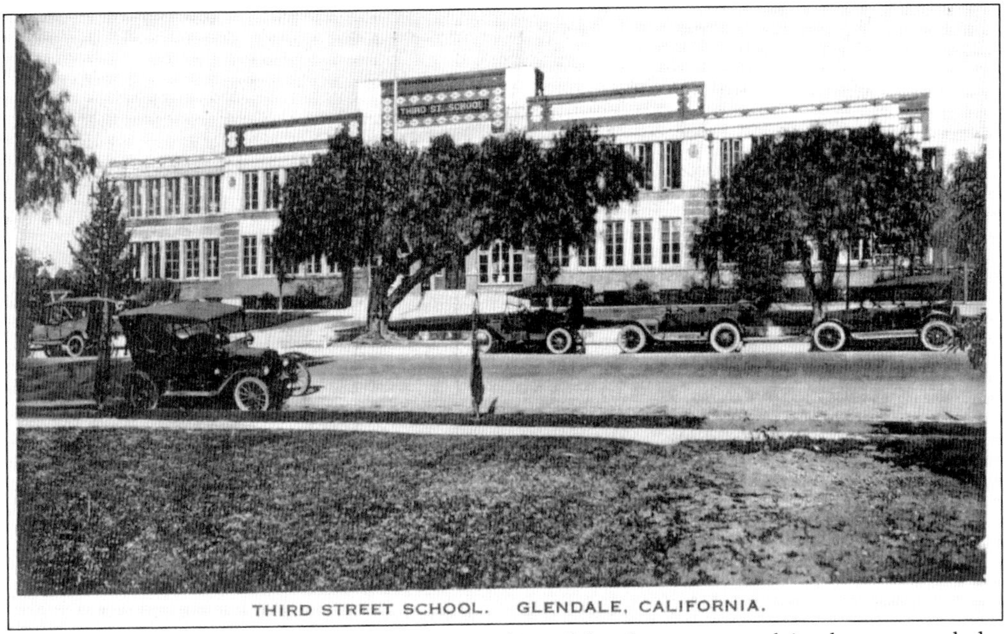

Classroom space in the Third Street Intermediate School soon proved inadequate, and the building was remodeled in 1915. Additional wings were added, along with a facade change. The building later served as the district office. This postcard was published by the Western Publishing and Novelty Company of Los Angeles. (Courtesy of the Special Collections Room, Glendale Public Library.)

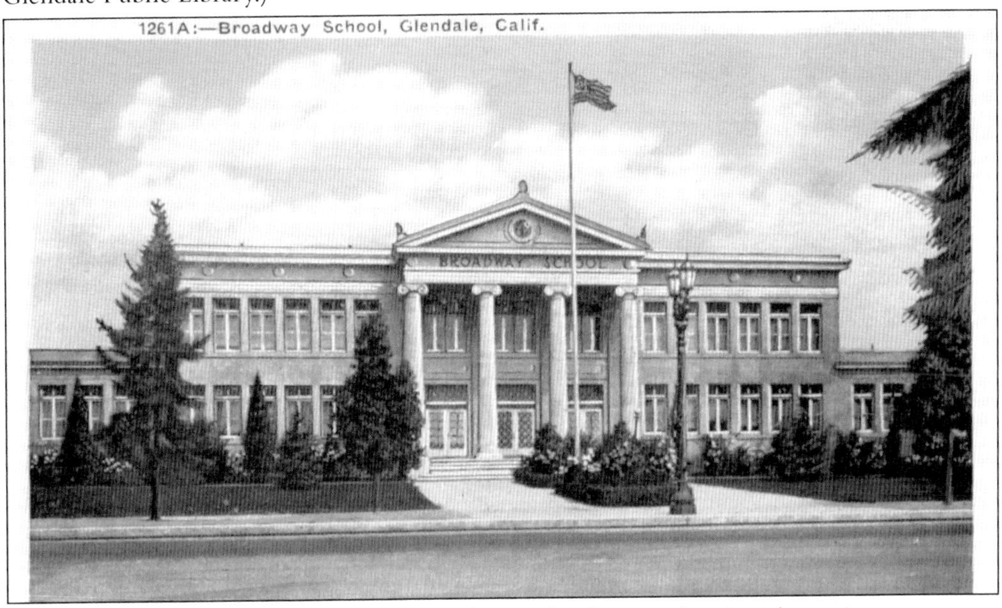

This two-story classical-style building, with grand columns adorning the main entrance on Broadway, was named the Broadway School. When the structure was declared a hazard after the 1933 Long Beach earthquake, the second floor and portico were removed, while the first floor was left intact. It later became John Marshall Elementary School. This postcard was published by the M. Kashower Company of Los Angeles about 1920. (Courtesy of the Bruce B. Herman Collection.)

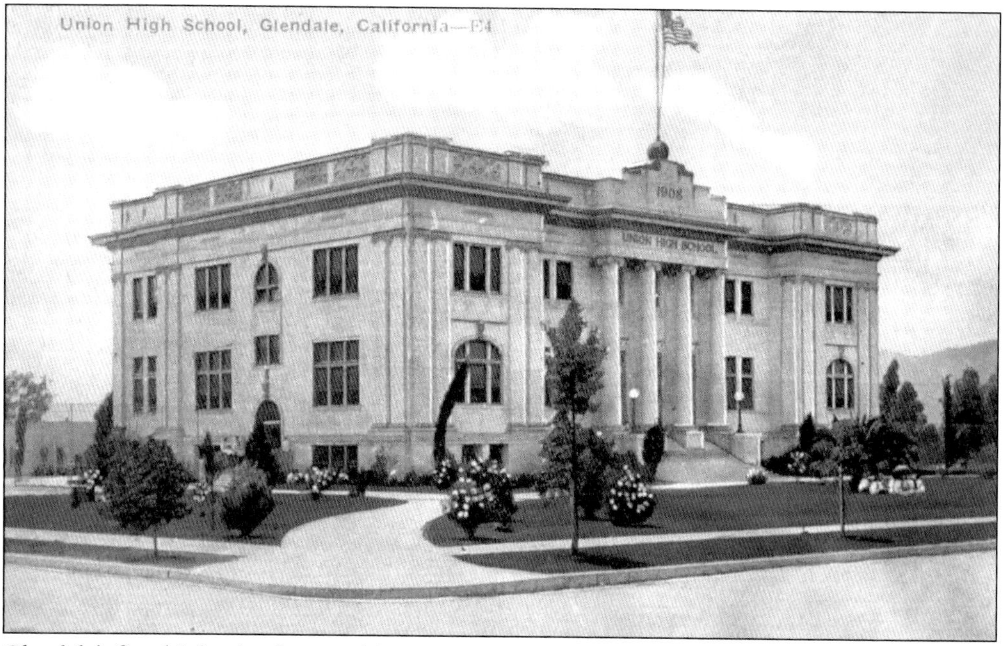

Glendale's first high school opened in 1901 in the old Glendale Hotel and averaged 23 students per day the first year. By the next year, the school had moved to a new, wood-frame building at Brand Boulevard and Broadway and had become Union High School—or more informally, "the Cheesebox." Population growth brought a bond measure in 1908 to construct a larger building (pictured) on Harvard Street. The cornerstone was laid that same year, and the school opened in 1909. This postcard was published by the Pacific Novelty Company of Los Angeles. (Courtesy of the Special Collections Room, Glendale Public Library.)

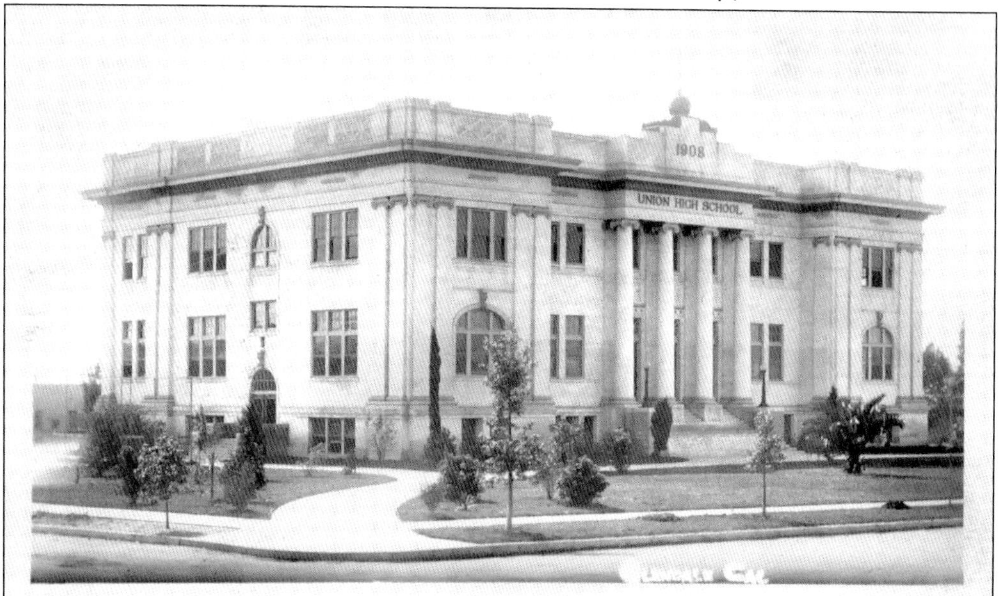

Glendale Union High School opened in 1909 at a cost of $75,000. The building, with its distinguished facade, was often referred to as "the White House." (Courtesy of the Special Collections Room, Glendale Public Library.)

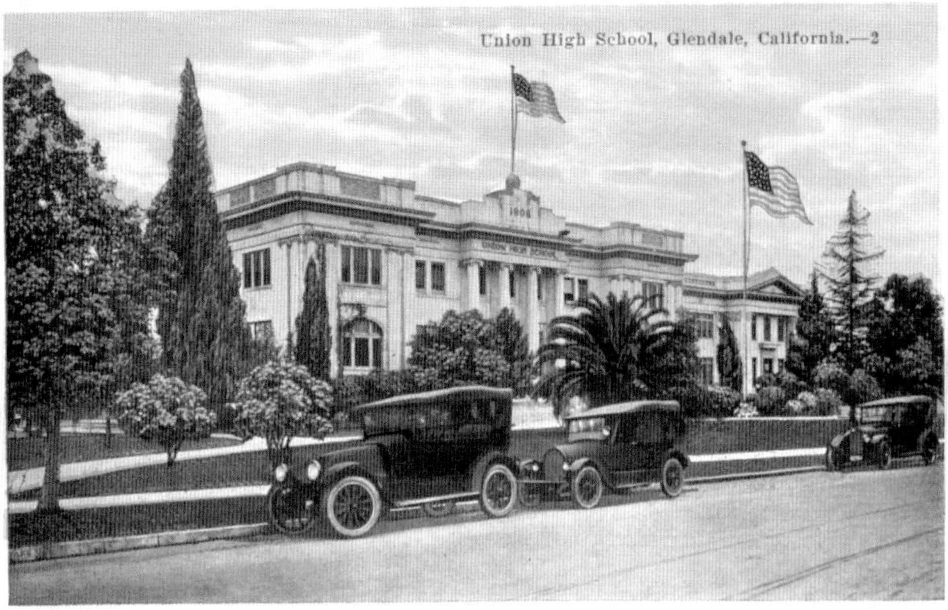

Within a short period of time, the two-story, white-brick high school became overcrowded. In 1914, Maryland Avenue, on the campus's west side, was vacated and additional classrooms were built. This postcard was published by S. H. Kress and Company. (Courtesy of the Special Collections Room, Glendale Public Library.)

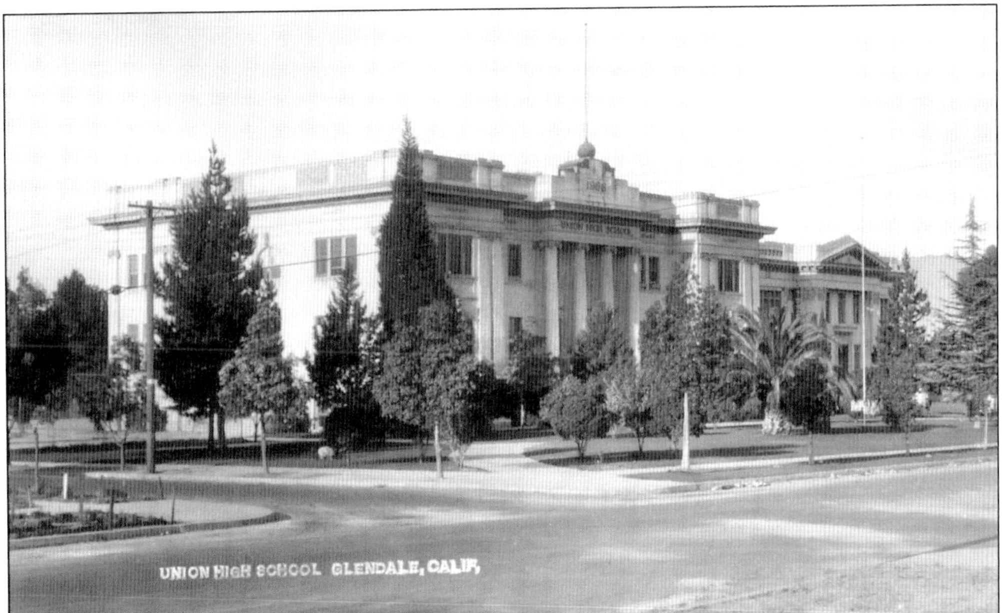

The first students at Glendale Junior College, which was formed in 1927, attended classes on the campus of the new Glendale High School on Broadway and Verdugo Road. In 1929, the collegians moved to classrooms in the old high school building on Harvard Street, seen here. They remained at that site until 1937, when their new college was built on Verdugo Road. (Courtesy of the Special Collections Room, Glendale Public Library.)

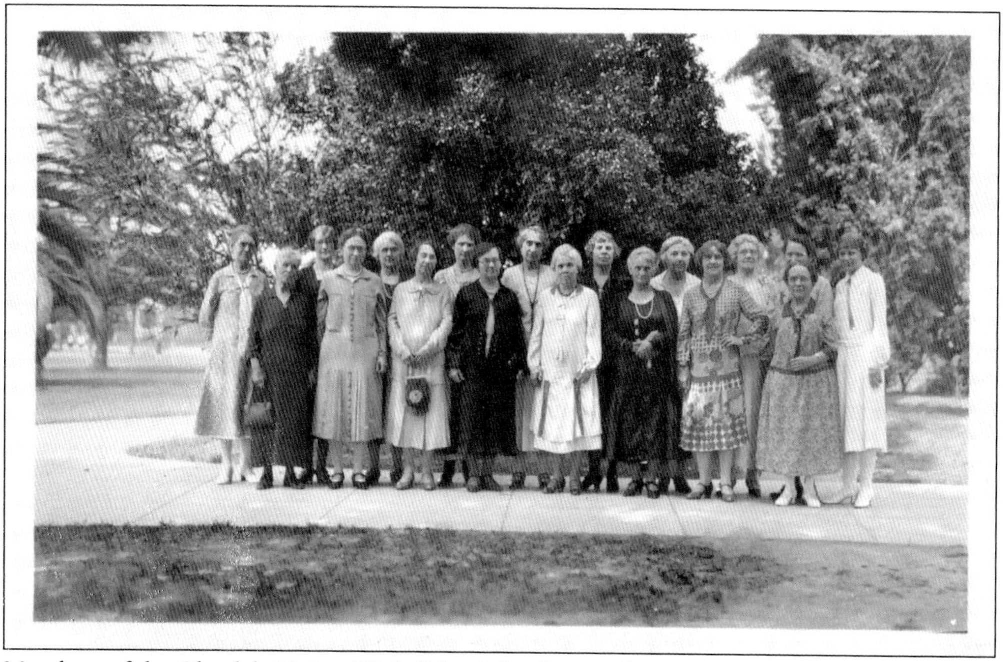

Members of the Glendale Union High School faculty are shown above in the 1920s. By then, high school enrollment had increased so rapidly that bungalows were erected on the Harvard Street campus to provide more classrooms. (Courtesy of the Special Collections Room, Glendale Public Library.)

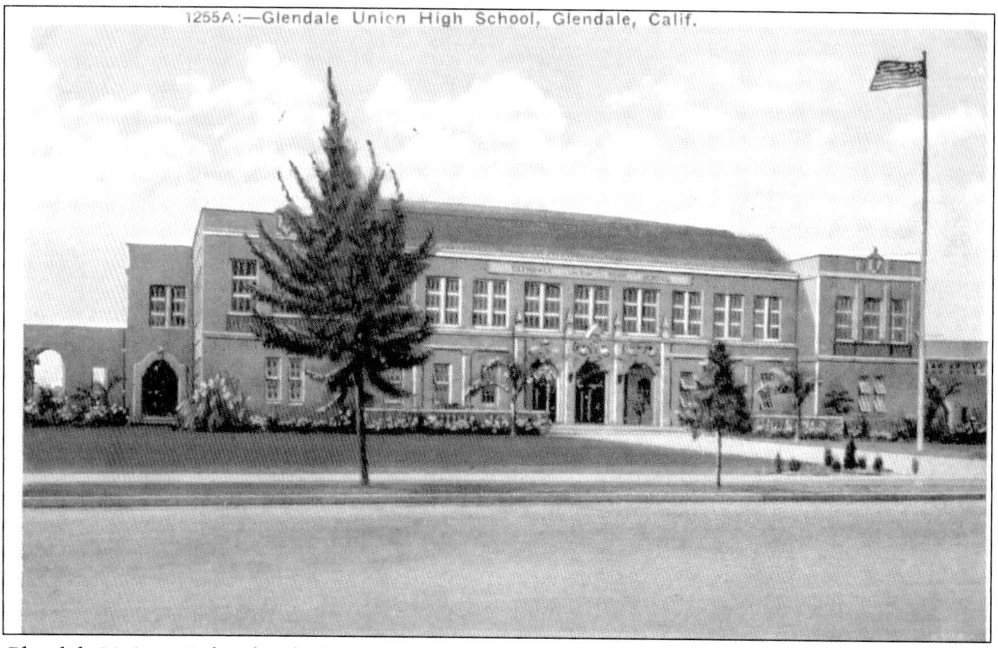

Glendale Union High School relocated to its new site at Broadway and Verdugo Road in February 1924. A $600,000 bond issue in 1922 funded construction and other costs. The high school's administration building is pictured here. This postcard was published by the M. Kashower Company of Los Angeles around 1925. (Courtesy of the George Ellison Collection.)

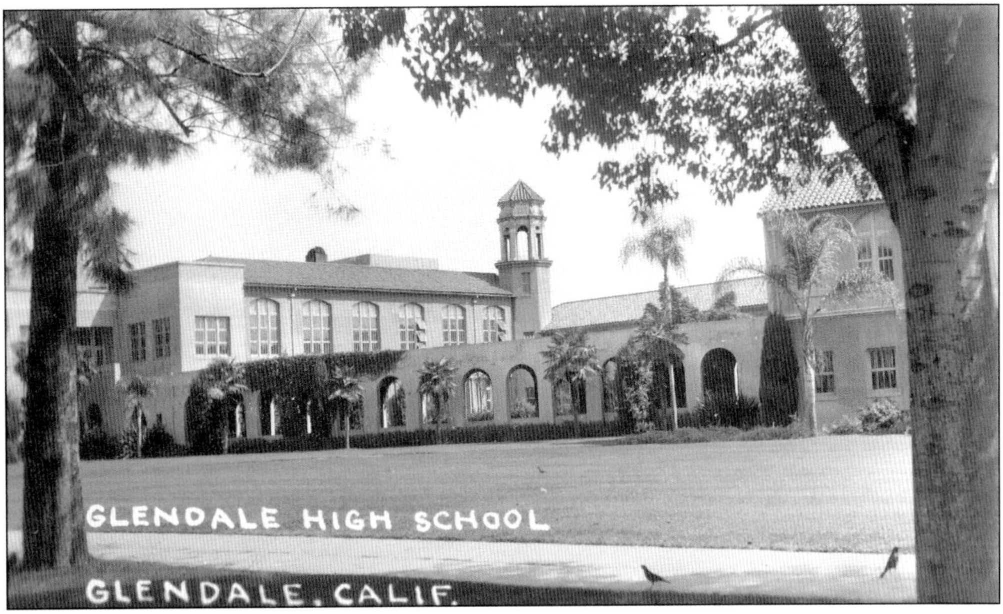

One of Glendale High's most illustrious alumni was Marion Morrison, later known as John Wayne. Morrison grew up in Glendale, attended local schools, and graduated from Glendale High in 1925. This postcard dates to about 1947. (Courtesy of the George Ellison Collection.)

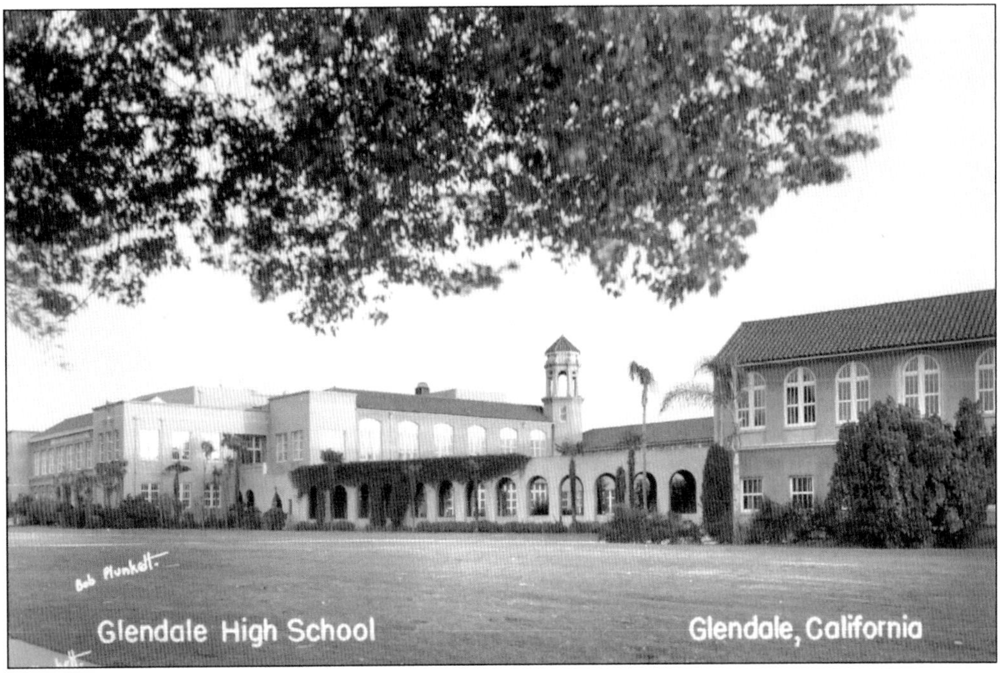

In 1964, some 40 years after it had opened, part of Glendale High School was severely damaged by fire. Students were relocated to other classrooms elsewhere on campus while the school was rebuilt. This postcard was published by the Angeleno Photo Service of Los Angeles around 1950. (Courtesy of the Special Collections Room, Glendale Public Library.)

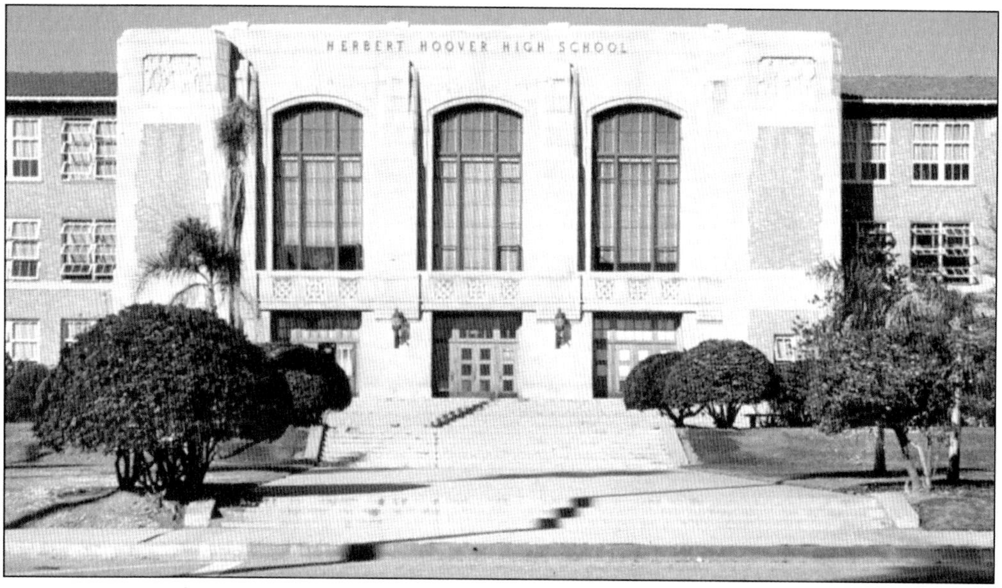

Just two years after Glendale High School was completed, the district purchased property on Glenwood Road in the northwest section of the city for another high school. Opened in 1929, it was named Herbert Hoover High in honor of the new president. Hoover, a Northern California resident, had visited Glendale the previous fall while campaigning for office. This postcard was published by Columbia Wholesale Supply of North Hollywood about 1956. (Courtesy of the Special Collections Room, Glendale Public Library.)

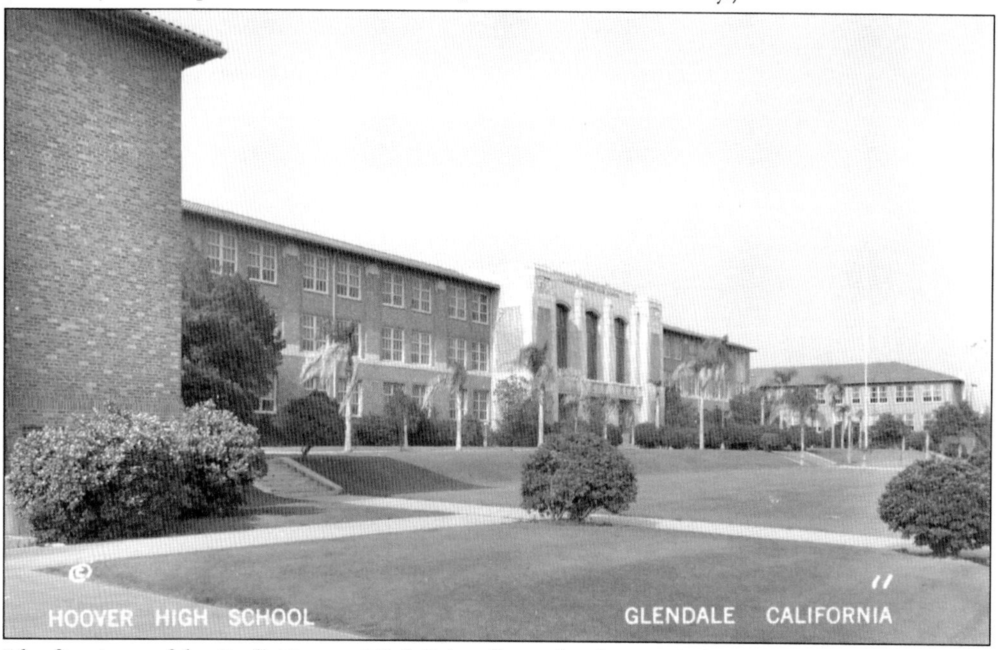

The first issue of the *Scroll*, Hoover High School's yearbook, was dedicated to President Hoover. It included copies of letters from the president and from his wife, Lou, who had visited the "tiny village of Glendale" when she was a child. This postcard was published by the Angeleno Photo Service of Los Angeles around 1950. (Courtesy of the Special Collections Room, Glendale Public Library.)

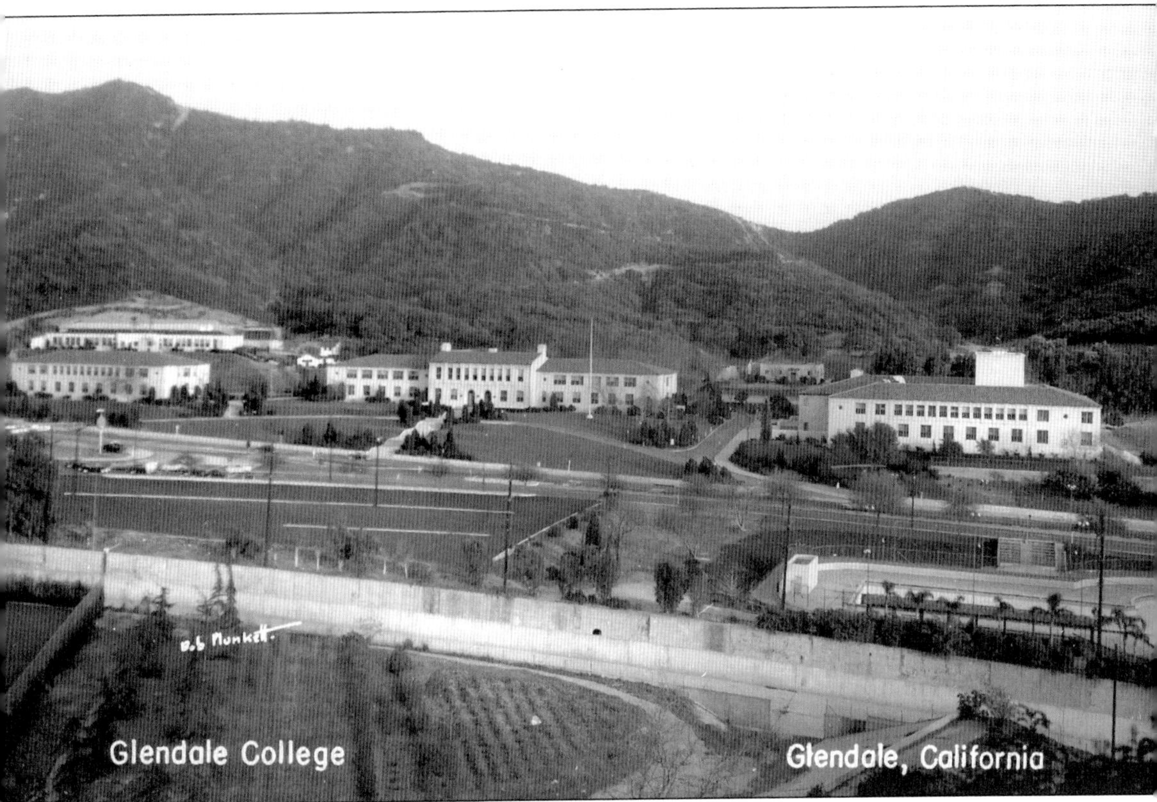

Glendale Junior College relocated to a 25-acre site on Verdugo Road in 1937 after extensive damage from the 1933 Long Beach earthquake had condemned its previous facility on Harvard Street. The science building (left) and the administration building (center) were the first two to be completed. A student union was soon added, with its costs divided between the district and the student body. The hillside was graded to provide athletic fields. The newly completed auditorium appears on the right, and in the foreground are the concrete-lined Verdugo Wash and an Olympic-sized outdoor pool, built in conjunction with the Civic Auditorium. This postcard was published by the Angeleno Photo Service of Los Angeles about 1950. (Courtesy of the Special Collections Room, Glendale Public Library.)

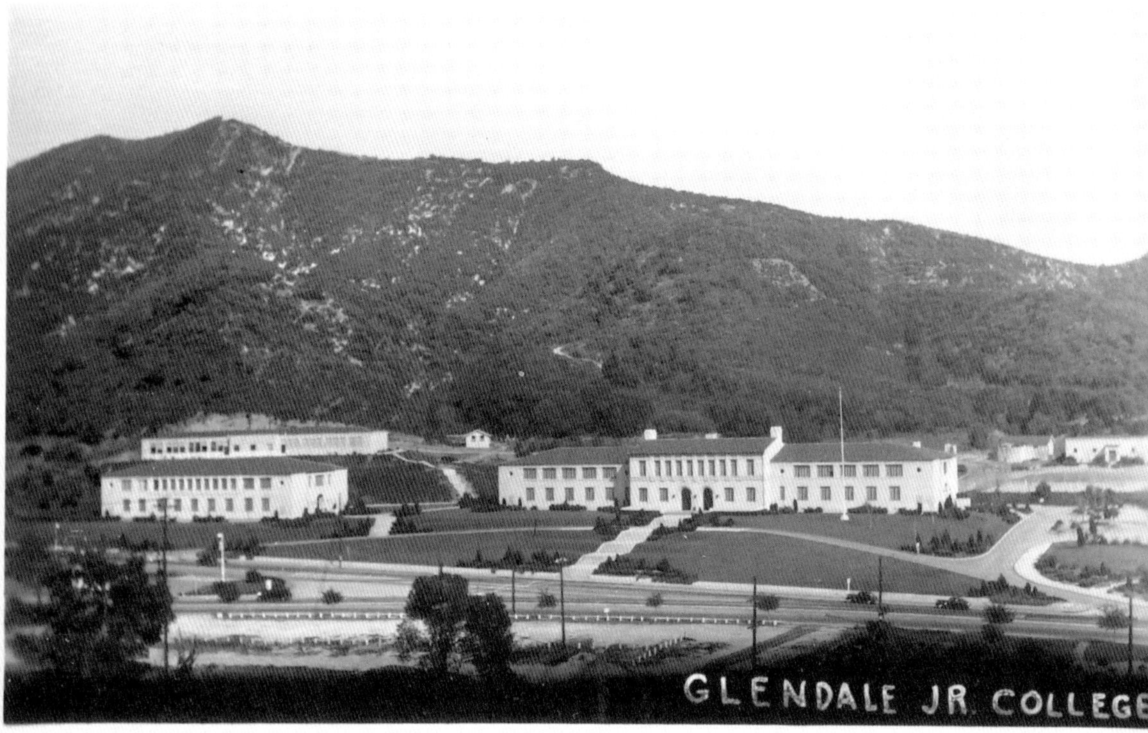

Glendale Junior College is located on Verdugo Road, one of the earliest streets in the city. It was originally a trail that the Verdugo family used to travel from the southern portion of their property north to the La Canada area. This postcard dates to about 1940. (Courtesy of the Special Collections Room, Glendale Public Library.)

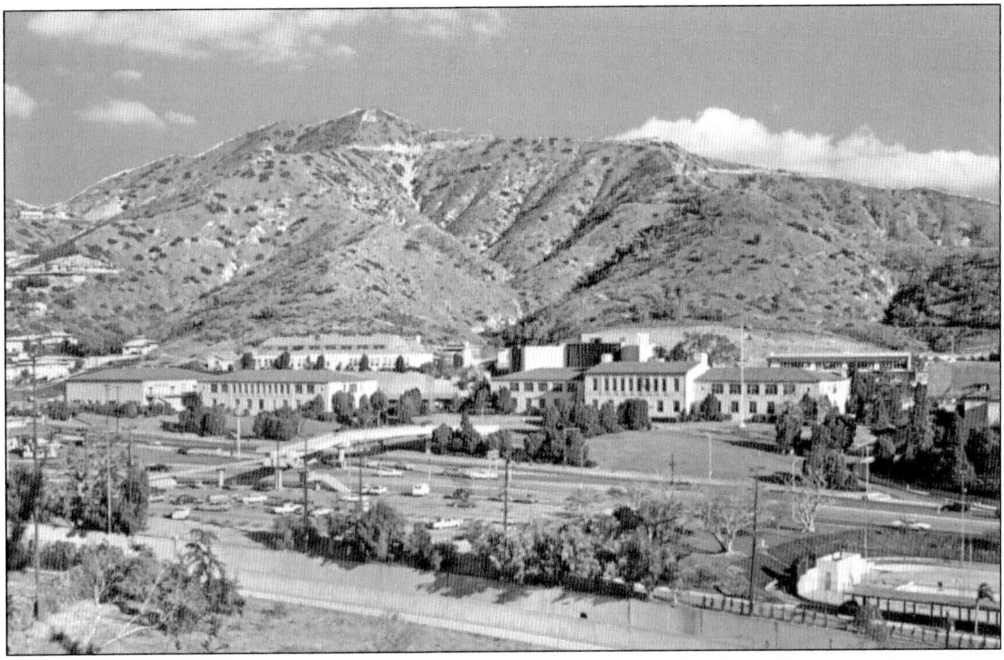

During the 1960s, a library and a women's gym were constructed at the college, and the parking lot was developed. The original science building was remodeled and another wing added. This postcard was published by Columbia Wholesale Supply of North Hollywood around 1967. (Courtesy of the George Ellison Collection.)

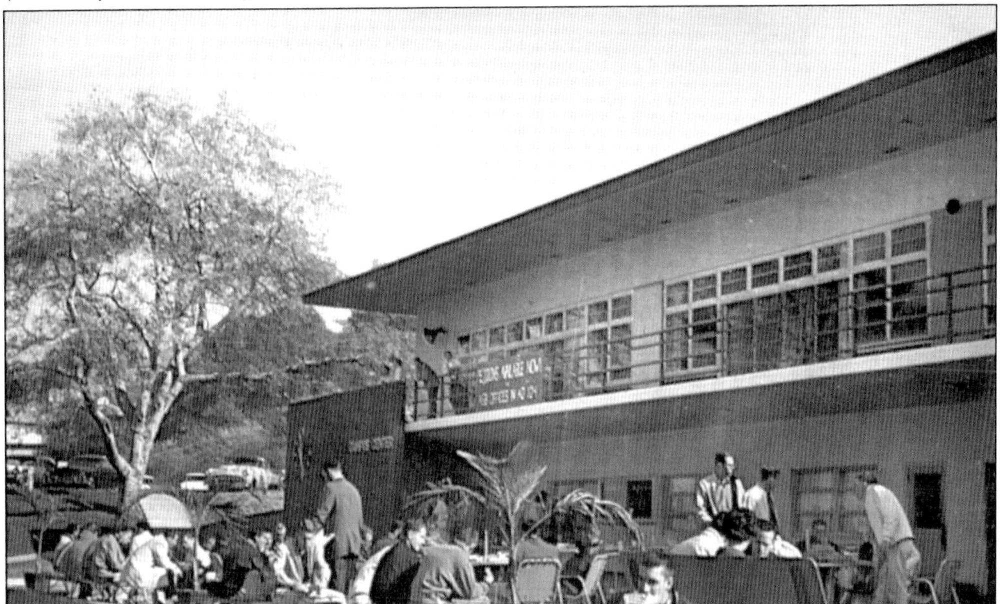

The 1950s were a time of growth at Glendale Junior College. A new Campus Center, seen here, was erected in 1957, along with carpentry and aviation shops. The men's gymnasium opened in 1955, and two bungalows were moved to the campus to provide more classroom space for a rapidly increasing student population. This postcard was published by Columbia Wholesale Supply of North Hollywood about 1958. (Courtesy of the George Ellison Collection.)

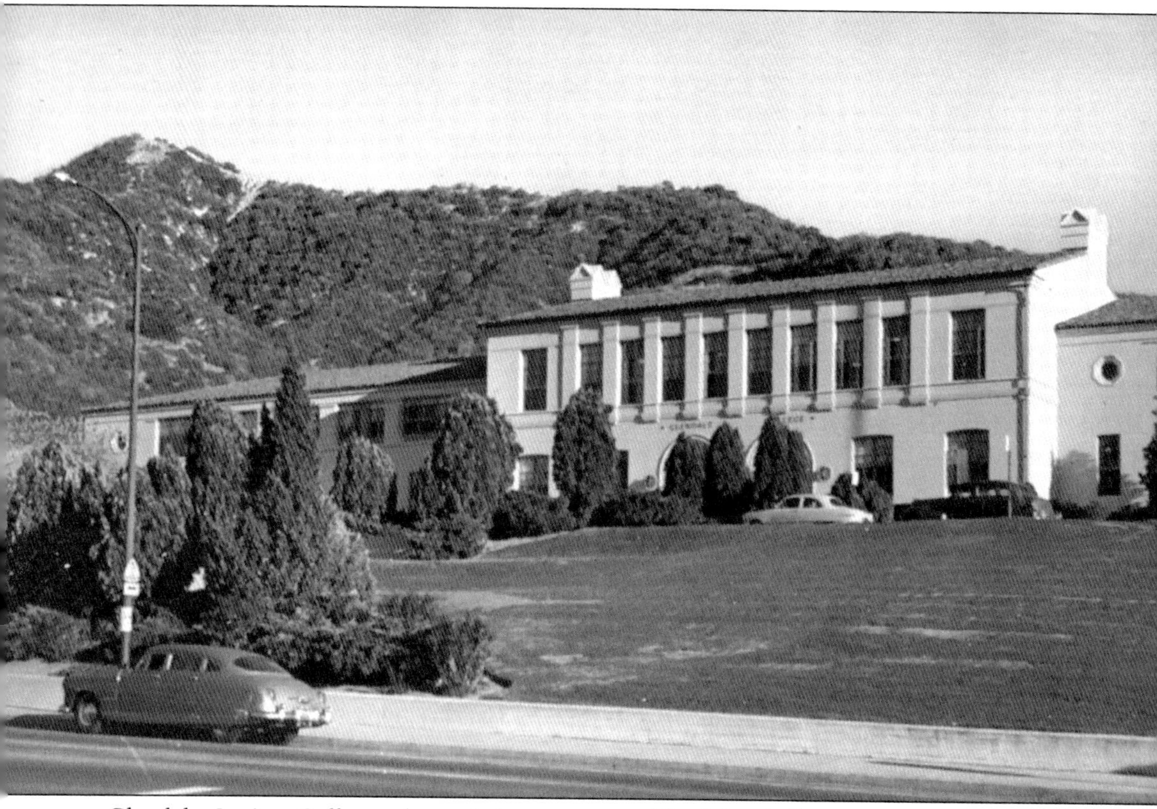

Glendale Junior College changed its name to Glendale College in 1944 and received accreditation from the Western College Association in 1953. The administration building is pictured on this postcard, published by Columbia Wholesale Supply of North Hollywood about 1952. (Courtesy of the George Ellison Collection.)

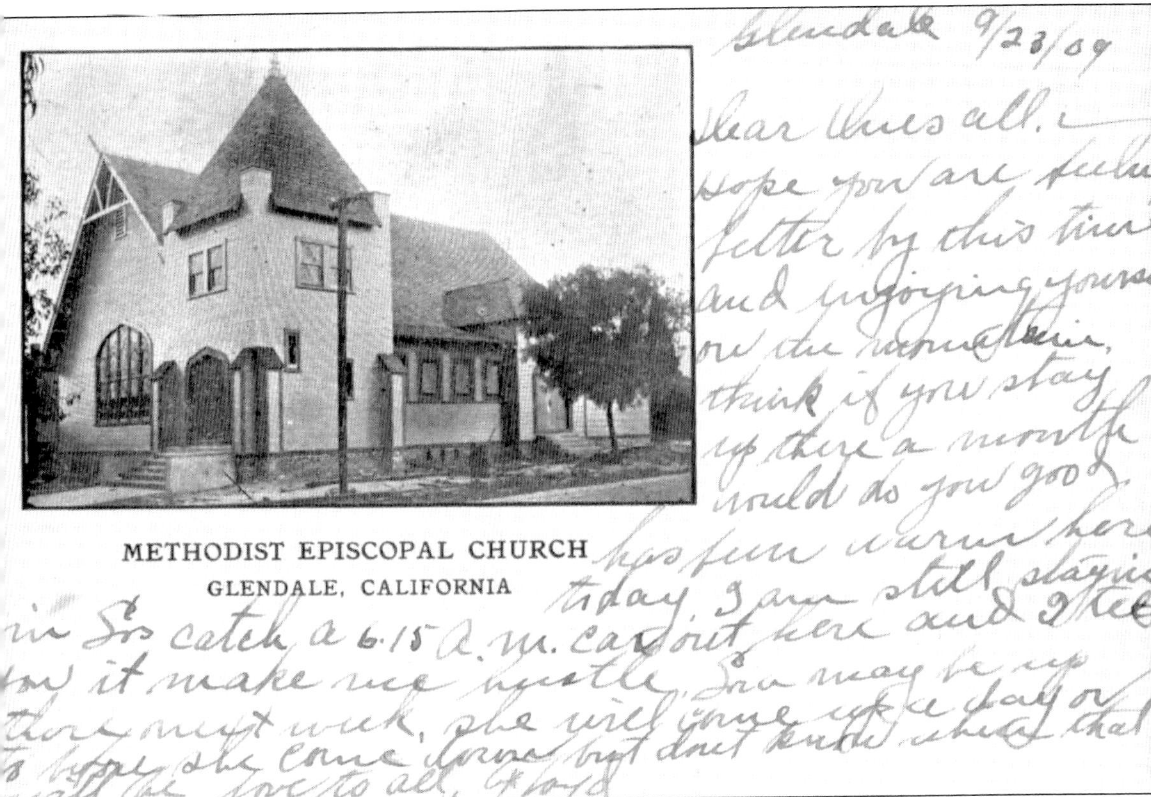

The Glendale Methodist Episcopal Church was organized in 1903 with its first meetings held at the Odd Fellows Lodge. The congregation's first sanctuary, the wood-frame structure pictured here about 1906, was erected at Third Street and Dayton Court in 1906. (Courtesy of the First United Methodist Church, Glendale.)

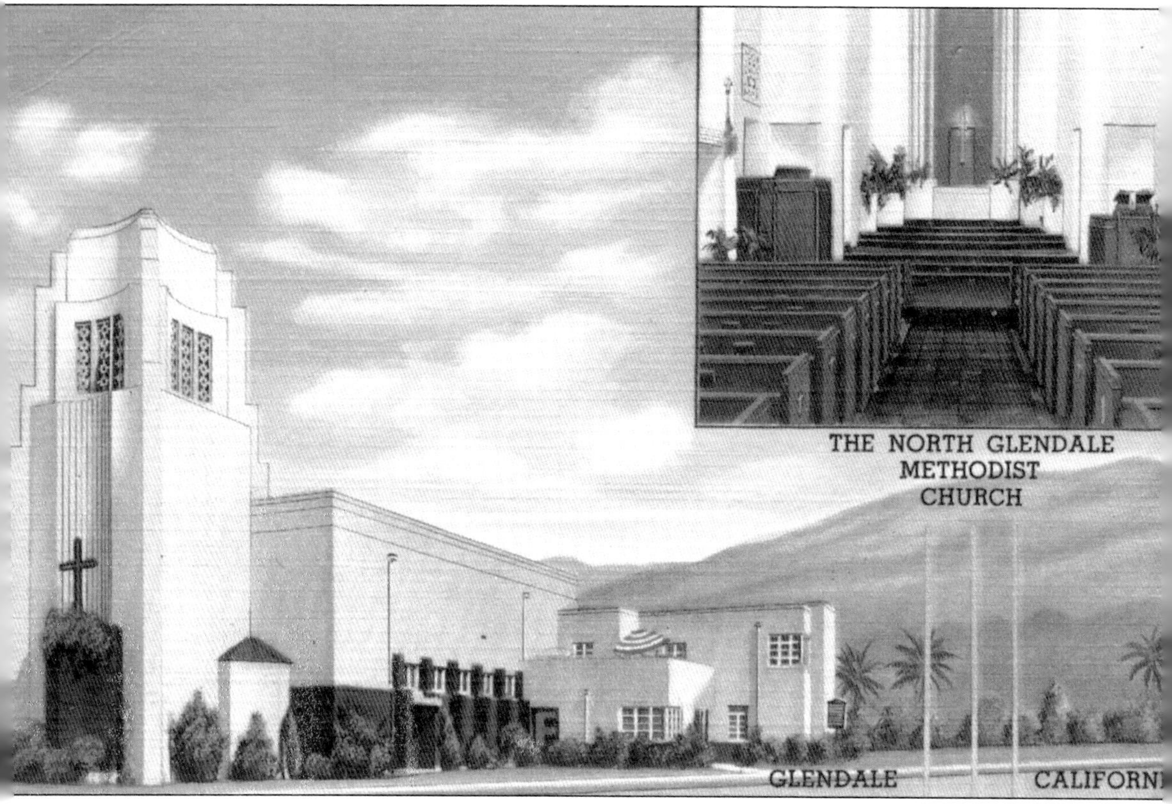

The North Glendale Methodist Church began in 1910. The congregation outgrew two smaller structures at North Central Avenue and Glenoaks Boulevard before hiring a young architectural student with only two years of training to design a modern building in 1942. The unique structure, with its "Tower of Light," was cited for its design by an interdenominational architectural board in New York City. The congregation was very active during World War II, forming a Saturday night canteen for servicemen who had no place to stay. More than 8,000 men spent the night there during the course of the war. This postcard was published by Genuine Curteich of Chicago. (Courtesy of the Special Collections Room, Glendale Public Library.)

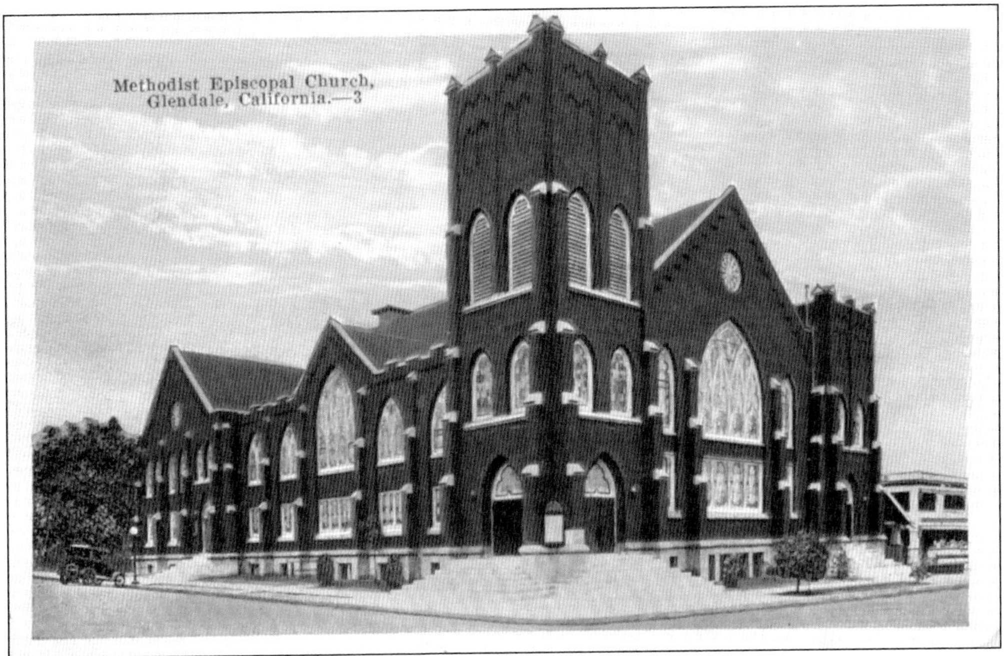

In 1917, the Methodist Episcopal Church dedicated a red-brick-veneer building at Wilson Avenue and Kenwood Street. The new structure had room for 500 Sunday school students. This postcard was published by the E. C. Kropp Company of Milwaukee around 1920. (Courtesy of the George Ellison Collection.)

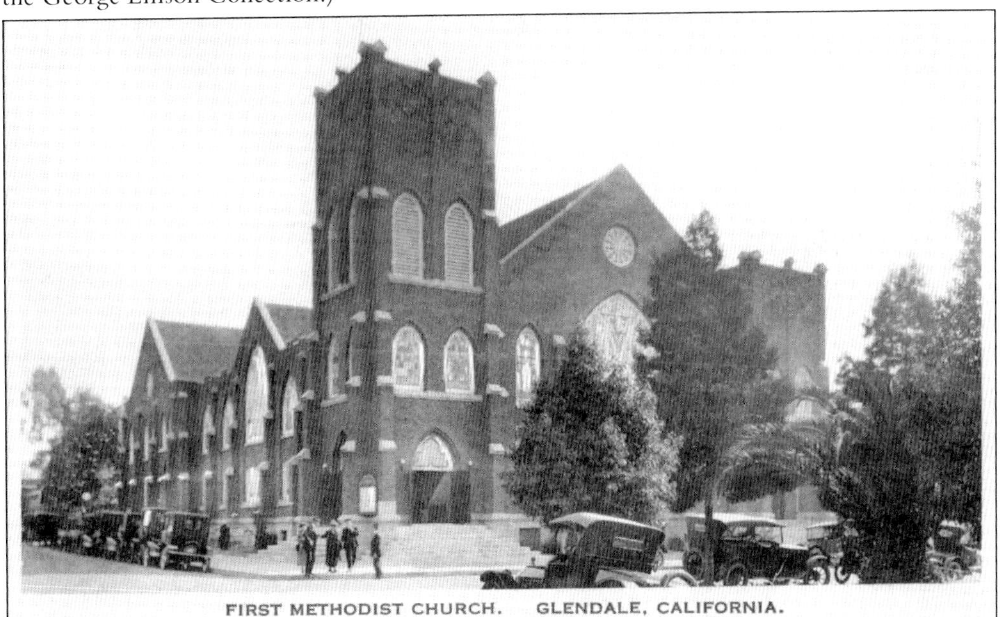

The First Methodist Church, built in 1917, included a spacious auditorium, which soon became the site of many community events. The Glendale Oratorio Society held community sings there, and it also served as a location for the Buster Keaton movie *The Three Ages* in 1923. This postcard was published by the Western Publishing and Novelty Company of Los Angeles. (Courtesy of the Special Collections Room, Glendale Public Library.)

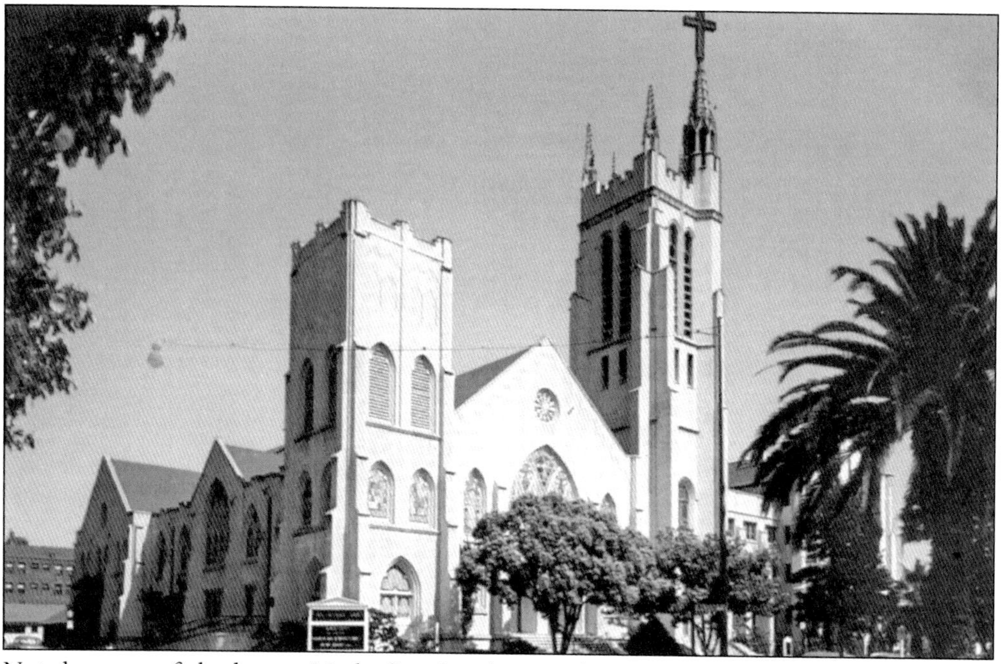

Noted as one of the largest Methodist churches on the West Coast, First Methodist had a Sunday school enrollment of 1,200 in 1924. A five-story building with a gym, classrooms, and a ladies parlor was completed in 1929. This postcard was published by the Mellinger Studio of Altadena around 1955. (Courtesy of the Special Collections Room, Glendale Public Library.)

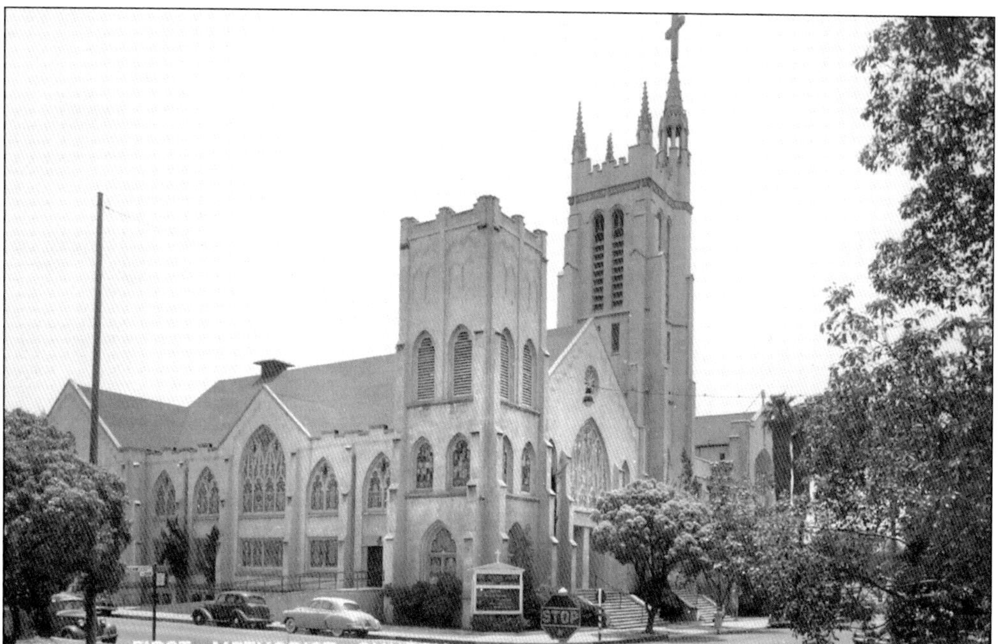

The First Methodist Church's Gothic-style tower, also completed in 1929, was topped with a revolving electric cross, which cast its light throughout the city. This postcard dates to about 1950. (Courtesy of the Special Collections Room, Glendale Public Library.)

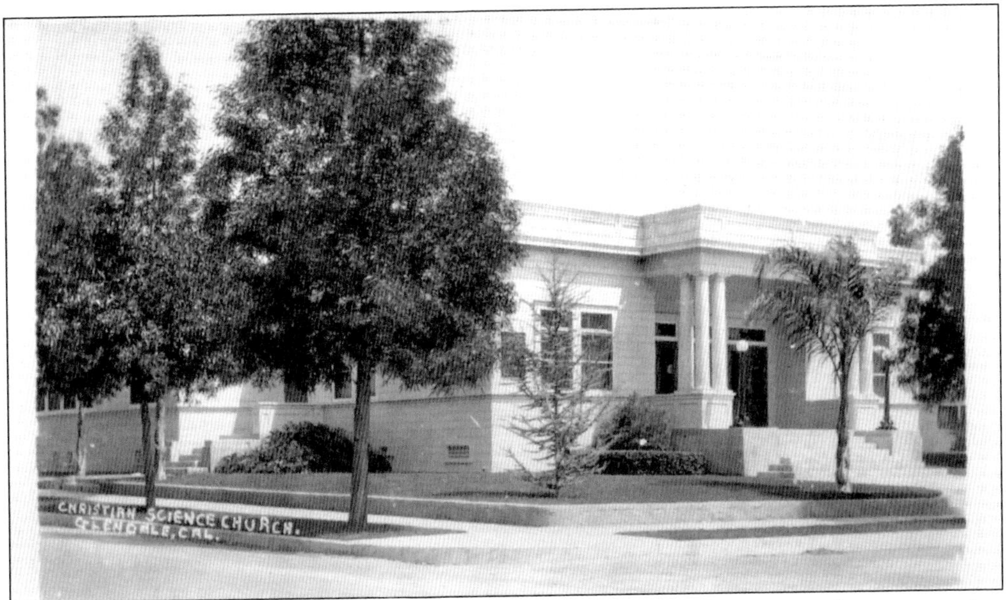

The First Church of Christ Scientist began holding services in 1912. In 1916, the congregation built its own church, seen here, at the corner of Maryland and California Avenues. (Courtesy of the Special Collections Room, Glendale Public Library.)

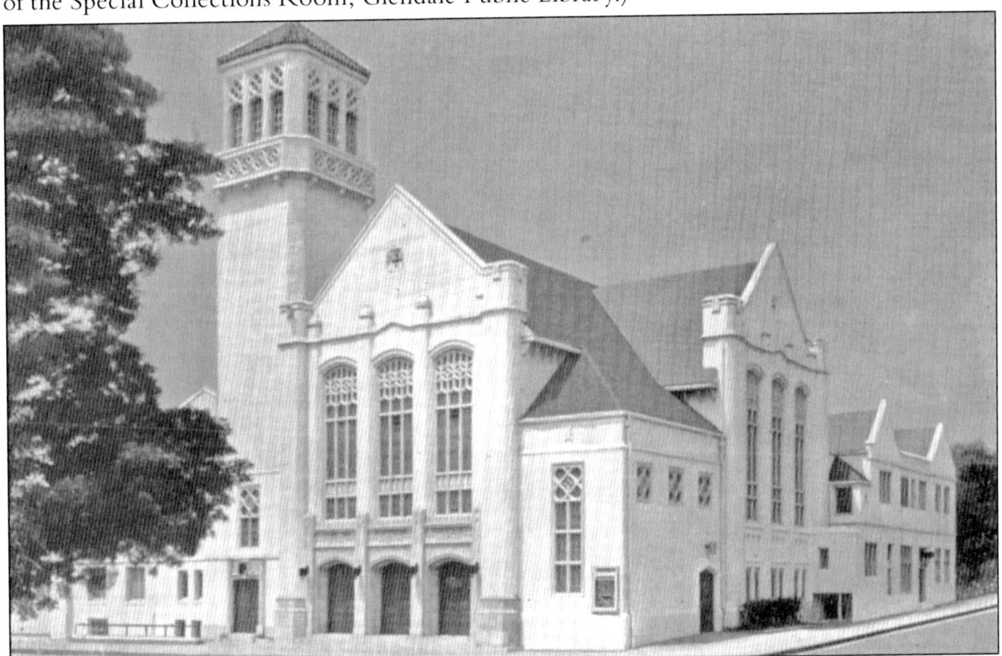

Located at Wilson Avenue and Louise Street, the First Baptist Church was one of the largest churches on the Pacific Coast, with over 3,000 members. The modern church building proved a popular gathering place for young people and offered a friendly atmosphere near the center of the aircraft industries. Rev. J. Whitcomb Brougher Jr. became pastor in 1927, the same year the new church (right) was constructed adjacent to a 1912 meeting hall (left). Brougher served as pastor for over 75 years. This postcard dates to around 1946. (Courtesy of the Special Collections Room, Glendale Public Library.)

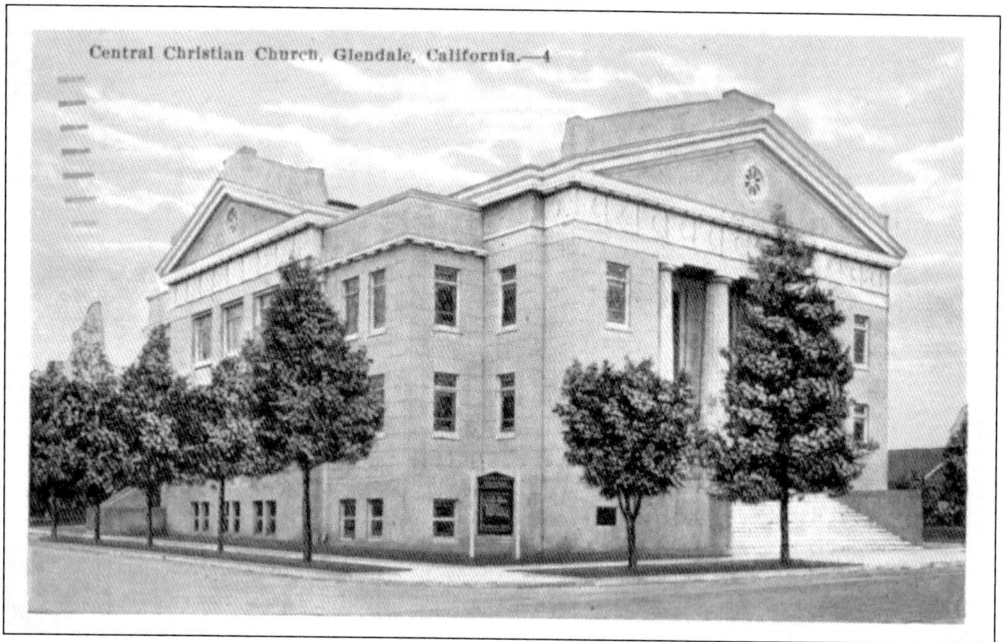

The Central Christian Church began in 1908, and the congregation built this sanctuary at the corner of Colorado and Louise Streets in 1922. This postcard was published by the E. C. Kropp Company of Milwaukee. (Courtesy of the George Ellison Collection.)

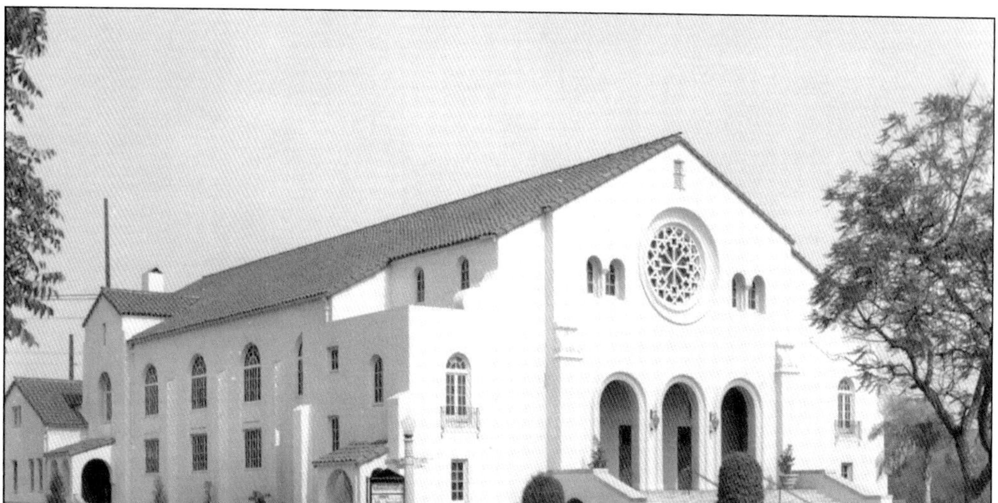

When its previous church at Isabel Street and California Avenue was destroyed by fire in 1930, the Seventh Day Adventist congregation built this sanctuary on the same site. It was dedicated in 1932. This souvenir postcard was issued in 1952 for the church's 20th anniversary. (Courtesy of the Special Collections Room, Glendale Public Library.)

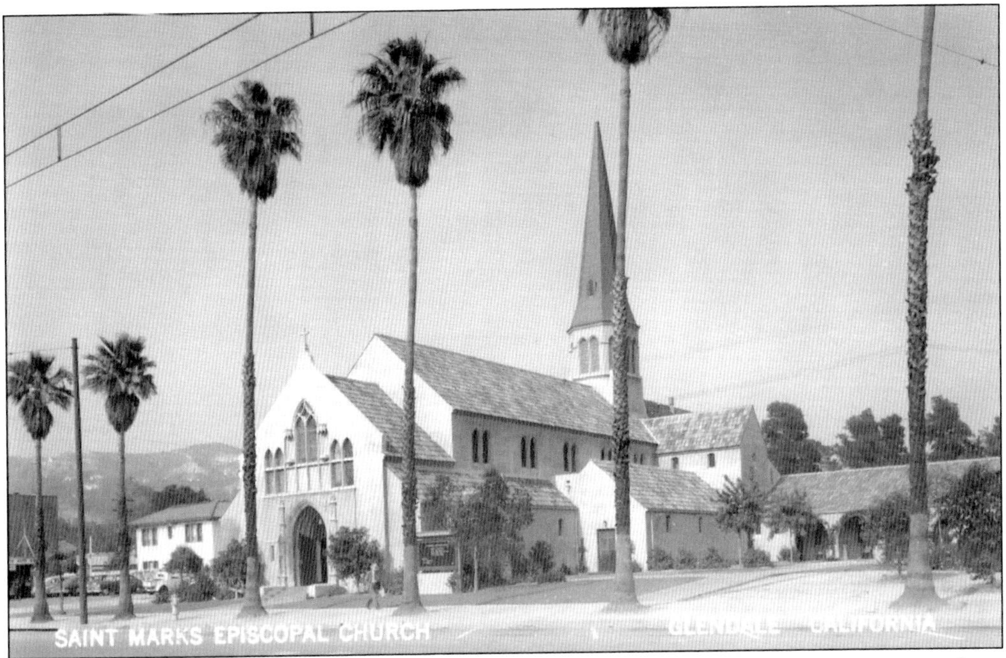

The new St. Mark's Episcopal Church on Brand Boulevard and Dryden Street opened on Christmas Eve in 1948. Founded in 1889, the church held its first services in St. Hilda's Hall, an Episcopal seminary for girls at the old Glendale Hotel. This postcard was published by the Angeleno Photo Service of Los Angeles around 1950. (Courtesy of the Special Collections Room, Glendale Public Library.)

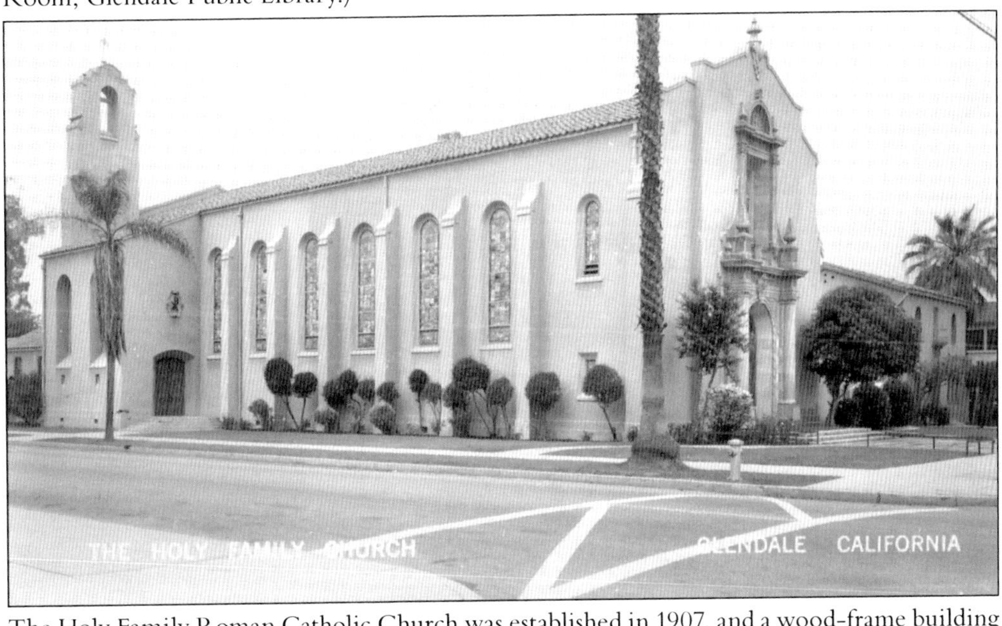

The Holy Family Roman Catholic Church was established in 1907, and a wood-frame building was constructed on Lomita Avenue in 1908. As the church grew, this new sanctuary was built at Elk Avenue and Louise Streets in 1921. Overcrowding brought a new wing in 1949. This postcard was published by the Angeleno Photo Service of Los Angeles about 1950. (Courtesy of the Special Collections Room, Glendale Public Library.)

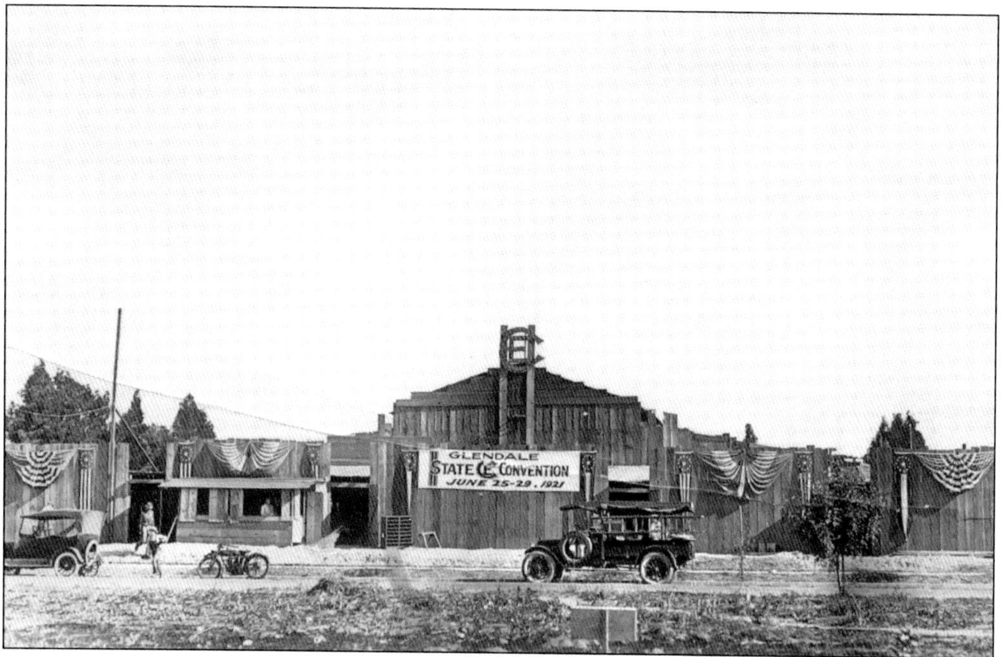

The 33rd Annual State Christian Endeavor Convention, held from June 25 to 29, 1921, brought more than 10,000 attendees to the city. Most stayed in private homes or camped in Verdugo Park. The auditorium, erected by the city at Harvard and Orange Streets, was torn down the day after the convention closed. (Courtesy of the Special Collections Room, Glendale Public Library.)

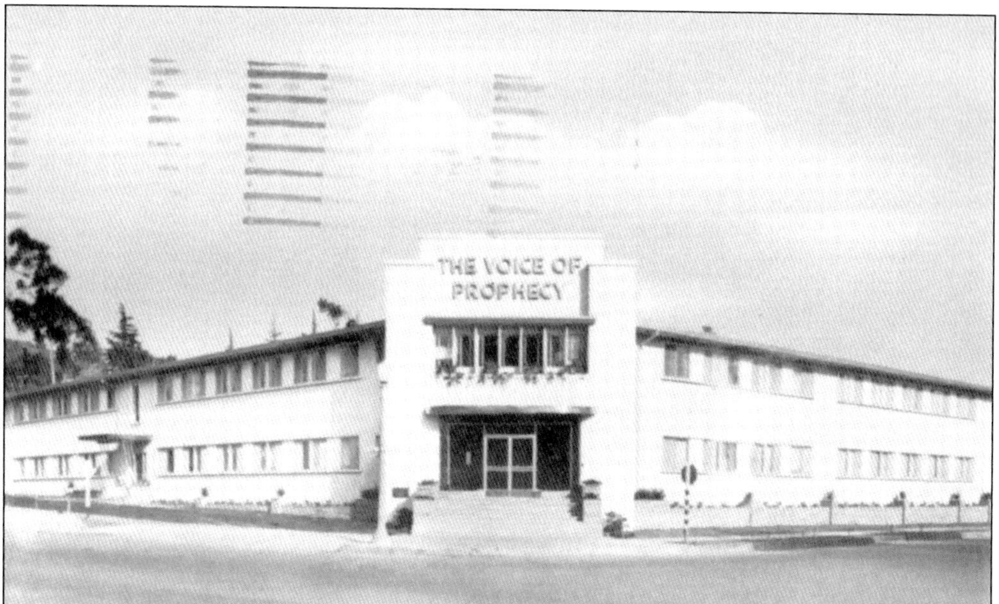

In 1943, Glendale became the headquarters for the Voice of Prophecy, the "radio arm" of the Seventh Day Adventist Church. In the early 1950s, the Adventists constructed a building on Chevy Chase Drive and from there produced a Christian program broadcast to listeners around the world. (Courtesy of the Special Collections Room, Glendale Public Library.)

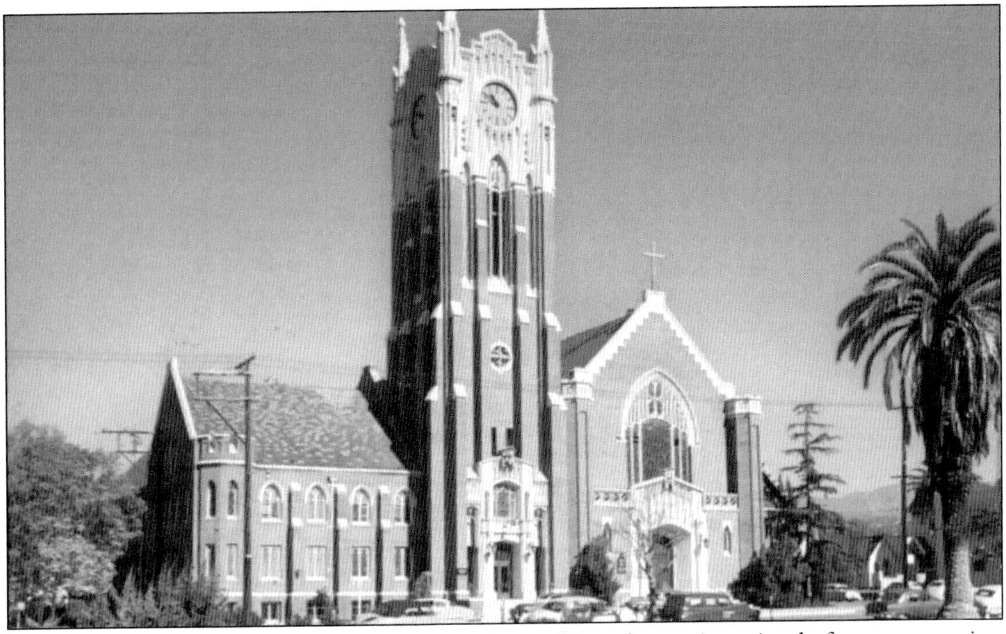

Members of the Glendale Presbyterian Church worshipped at various sites before constructing this church at the corner of Harvard and Louise Streets in 1923. Shockwaves from the 1971 earthquake caused so much internal damage that the building had to be demolished. A new church was later built on the same site, on top of the existing basement. This postcard was published by Columbia Wholesale Supply of North Hollywood around 1953. (Courtesy of the Special Collections Room, Glendale Public Library.)

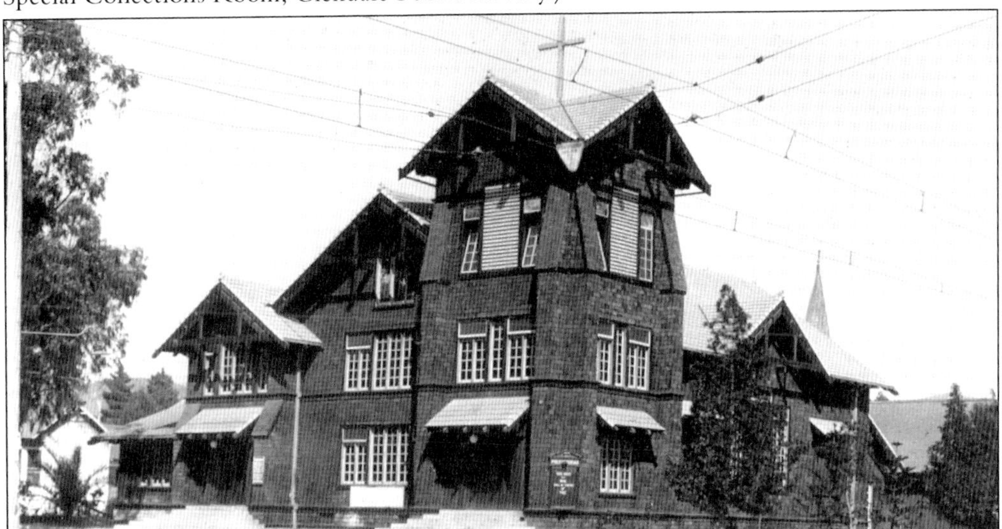

The Glendale Presbyterian Church was formed in 1884. Members held a Christmas Eve supper that year, raising $40—enough to inspire a building project near Tropico. In 1888, when the congregation realized the fast-growing town of Glendale was spreading northward, it moved the small sanctuary (visible behind the larger church) to the corner of Broadway and Cedar Street. In 1912, the small church was moved to the back of the lot and the larger church was built. This postcard dates to about 1920. (Courtesy of the Special Collections Room, Glendale Public Library.)

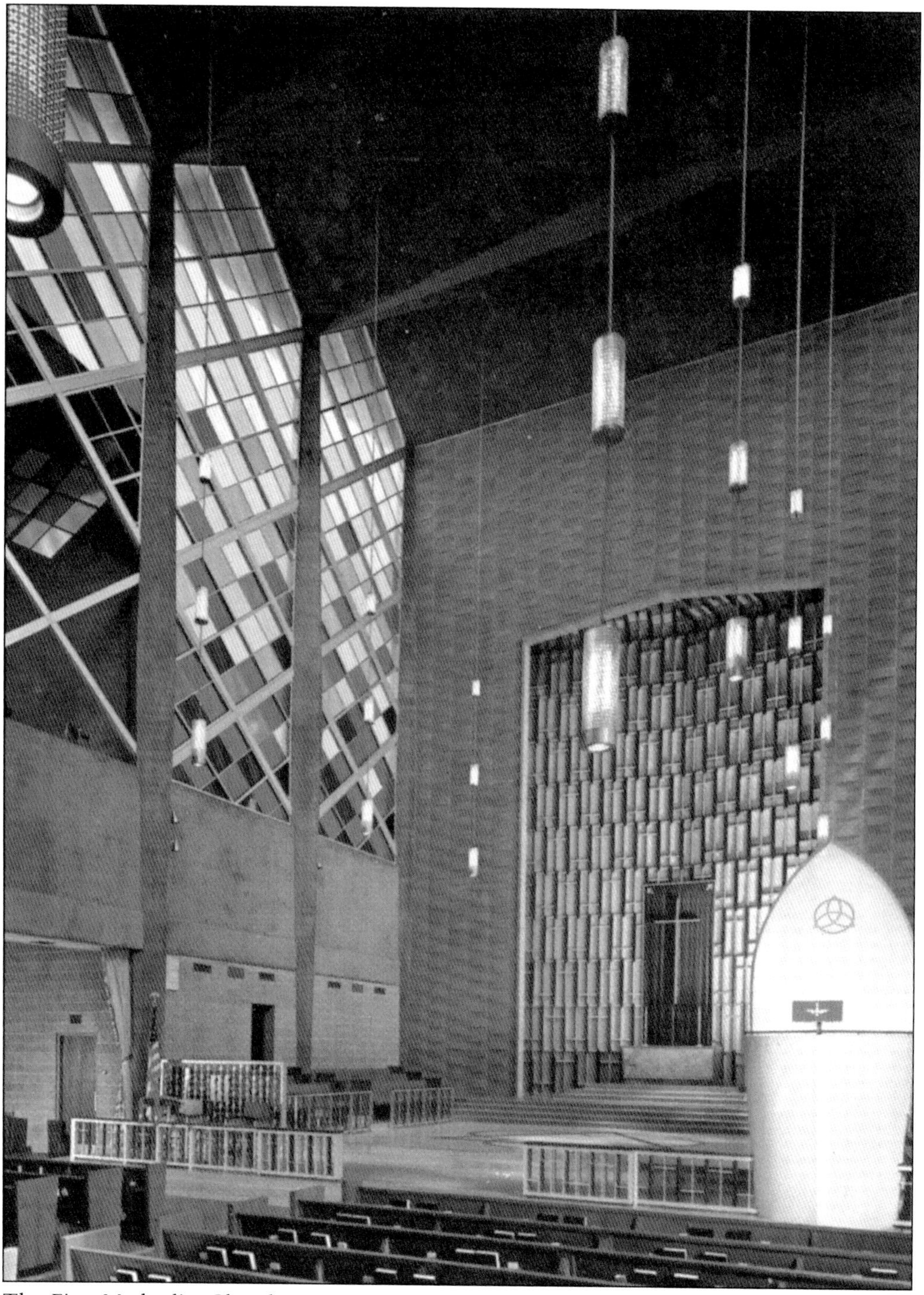

The First Methodist Church opened its new sanctuary at Broadway and Kenwood Street in 1961. The $1.3-million cathedral, called the "Cathedral of the West," seats 1,320. The nave soars to nearly 100 feet, while large stained-glass windows provide a changing light mosaic. This postcard was published around 1961. (Courtesy of the Special Collections Room, Glendale Public Library.)

Three

Public Buildings

Both government and quasi-public buildings served as iconic features of the city that represented grandeur without opulence. Glendale residents often advocated for fiscal conservatism, little government spending, and self-reliance on the community for the public good. Glendale's city hall has always been handsome and stately without being overly exaggerated. The first city hall was built in 1912. As government grew, a second city hall replaced the original building and, since its establishment in 1940, has remained the anchor as newer government buildings sprouted up around this center, such as the 1960s modern municipal services building originally considered a city hall annex.

Public buildings included the homes of prominent organizations like the Elks Club and the women's Tuesday Afternoon Club. Social clubs were distinctly segregated between men and women. Historic landmarks such as the two adobes from Glendale's Spanish history, adored by residents, spawned the decades-long Days of the Verdugos festivities. Residents won the fight to save the old adobe of the Sanchez family from demolition and renamed it the Casa Adobe de San Rafael in honor of the area's heritage.

Always a valuable part of Glendale's history, medical institutions included both large and small facilities for the care of the old and the sick. The up-to-date Glendale Adventist Medical Center serves the local area today, but as the descendant of the old Glendale Sanitarium, it once offered medical help to the ailing from across the country. The Glendale Library was one of the town's earliest institutions, beginning in the early 1900s and expanding over the years to include an ever-increasing central library and friendly neighborhood branches. Other public buildings, like the impressive Glendale Post Office, were built with the help of the federal government in the face of the Depression.

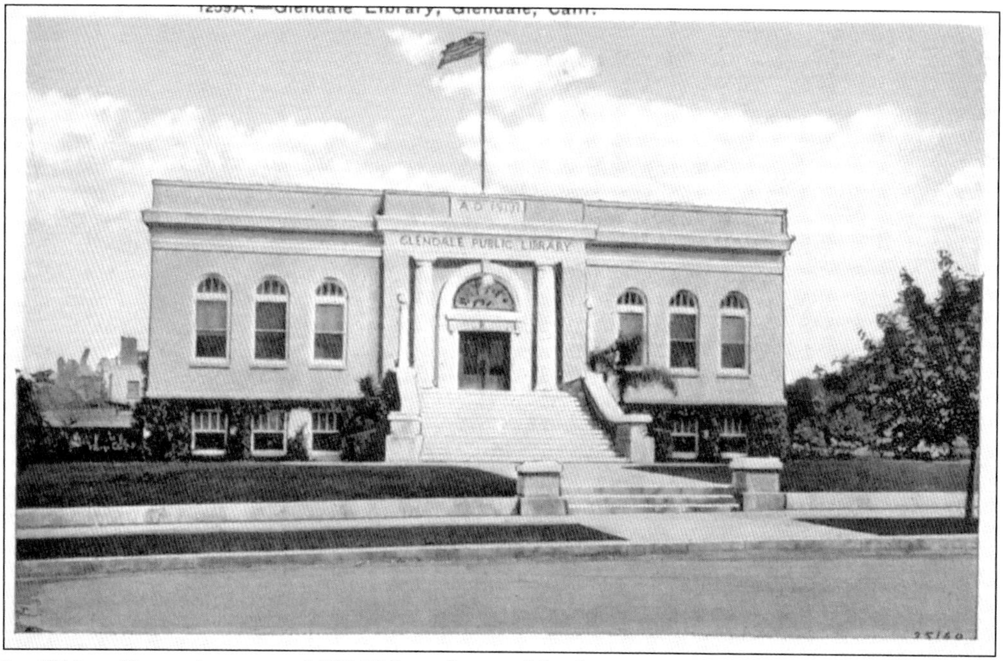

In 1913, a Carnegie grant of $12,500 made possible the construction of the Glendale Public Library at the corner of Kenwood and Harvard Streets. It was dedicated in 1914. This postcard was published by the M. Kashower Company of Los Angeles about 1920. (Courtesy of the Special Collections Room, Glendale Public Library.)

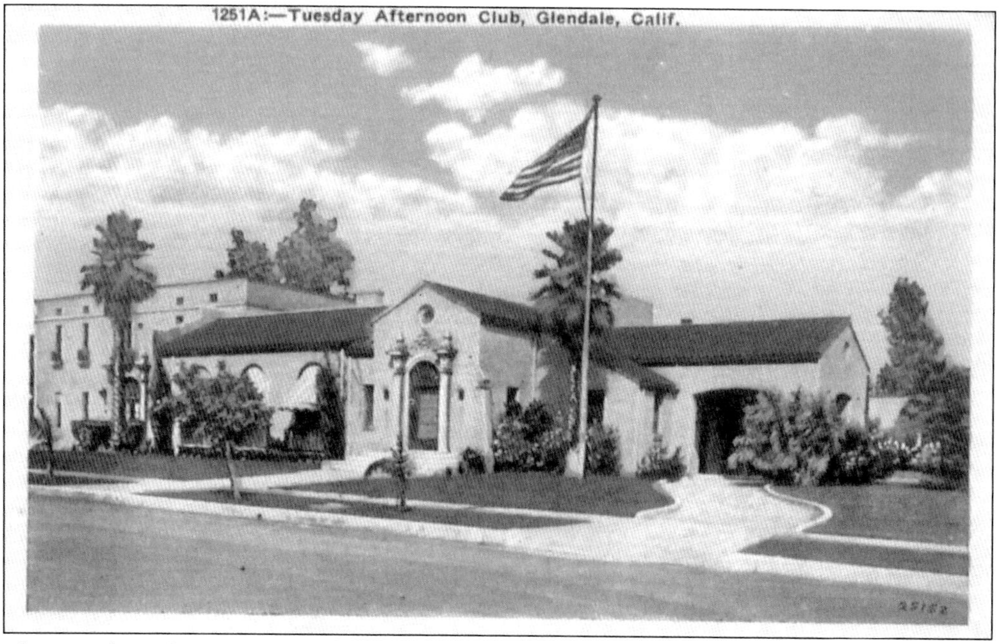

The Tuesday Afternoon Club began in 1888 when a small group gathered for friendship and later for book discussions. In 1904, the friends organized as the Tuesday Afternoon Club and built this clubhouse, designed by local architect Alfred F. Priest, at Central Avenue and Lexington Drive in 1923. (Courtesy of the Glendale Historical Society.)

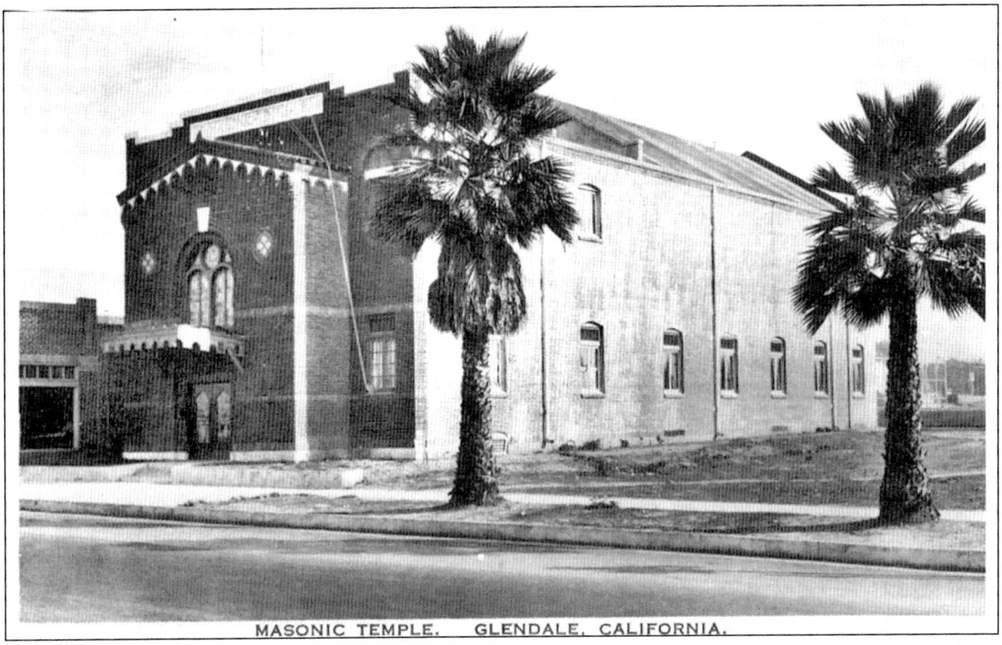

The first Masonic Lodge, Unity Lodge No. 368, was established in 1905. In 1910, members built this two-story Masonic Temple at 232 South Brand Boulevard. It served as a meeting place for the Masons until 1928, when it was demolished and replaced by a larger structure. This postcard was published by the Western Publishing and Novelty Company of Los Angeles around 1914. (Courtesy of the Special Collections Room, Glendale Public Library.)

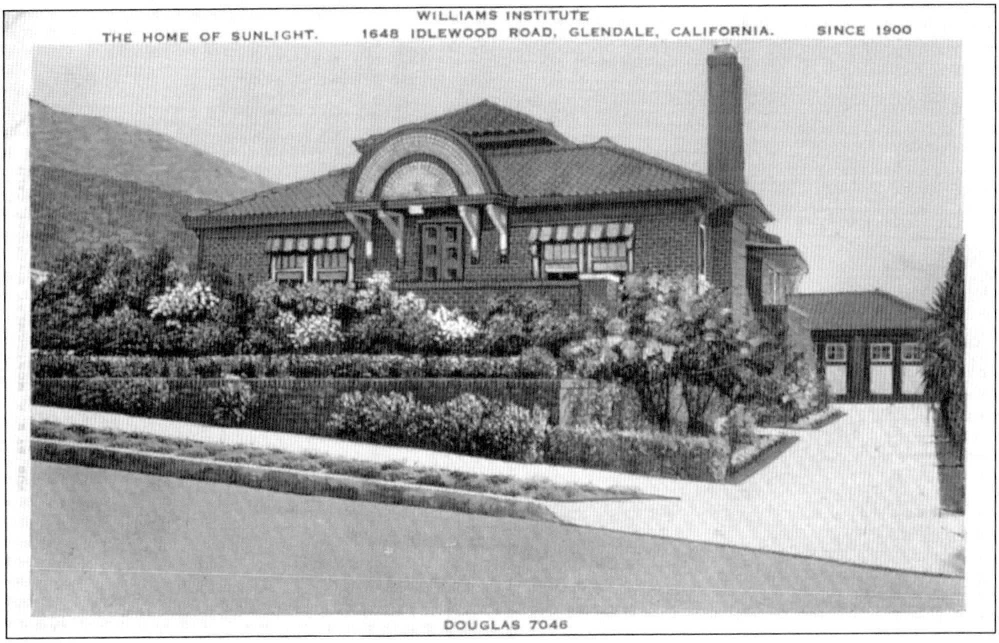

Osteopathic physician Robert H. Williams operated the Williams Institute from his Idlewood Road residence. Williams, who used natural light to treat his patients, called it "the Home of Sunlight." Built in 1924, the house continues to be privately owned. (Courtesy of the Special Collections Room, Glendale Public Library.)

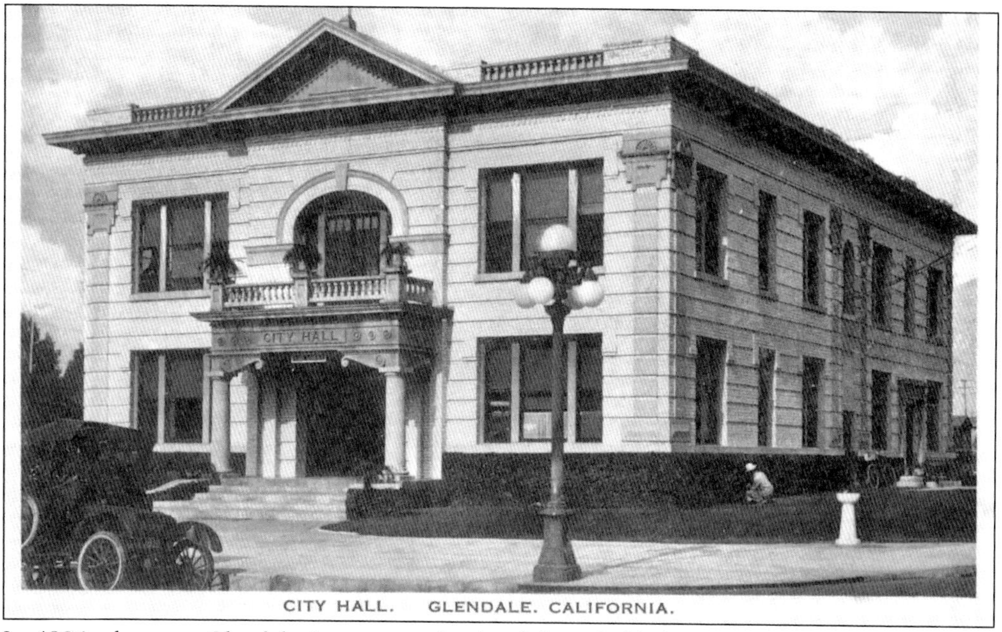

In 1906, the year Glendale incorporated, city fathers held their first official meeting at a private home, then moved to a building housing the *Glendale News*, which had been a strong supporter of incorporation. City hall, pictured here, was built at the corner of Broadway and Howard Street in 1912. The cost of $7,047 did not include any heating facilities. This postcard was published by the Western Publishing and Novelty Company of Los Angeles about 1922. (Courtesy of the George Ellison Collection.)

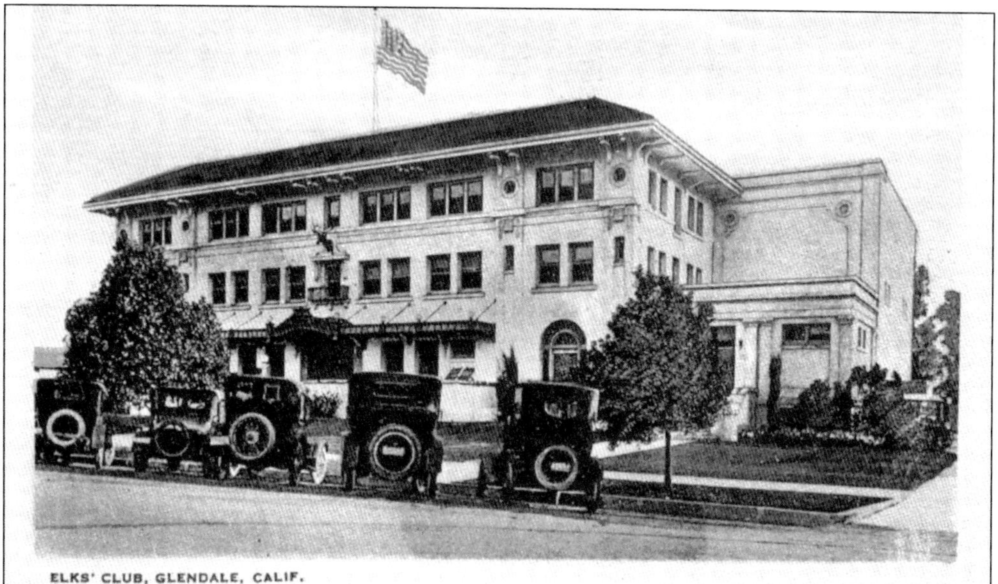

The Glendale Elks Lodge was instituted in 1912, and rapid growth encouraged members to purchase land at 120 East Colorado Street in 1913. The ground-breaking, delayed by World War I, took place in 1917, and the clubhouse opened in 1918. This postcard was published by the Artochrom Lithograph Company of Los Angeles around 1923. (Courtesy of the Special Collections Room, Glendale Public Library.)

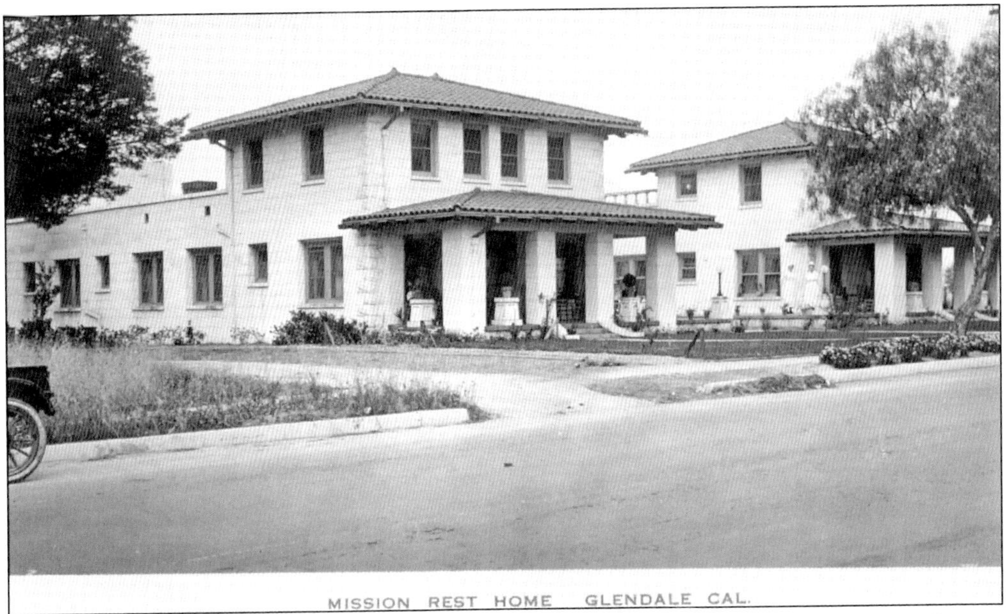

The Mission Rest Home, on San Fernando Road near Chevy Chase Drive, was one of many such facilities built in the city. Glendale's healthy climate encouraged the development of hospitals, medical facilities, and sanitariums. This postcard dates to about 1923. (Courtesy of the Special Collections Room, Glendale Public Library.)

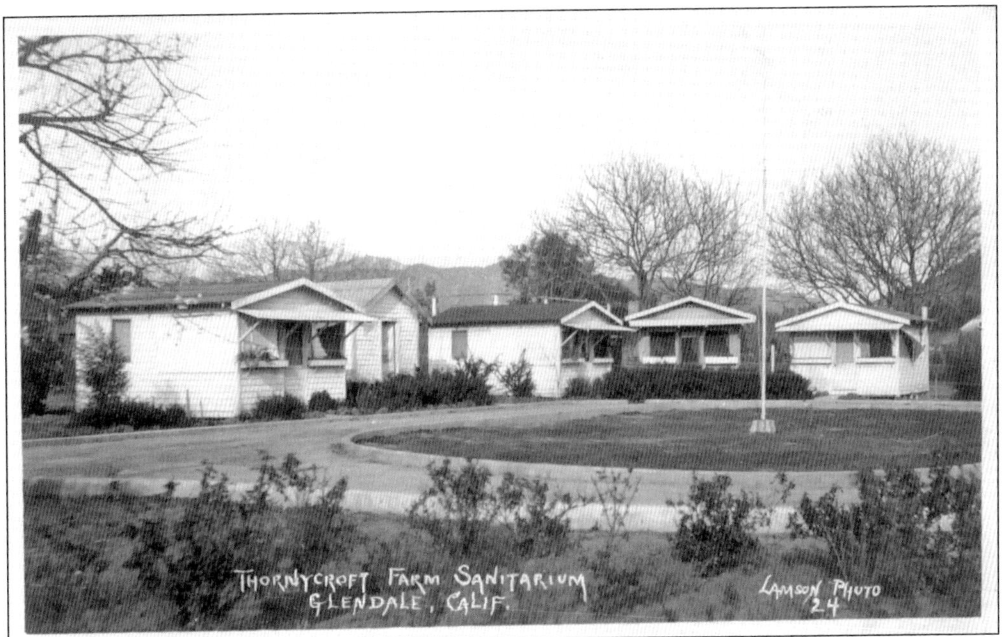

By the 1890s, Thornycroft Farm was operating near Windsor Road and Adams Street, which was then open country. Owner Maxwell "Nannie" Miller stressed the region's healthy climate, which brought patients from around the world. The sanitarium's most striking features were its 15 cottages, set amongst a large garden and six acres of fruit trees. Thornycroft was the forerunner of the Glendale Community Hospital. (Courtesy of the Glendale Historical Society.)

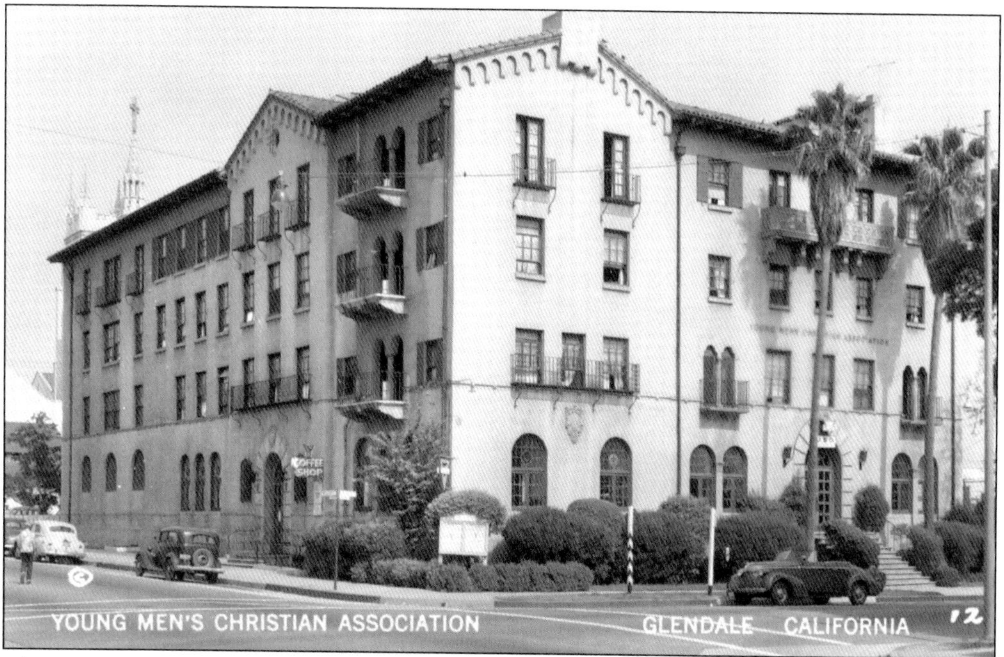

The YMCA was founded in 1919. A campaign to raise funds for a building was held in 1924, and pledges for the entire cost of $275,000 were received within eight days. After a site was secured at Wilson Avenue and Louise Street, the cornerstone was laid in 1926. This postcard was published by the Angeleno Photo Service of Los Angeles around 1950. (Courtesy of the Special Collections Room, Glendale Public Library.)

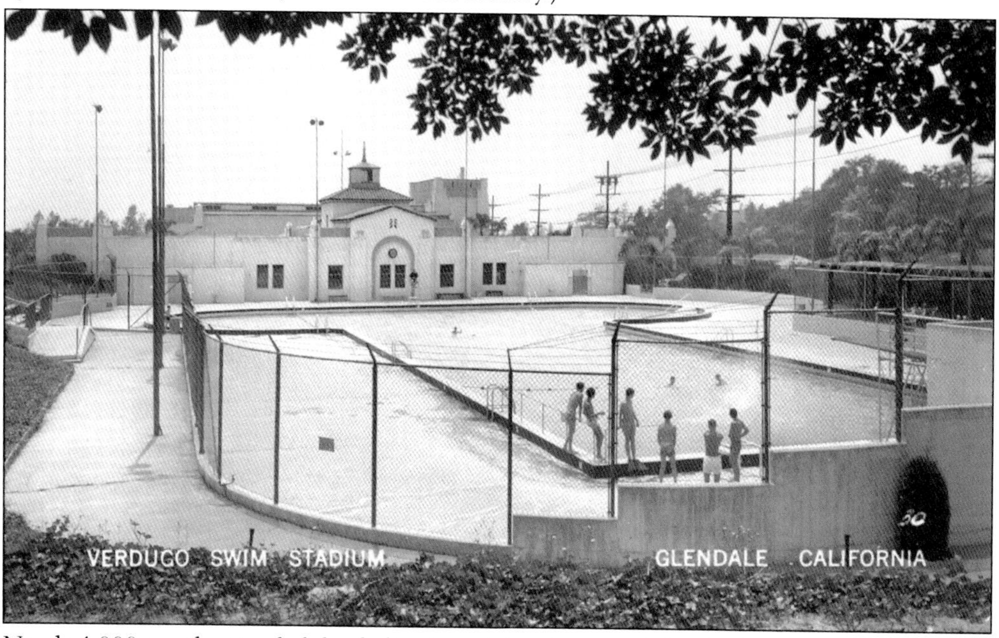

Nearly 1,000 people attended the dedication of the Verdugo Swim Stadium in 1938. When the pool opened, it was called one of the finest municipal plunges in the country. This postcard was published by the Angeleno Photo Service of Los Angeles about 1950. (Courtesy of the Bruce B. Herman Collection.)

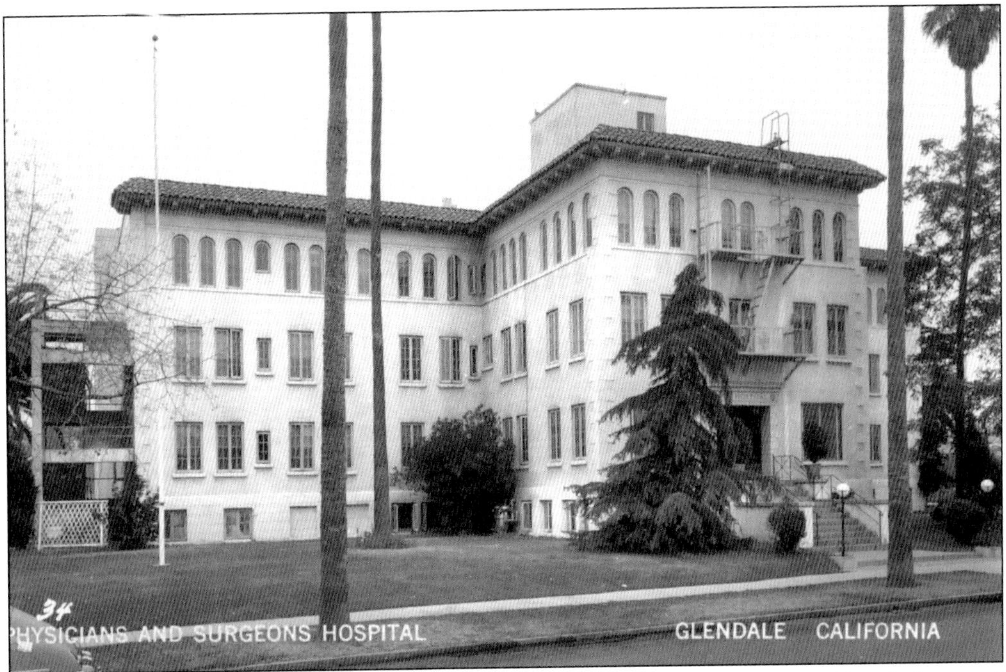

Built of steel and concrete at a cost of $225,000, the Physicians and Surgeons Hospital opened in 1926 with all the latest equipment. In 1955, its name was changed to the Memorial Hospital of Glendale. This postcard was published by the Angeleno Photo Service of Los Angeles. (Courtesy of the Special Collections Room, Glendale Public Library.)

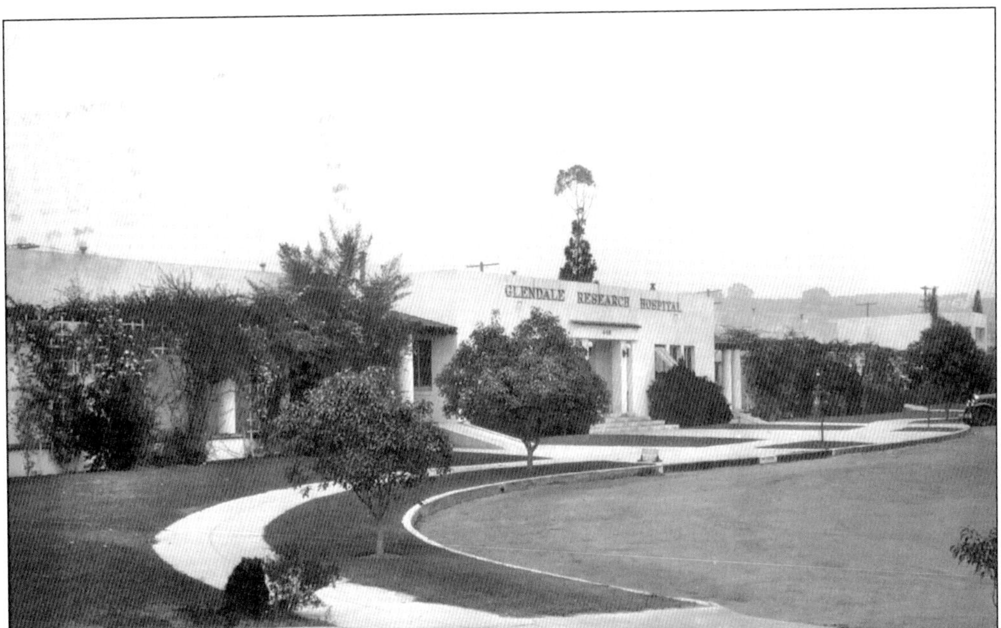

The Glendale Research Hospital was constructed in 1920. Later renamed Behrens Memorial Hospital, it was the forerunner of the Verdugo Hills Hospital. This postcard dates to about 1930. (Courtesy of the Special Collections Room, Glendale Public Library.)

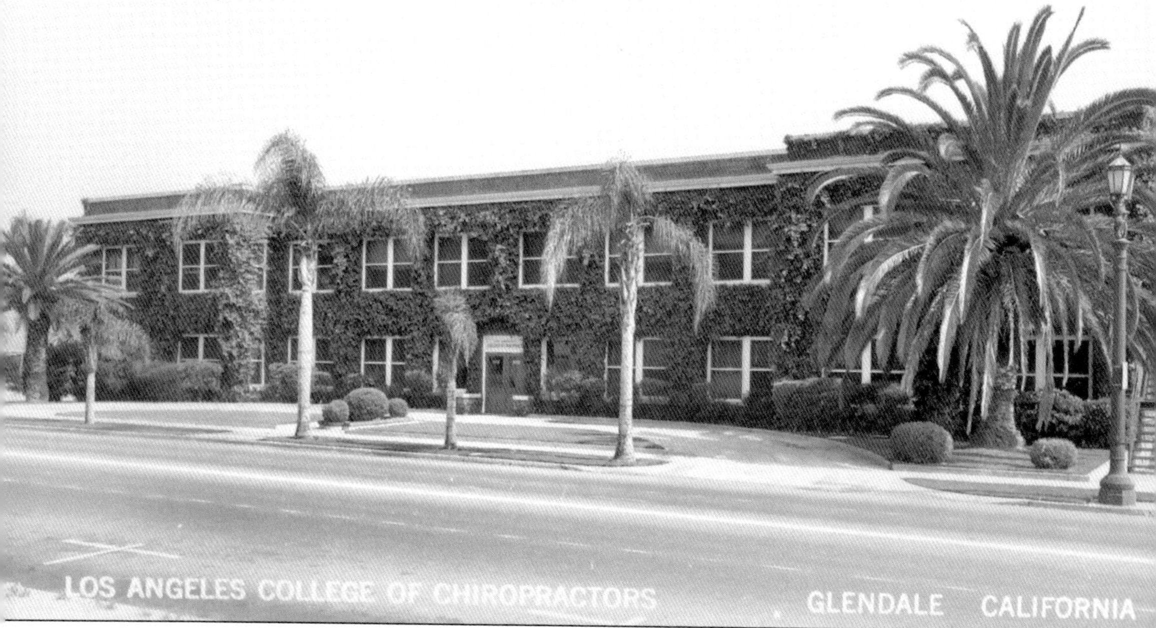

This structure, once housing the Los Angeles College of Chiropractors, was built as the Harrower Laboratory and Clinic. Dr. Harrower, whose theories on endocrinology created controversy and publicity, established his business in 1918. By 1920, sales of his Sani-tate potion had flourished, and he built this facility at 920 East Broadway. At the time, Harrower Lab was the largest non-institutional employer in Glendale, with 50 employees. After Dr. Harrower's death, the building was sold to a pharmaceutical company and then to Cecil B. DeMille, who sold it to the college in 1949. This postcard was published by the Angeleno Photo Service of Los Angeles around 1950. (Courtesy of the Special Collections Room, Glendale Public Library.)

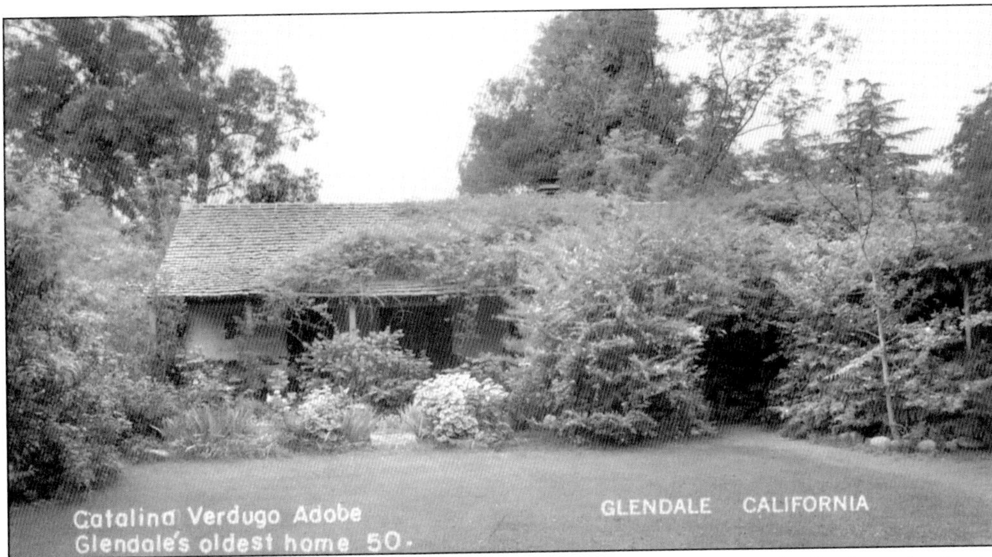

Teodoro Verdugo, the grandson of Spanish land grant owner Jose Maria Verdugo, built the Verdugo Adobe around 1860. Teodoro invited his aunt Catalina, who was blind from smallpox and had never married, to live with his family. Since Catalina was the daughter of Jose Maria Verdugo and had inherited half of the land grant, many assumed that she also owned the adobe; as a result, for many years it was known as the Catalina Adobe. The location is now a city museum and park at 2211 Bonita Drive. This postcard was published by the Angeleno Photo Service of Los Angeles about 1950. (Courtesy of the Special Collections Room, Glendale Public Library.)

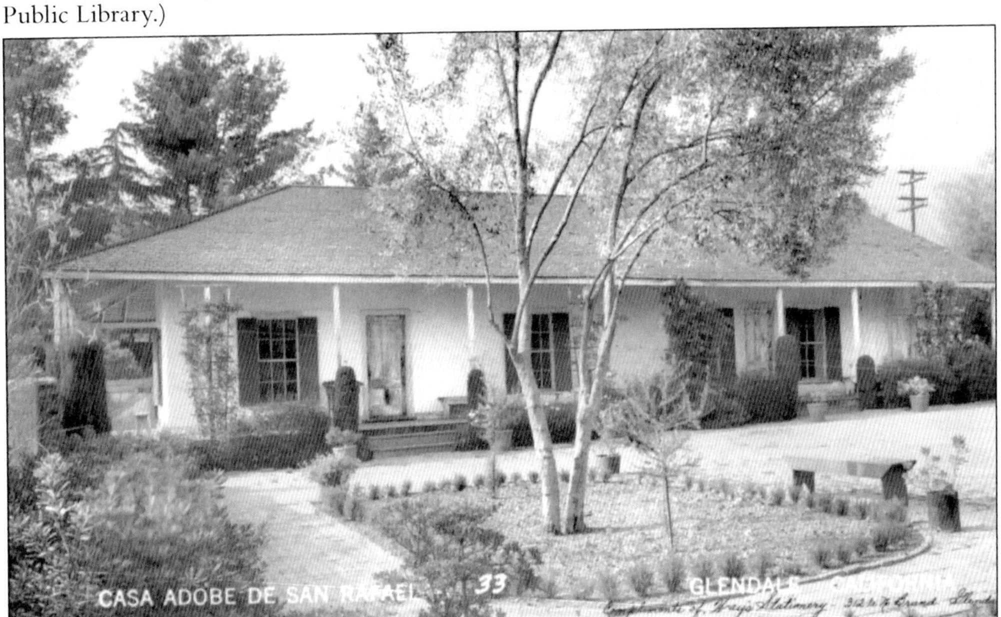

Tomas Sanchez and his wife, Maria, built Casa Adobe de San Rafael in 1870. A third-generation Californian, Sanchez served as sheriff of Los Angeles County from 1859 to 1867. The site is now a city-owned museum and park on Dorothy Drive. This postcard was published by the Angeleno Photo Service of Los Angeles around 1950. (Courtesy of the Special Collections Room, Glendale Public Library.)

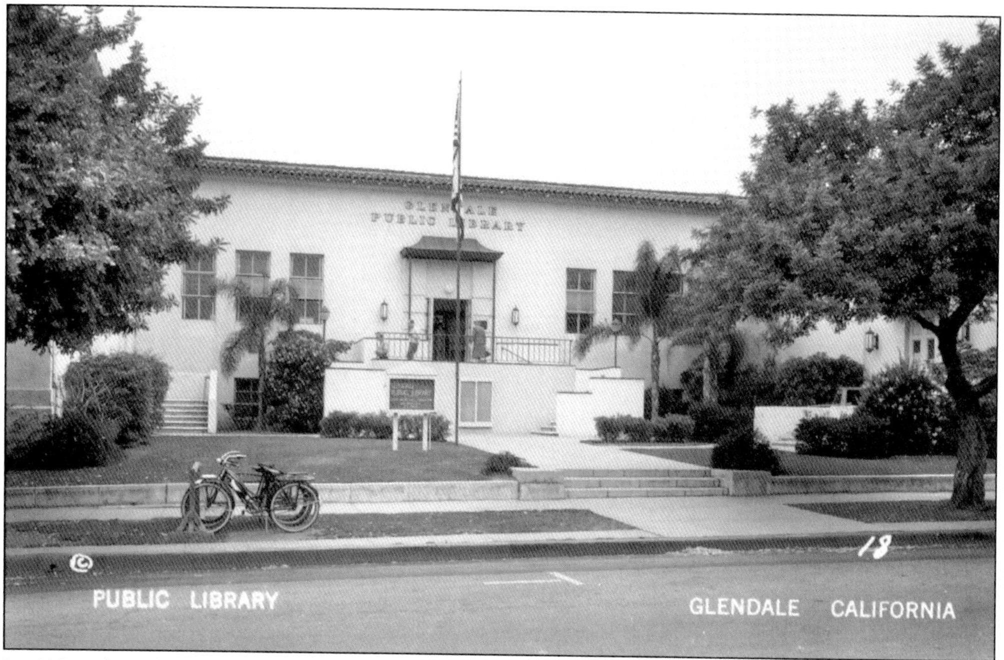

In 1926, the Glendale Public Library on Harvard Street was enlarged to create additional space along the rear of the building. By 1942, wings had been added on either side of the original structure, but space continued to be at a premium. A new library was built across the street in 1973. This postcard dates to about 1950. (Courtesy of the Special Collections Room, Glendale Public Library.)

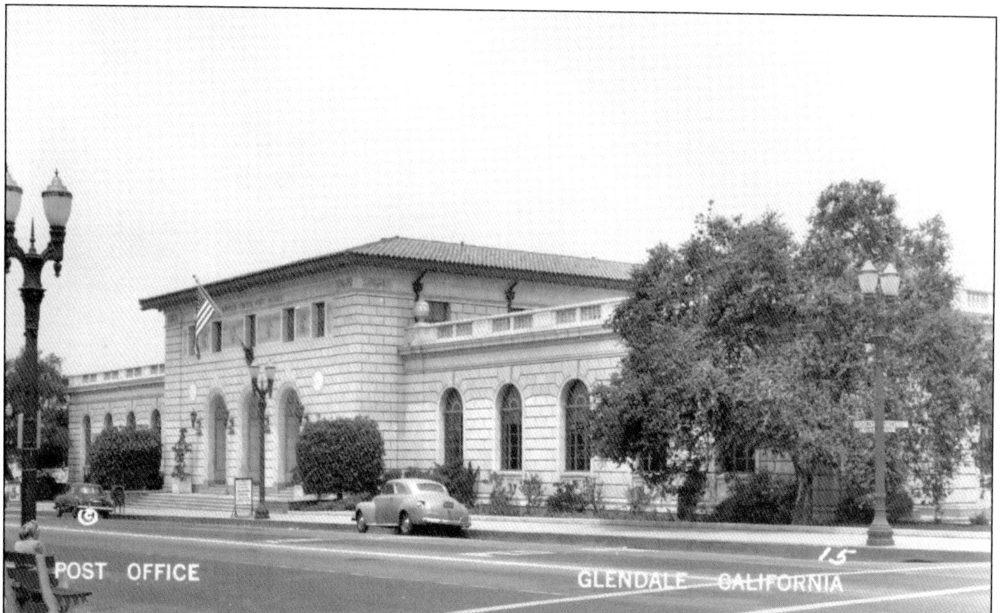

The U.S. Post Office, built on Broadway between Louise and Kenwood Streets, was completed in 1934. Max Green, who was appointed postmaster in 1935, served in that position until retiring in 1960 at age 70. This postcard was published by the Angeleno Photo Service of Los Angeles around 1950. (Courtesy of the Special Collections Room, Glendale Public Library.)

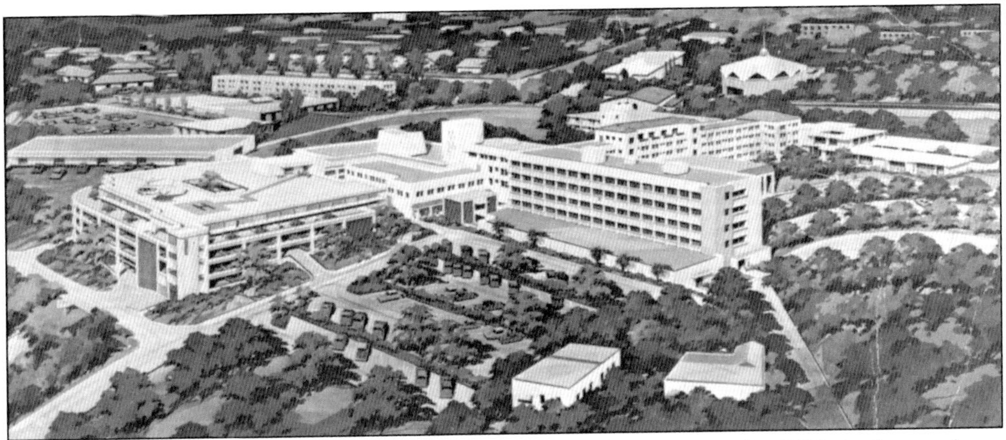

The Glendale Adventist Hospital, which opened on Wilson Terrace in 1924, is shown above in a *c.* 1967 artist's rendering of a planned expansion to 16 buildings. (Courtesy of the Special Collections Room, Glendale Public Library.)

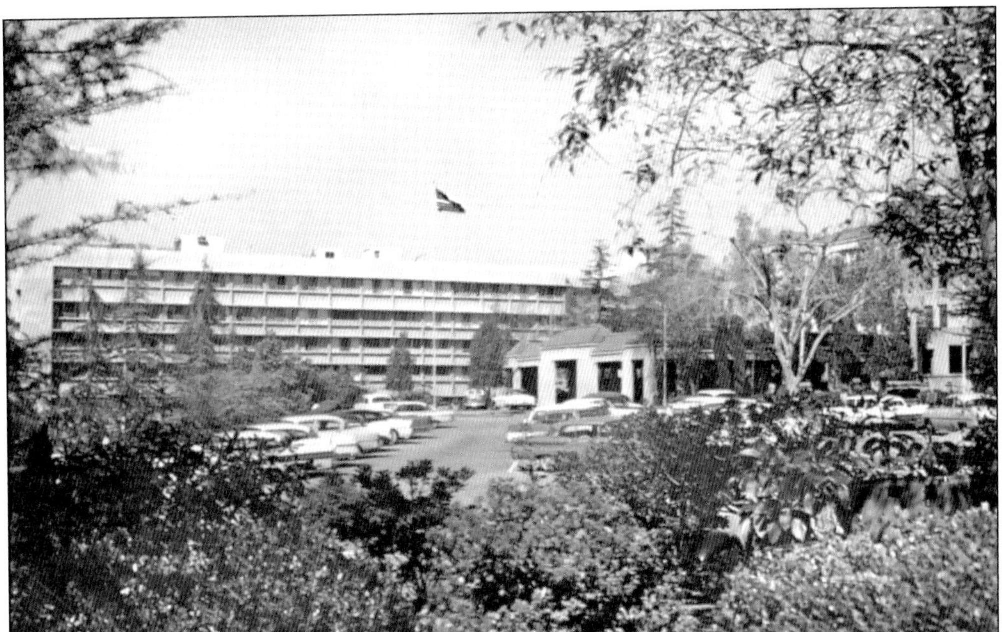

Set on 32 acres, the Glendale Adventist Hospital offered more than 300 beds in spacious rooms to meet the needs of their patients. (Courtesy of the Special Collections Room, Glendale Public Library.)

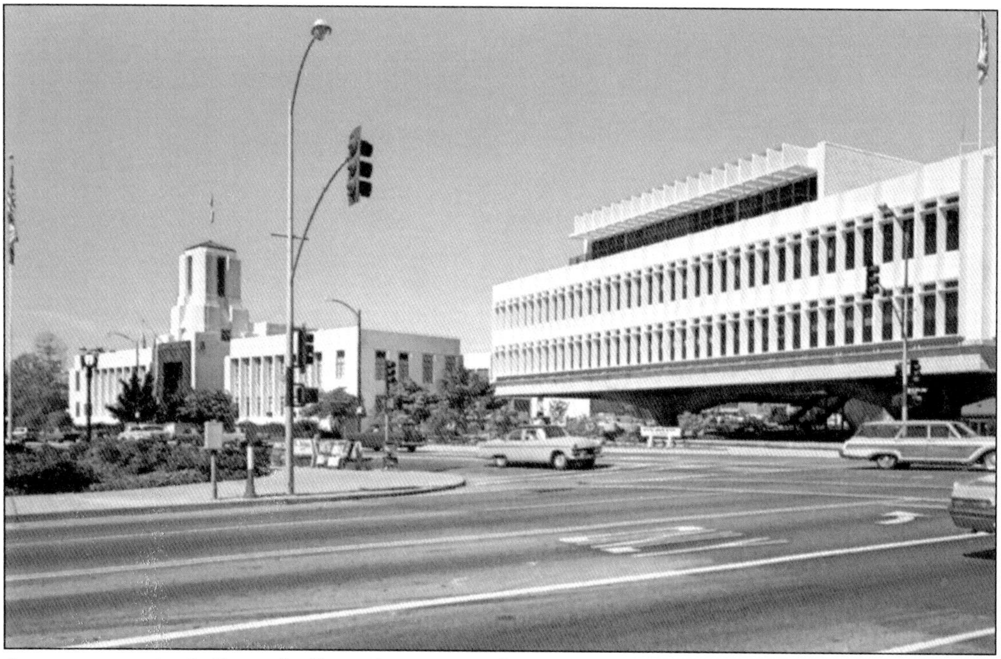

An annex to city hall was built at the corner of Broadway and Glendale Avenue in 1966. The futuristic-style municipal services building stands high above a public plaza. This postcard was published by Columbia Wholesale Supply of North Hollywood around 1967. (Courtesy of the George Ellison Collection.)

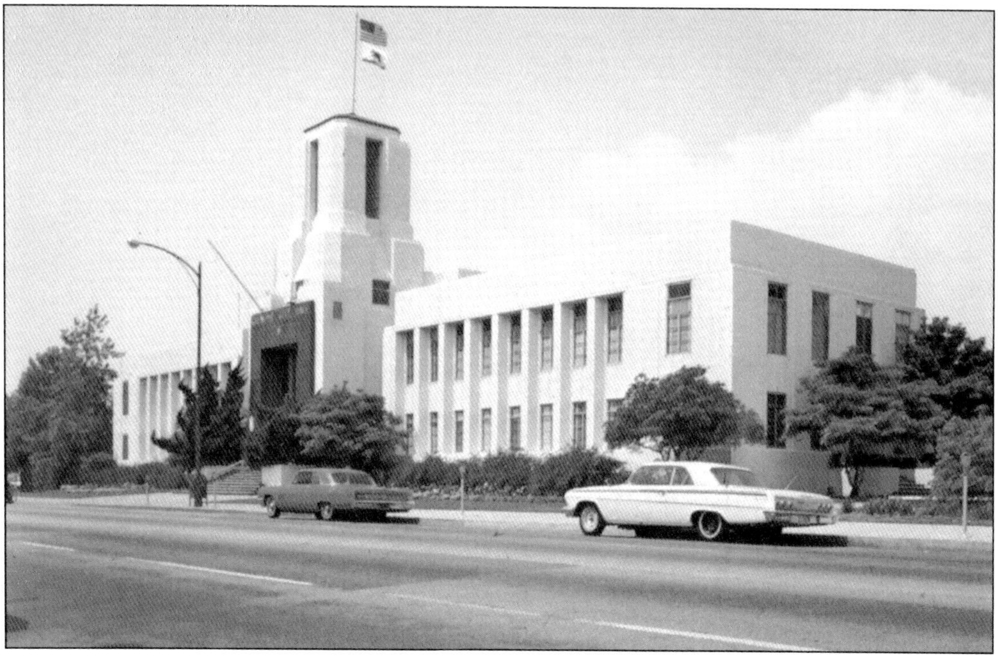

A new city hall was designed by Glendale architect Albert E. Hansen and constructed at 613 East Broadway between 1940 and 1942 by the Works Progress Administration. This postcard was published by the Western Publishing and Novelty Company of Los Angeles about 1967. (Courtesy of the George Ellison Collection.)

Four

Commercial Buildings

Glendale's most prominent commercial buildings were its banks, hotels, and theaters. The towering 1959 Glendale Federal Saving and Loan building rushed to establish Glendale as a banking center of California during a time when banking was becoming highly institutionalized. The building's movable aqua-blue fins were designed with light, temperature, and the environment in mind. Three of the four corners of Brand Boulevard and Broadway held the community's most substantial banks for a long period of time, and today the bank at the northeast corner is a remnant of that financial center.

Glendale did not have the grand lodgings found in Los Angeles and Pasadena, but the Hotel Glendale, the California Hotel, and the Maryland Hotel were premier hotels of the 1920s and provided an elegant image of a city that was not a tourist destination. The Hotel Glendale was rumored to have a speakeasy in the basement during Prohibition.

The Alexander Theatre was Glendale's most opulent theater, while smaller theaters along Brand Boulevard and throughout the neighborhoods gave residents many movie-viewing options. The city had a large number of movie theaters compared to other California communities of the same size. Glendale's spot as an early filming location and as a home to some large studios, along with its idyllic residential base, may be the reason for this disproportion. Nearly all of the neighborhood theaters are gone today, but the Alex Theatre was rehabilitated in the early 1990s, at a time when redevelopment was the norm. Commercial buildings in Glendale have not been grand; they were established primarily to serve the local residents. In the 1950s and 1960s, stylish, one-story, low-profile coffee shops, bowling alleys, and motels continued to serve local residents and the surroundings.

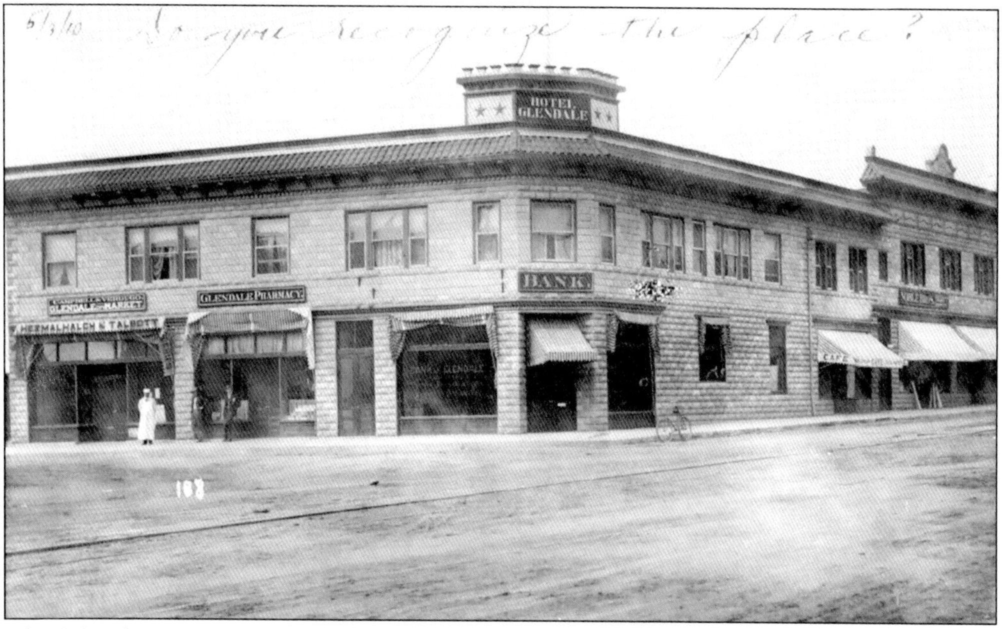

Glendale's first intersection, at Wilson and Glendale Avenues, held the city's first bank, first hotel, and a post office (the first to bear the Glendale name). A lumberyard, livery, and barber were also nearby. (Courtesy of the Special Collections Room, Glendale Public Library.)

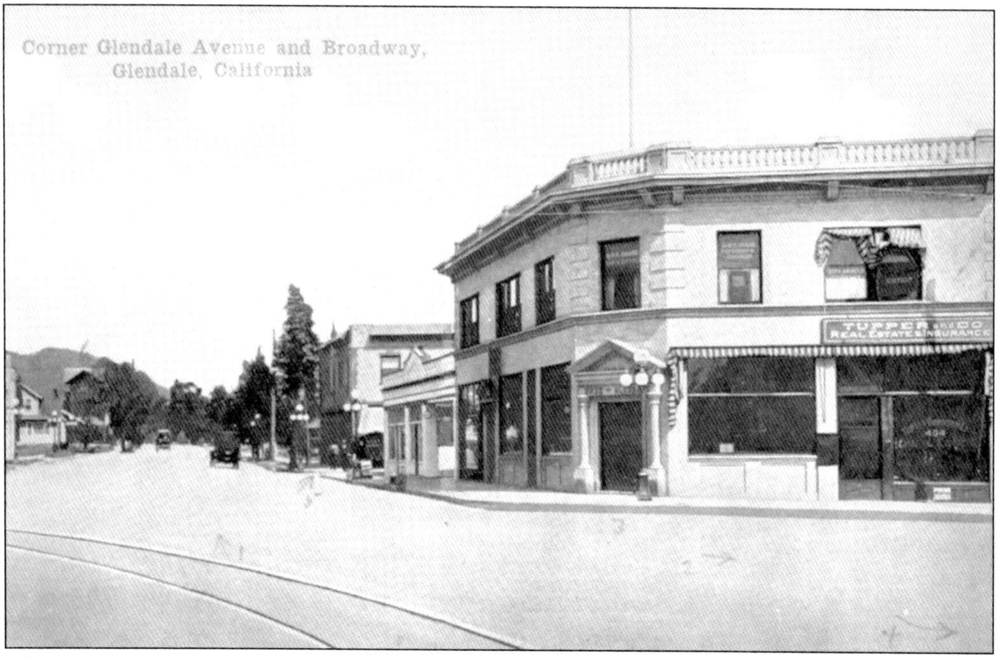

The Bank of Glendale built a two-story structure at the southeast corner of Glendale Avenue and Broadway in 1909. This postcard was published by the Van Ornum Colorprint Company of Los Angeles around 1919. (Courtesy of the Special Collections Room, Glendale Public Library.)

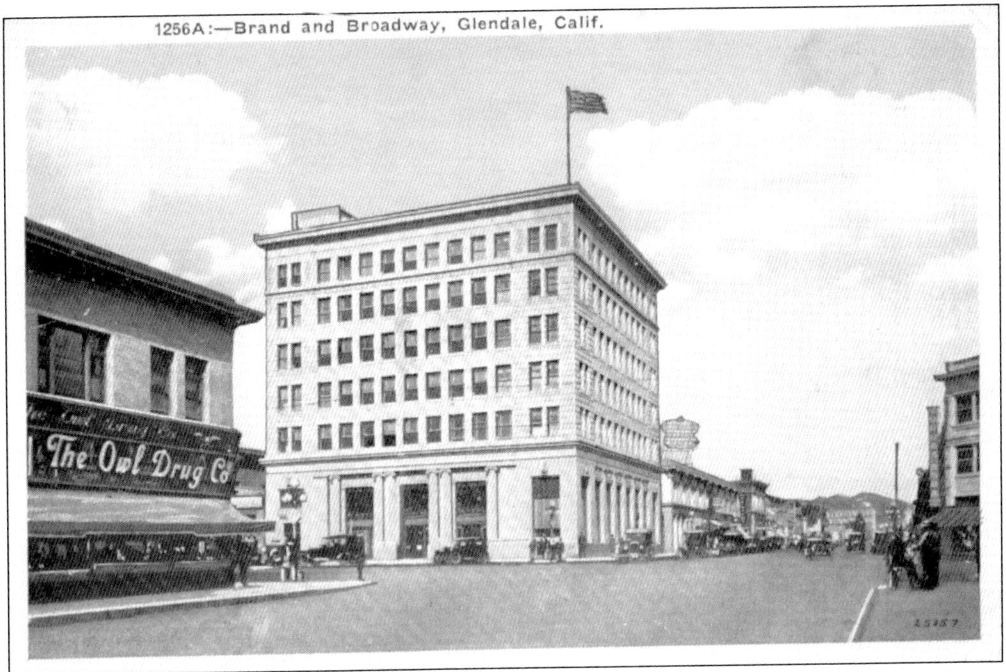

Constructed at Brand Boulevard and Broadway in 1924, the Security Trust and Savings Bank was the city's first six-story building. It later became the Security First National Bank. The ground floor of the 1911 Rudy Building (opposite) was occupied by a series of drugstores, including the Owl Drug Company. This postcard view, looking east on Broadway, was published by the M. Kashower Company of Los Angeles. (Courtesy of the George Ellison Collection.)

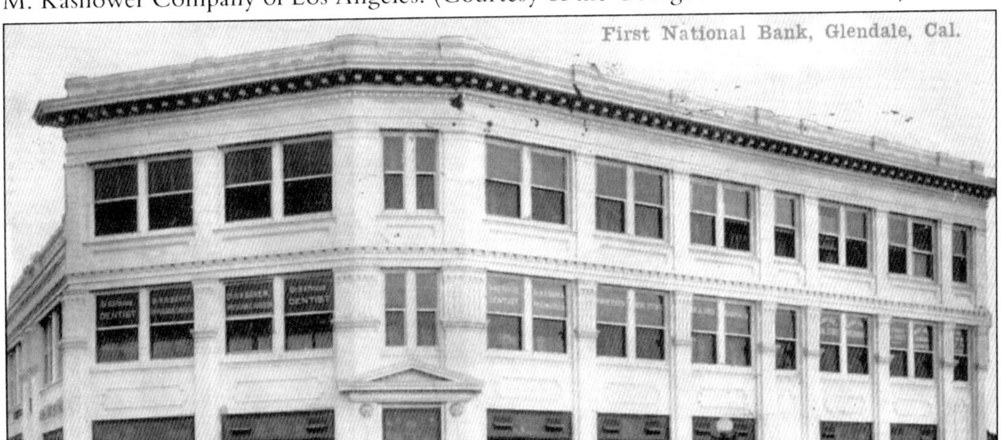

The First National Bank of Glendale, with Leslie C. Brand as the principal stockholder, was the second bank to open in the city. The bank later moved to the pictured location at the corner of Brand Boulevard and Broadway. This postcard was published by the Van Ornum Colorprint Company of Los Angeles about 1922. (Courtesy of the Bruce B. Herman Collection.)

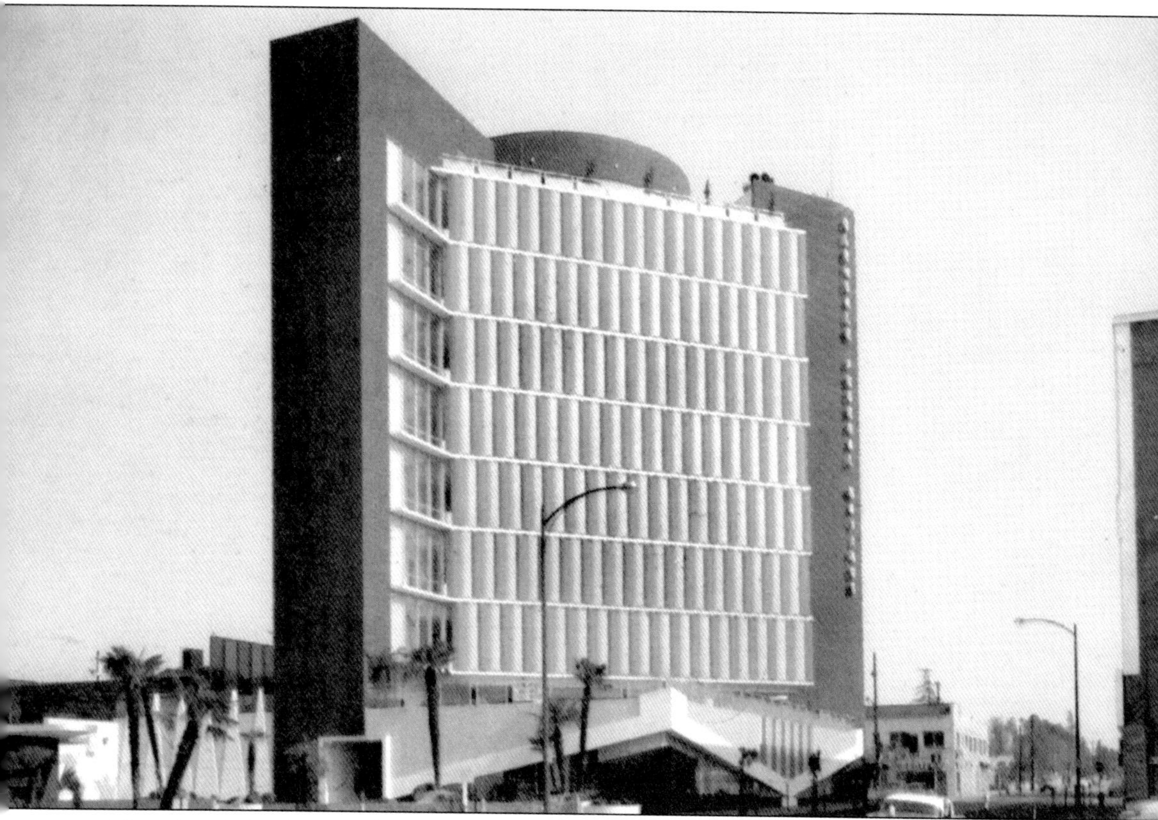

The Glendale Federal Savings and Loan Association's flagship building was designed by W. A. Sarmiento and opened on Brand Boulevard in 1959. Distinctive, blue-enameled mechanical louvers controlled the interior light. A lighted Christmas tree topped the building from 1962 until the early 1980s. This postcard dates to about 1960. (Courtesy of the George Ellison Collection.)

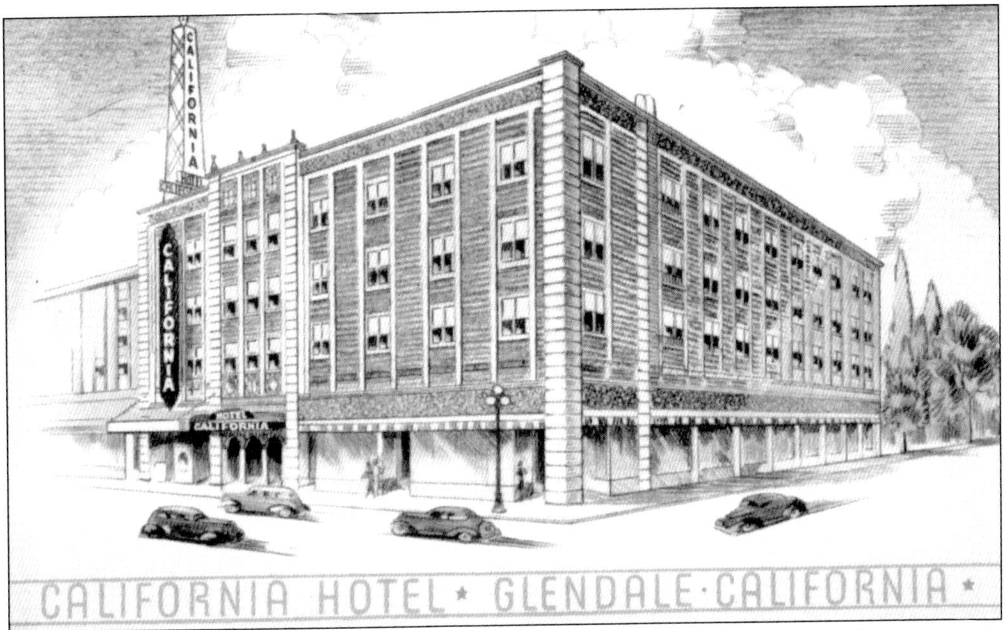

Operated by the Eastman Hotel Company, the Hotel California offered an adjacent movie theater providing entertainment for guests and the public alike. This postcard was published by B. R. Montgomery of Riverside. (Courtesy of the Special Collections Room, Glendale Public Library.)

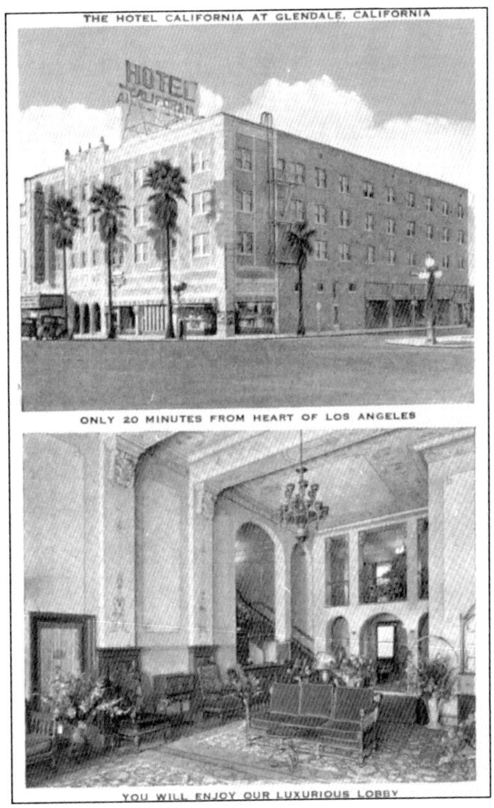

The Hotel California, at the corner of Brand Boulevard and Lexington Drive, advertised itself as Glendale's "newest and finest" hotel with steam heat, good ventilation, and a location only 20 minutes from the heart of Los Angeles. (Courtesy of the Bruce B. Herman Collection.)

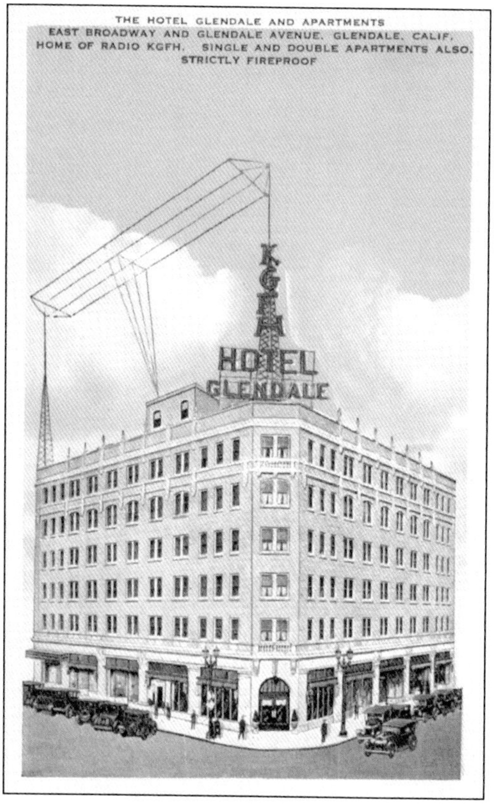

The Hotel Glendale, standing at the corner of Glendale Avenue and Broadway, was also the home of KGFH radio from 1927 to 1929. This postcard was published by B. R. Montgomery of Riverside around 1929. (Courtesy of the Special Collections Room, Glendale Public Library.)

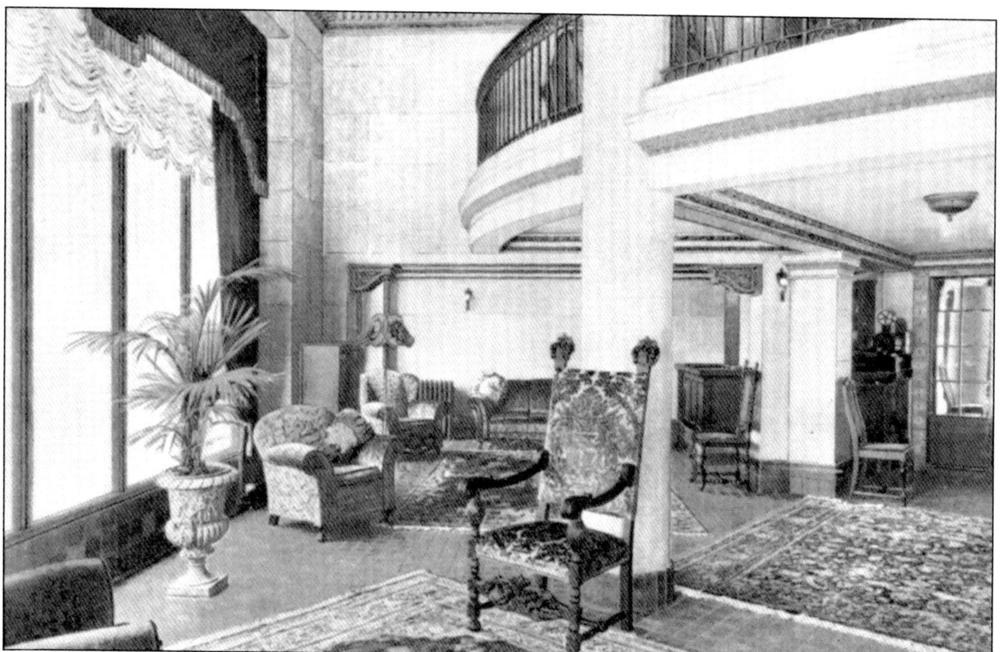

The expansive lobby of the Hotel Glendale set it apart from the many hotels constructed in the suburbs of Los Angeles during the 1920s. This postcard was published by the Neuner Corporation of Los Angeles. (Courtesy of the Special Collections Room, Glendale Public Library.)

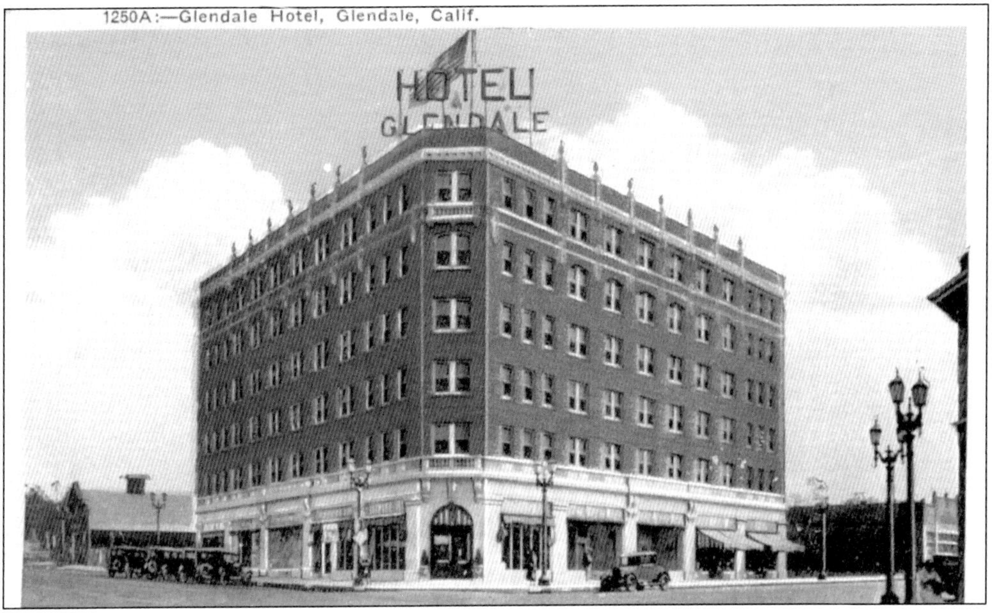

Charles W. Ingledue and his associates built the Hotel Glendale in 1924. Ingledue, a businessman and civic leader, served on the city's charter committee in the early 1920s and on the board of the Merchant's Association in 1940. This postcard was published by the M. Kashower Company of Los Angeles about 1927. (Courtesy of the Special Collections Room, Glendale Public Library.)

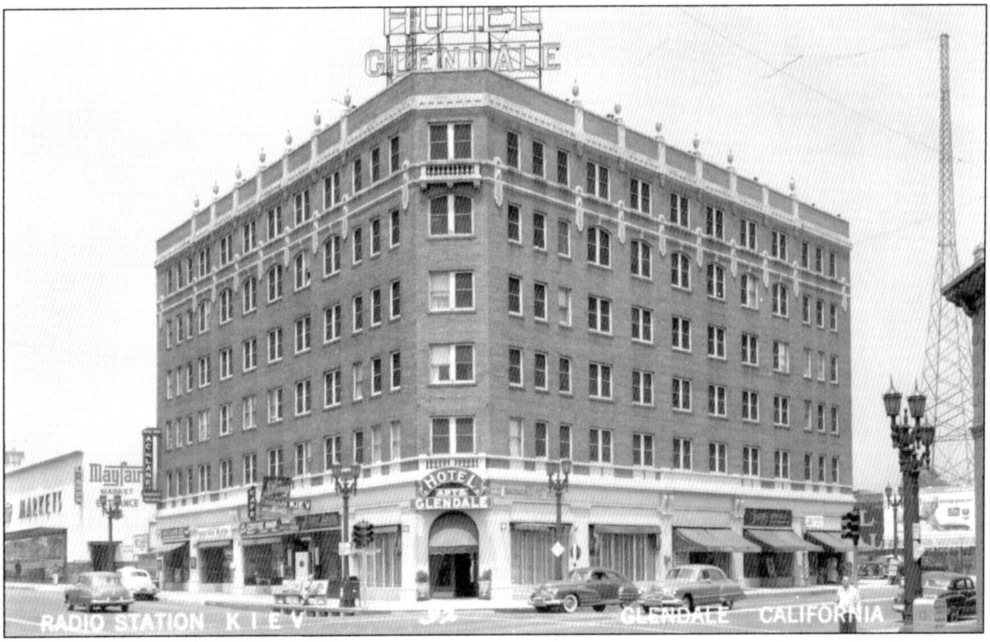

Owned by Reed Callister and David Cannon, the radio station KIEV was located in the Hotel Glendale's basement for 30 years. The station came on the air in 1931, and its twin steel towers, purchased from KNX, soon became a local landmark. This postcard was published by the Angeleno Photo Service of Los Angeles around 1950. (Courtesy of the Special Collections Room, Glendale Public Library.)

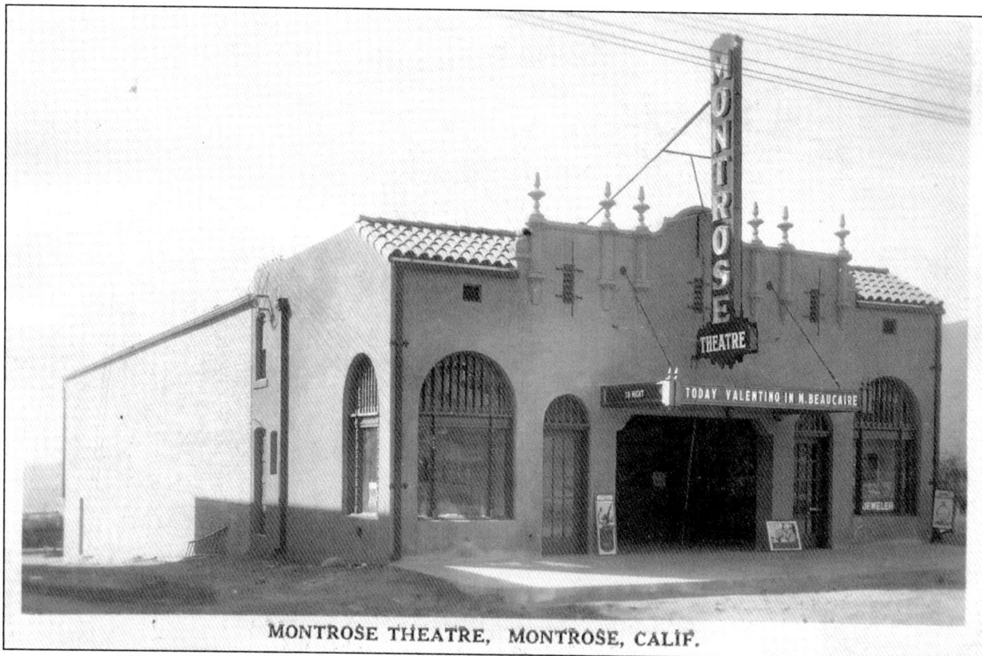

Montrose merchants, seeking to bring residents to Honolulu Avenue, built the Montrose Theatre, which held its grand opening in October 1924. The Spanish-style theater offered Saturday matinees for 10 to 15¢. (Courtesy of the Special Collections Room, Glendale Public Library.)

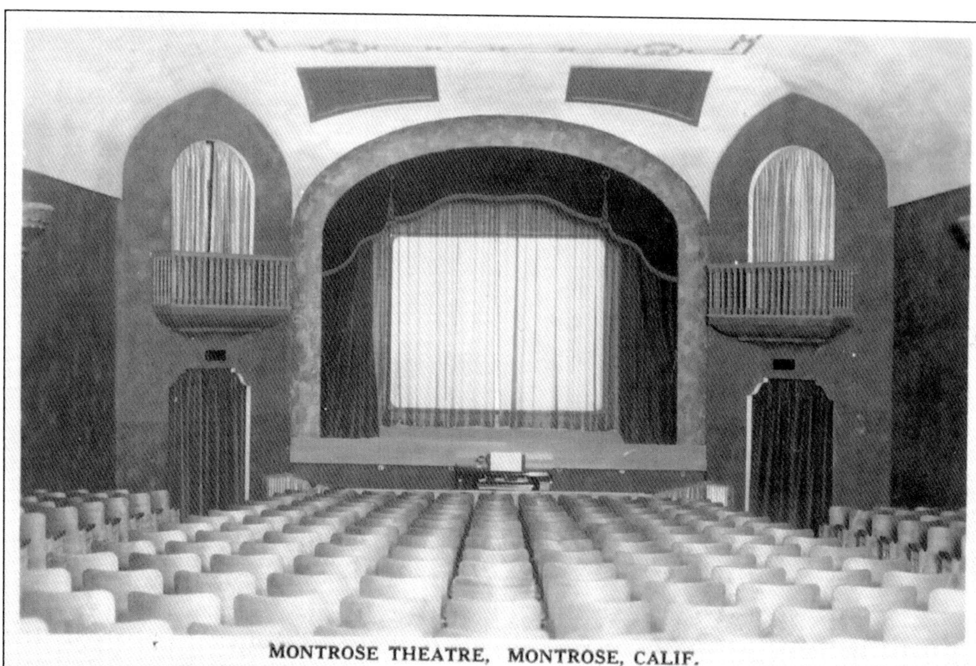

The interior of the Montrose Theatre, decorated in shades of blue and orange, was also designed for vaudeville shows. It offered local residents a place for fashion shows, cooking classes, and town events. (Courtesy of the Special Collections Room, Glendale Public Library.)

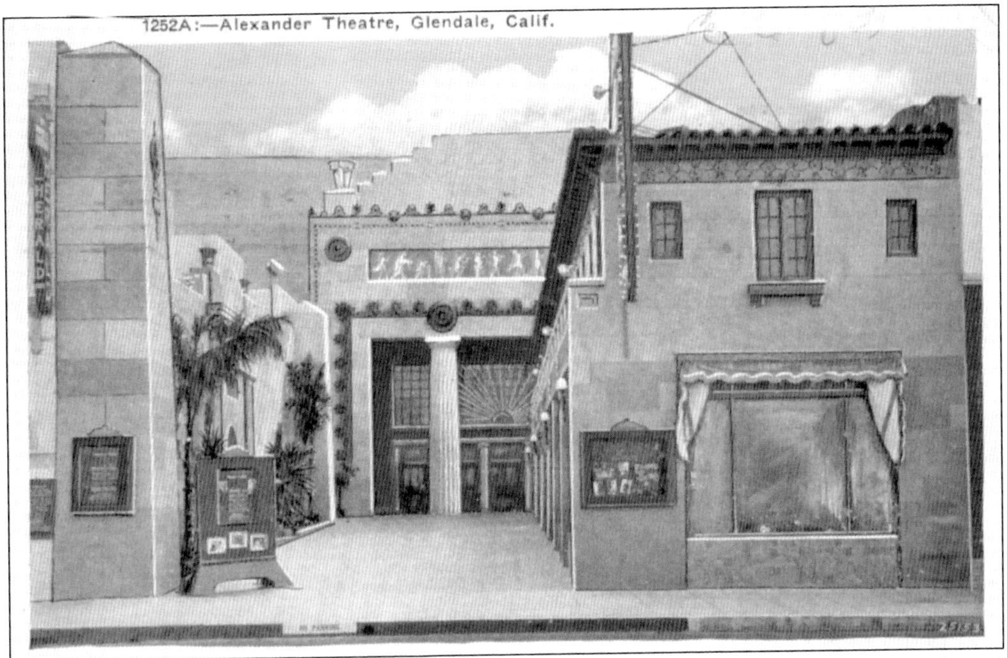

A row of shops lined the entrance to the Alexander Theatre, which opened on Brand Boulevard in 1925. Designed in a neo-Greek and Egyptian style, it was named after Alexander Langley, the son of an official in the Langley Theater chain. This postcard was published by the M. Kashower Company of Los Angeles about 1926. (Courtesy of the Bruce B. Herman Collection.)

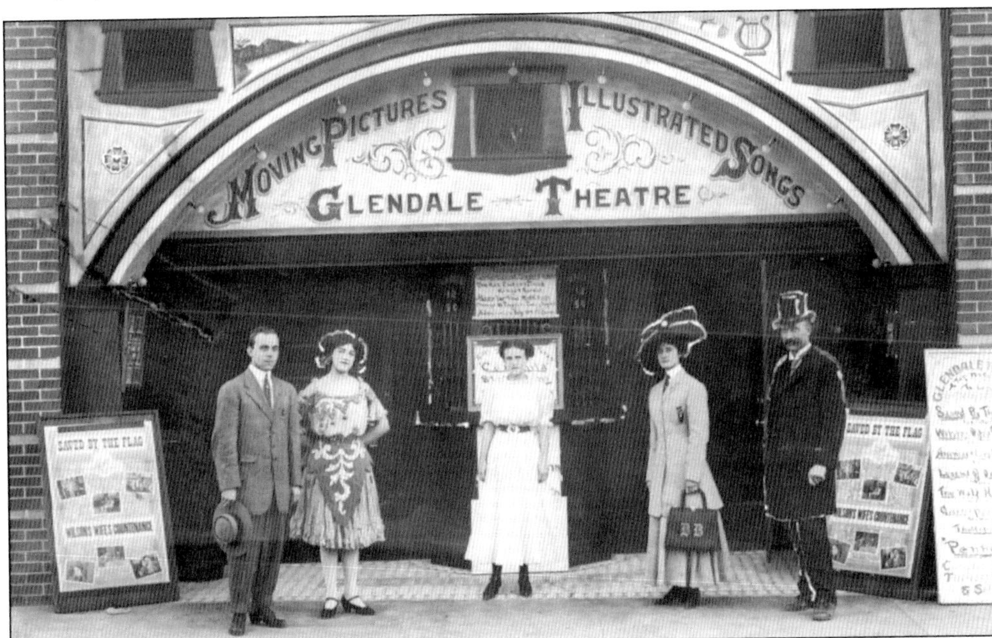

Opening in 1910, the Glendale Theatre stood on Broadway near Isabel Street and across from the Victorian-style Glendale Hotel. It was owned and managed by Bush family members, pictured here. The theater closed in 1914, when the new Palace Grand Theatre proved to be too much competition. (Courtesy of the Special Collections Room, Glendale Public Library.)

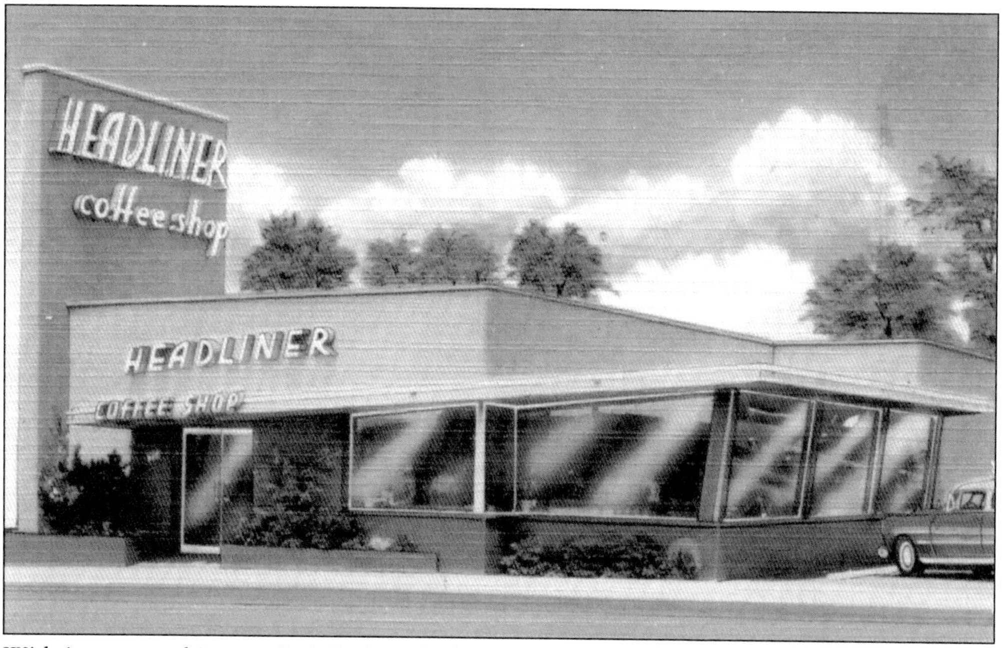

With its eye-catching vertical signboard, the Headliner Coffee Shop at 915 Glendale Avenue was designed to capture the attention of passing motorists. The late modern Googie style was also used in other local coffee shops. This postcard was published by Colorpicture. (Courtesy of the George Ellison Collection.)

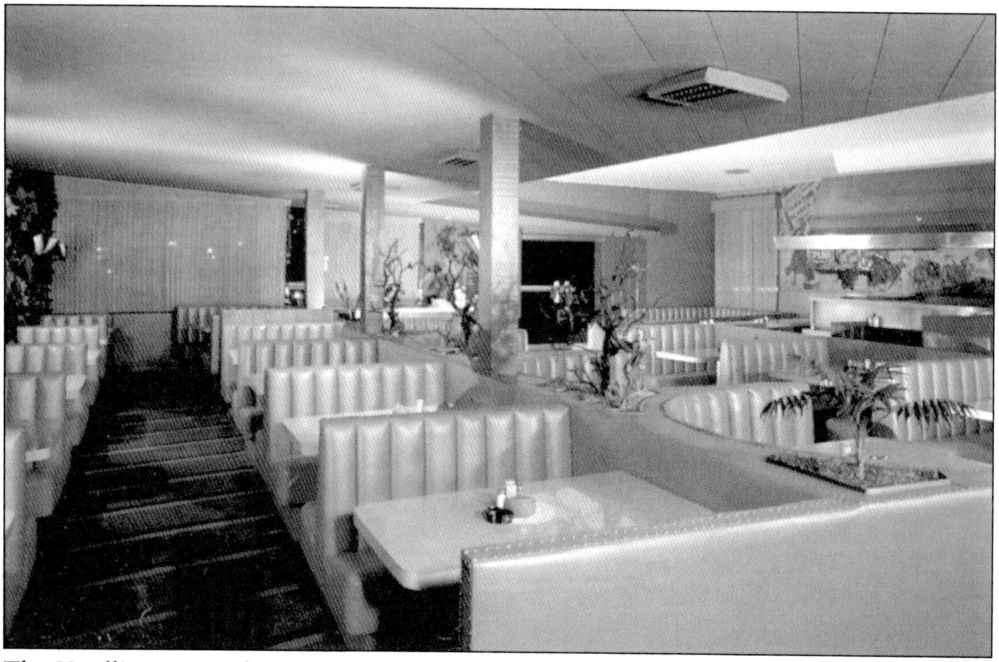

The Headliner covered one of its interior walls with newspaper, in keeping with its name. The red Naugahyde-vinyl-upholstered booth benches were typical of coffee shops of that era. This postcard was published by the Mellinger Studio of Altadena. (Courtesy of the George Ellison Collection.)

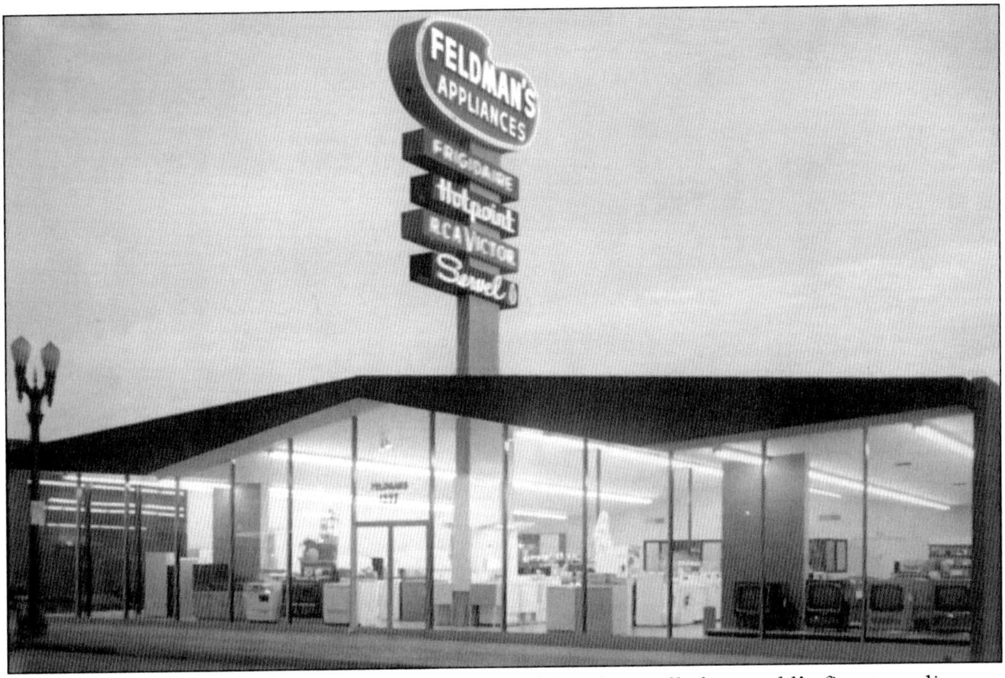

Feldman's Appliance Store on Colorado Street claimed to sell the world's finest appliances, televisions, furniture, and carpeting at the world's lowest prices. This postcard was published by the Mellinger Studio of Altadena. (Courtesy of the George Ellison Collection.)

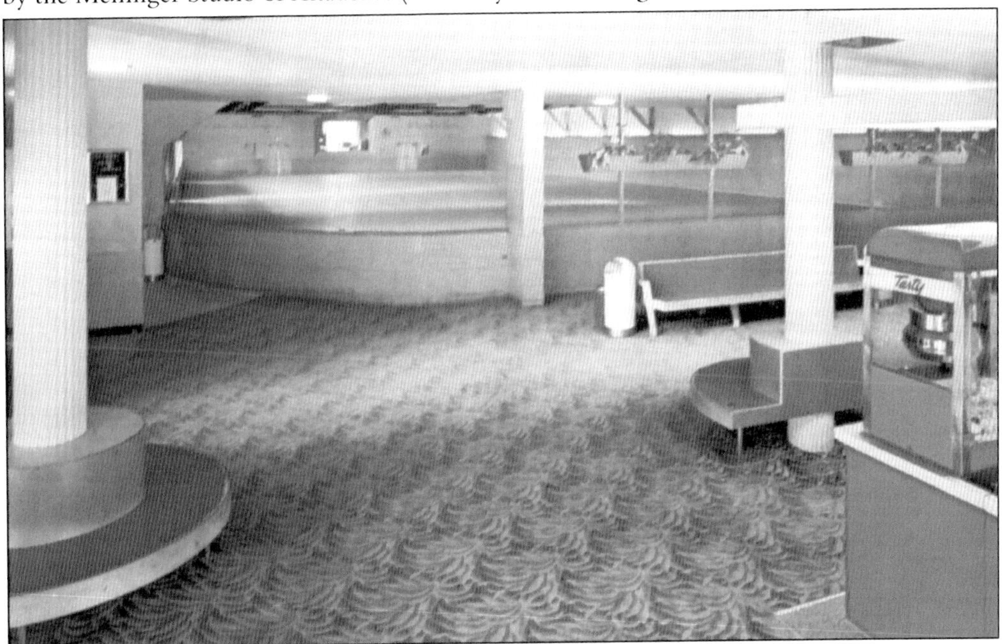

Constructed in the 1940s as a foundry for World War II aircraft parts, this building was converted to Harry's Roller Rink in 1950. With a 170-by-70-foot maple floor that was 2.5 inches thick, Harry's, on San Fernando Road, was considered one of the finest roller rinks on the West Coast. It later became Moonlight Rollerway. This postcard was published by the Mellinger Studio of Altadena around 1958. (Courtesy of the Bruce B. Herman Collection.)

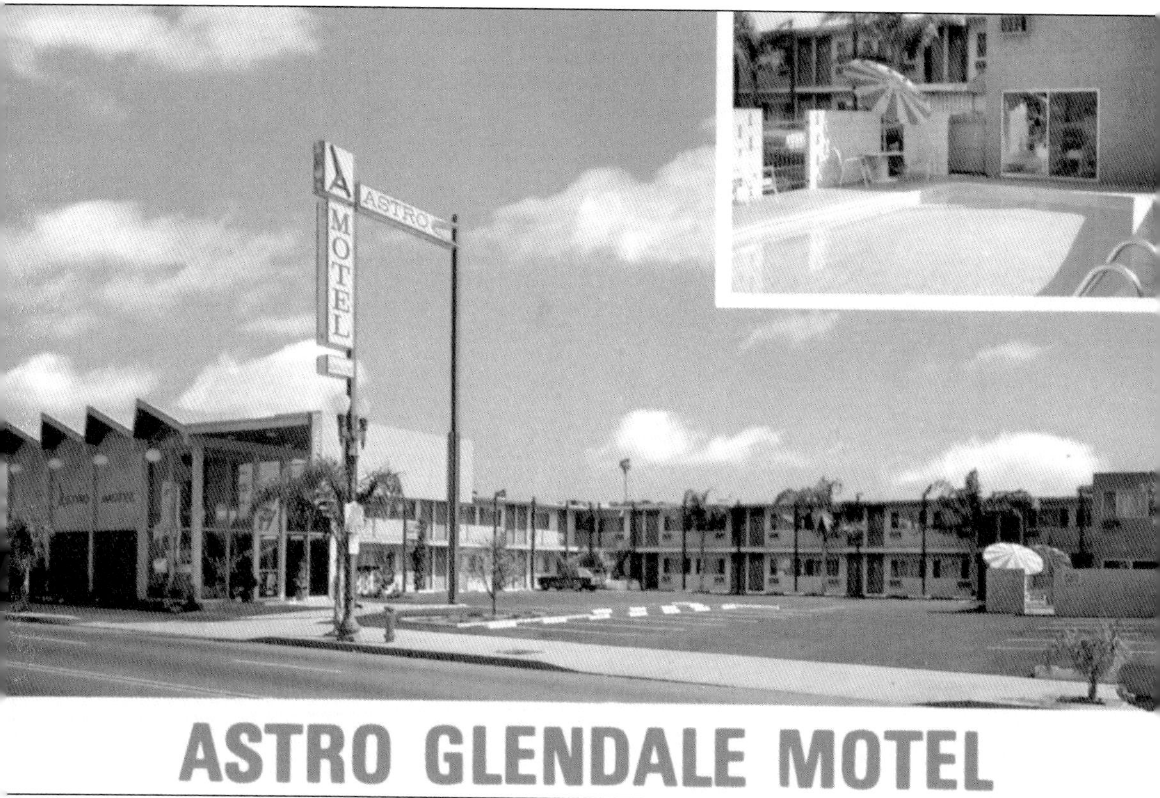

The Astro Motel on Colorado Street, with its futuristic signage, fins, space-age lettering, and colorful paint scheme, typified the Googie style. Before the advent of the freeways, Colorado Street was an important travel corridor from Route 66 to Glendale and held many roadside motels. (Courtesy of the Juliet M. Arroyo Collection.)

Five

Street Scenes and Brand Boulevard

Broadway, originally named Fourth Street, and Glendale Avenue provided the first commercial center for the city. Commercial development along Broadway surpassed commercial development along Glendale Avenue, and by the second decade of the 20th century, Broadway was completely developed. The section between Brand Boulevard and Glendale Avenue contained two-story brick buildings with offices and shops. Many of the structures that remained into the 1960s were lost during the Sylmar earthquake of 1971 or through modern redevelopment. Postcard views of various sparsely developed neighborhoods during the early 1900s were very common, showing nice tree-lined streets with uniform street curbs and houses that sat off walkways.

Brand Boulevard competed with Broadway as Glendale's main street until 1921, when the newness of Brand brought together everyone across the city, including residents from neighboring Montrose and La Crescenta. Entertainment and shopping destinations lined both sides of the wide avenue, while the Pacific Electric cars headed south to downtown Los Angeles or north up and over to northern Glendale and west to Burbank. Brand Boulevard was named in honor of Leslie C. Brand, Glendale's flamboyant booster, who had the capital to provide the tiny town with the infrastructure needed to expand.

The first buildings on the street emerged in 1905, and within 10 years, the commercial center was radiating out from the Brand Boulevard and Broadway intersection. By 1955, the electric streetcars had left Glendale to be replaced by buses and cars as the remaining transportation mode. By the 1960s and 1970s, new shopping centers across the Los Angeles area took shoppers away from Brand Boulevard's main street appeal only to be lured back by redevelopment in the 1980s. Brand Boulevard was always a popular postcard view, representing Glendale from 1908 to the 1970s.

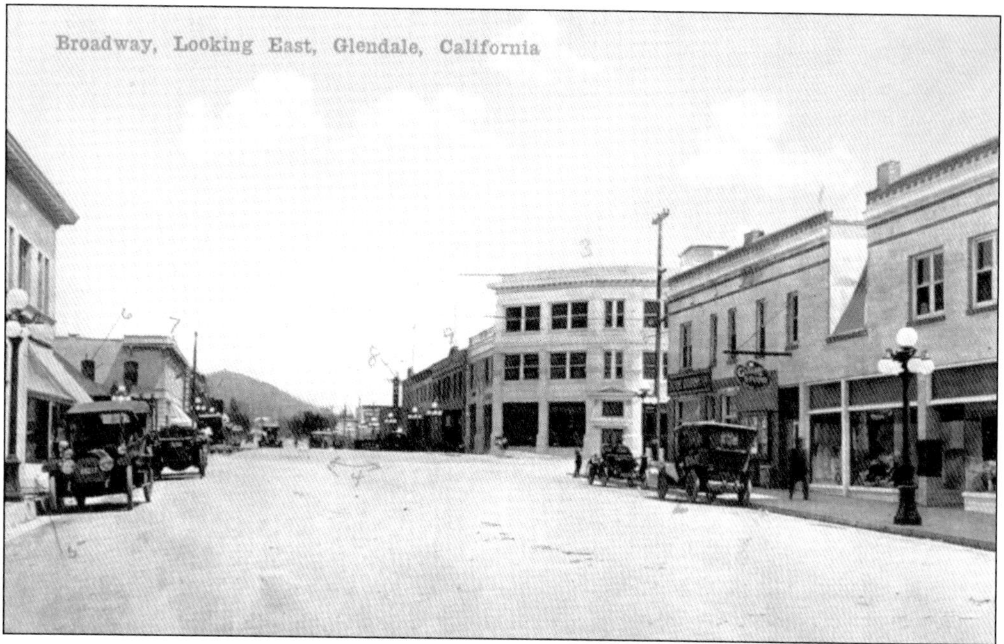

Broadway, seen in this eastward view toward Brand Boulevard, was originally called Fourth Street. It was renamed to reflect its status as one of the few "broad ways" in town. This postcard was published by the Van Ornum Colorprint Company of Los Angeles about 1917. (Courtesy of the Special Collections Room, Glendale Public Library.)

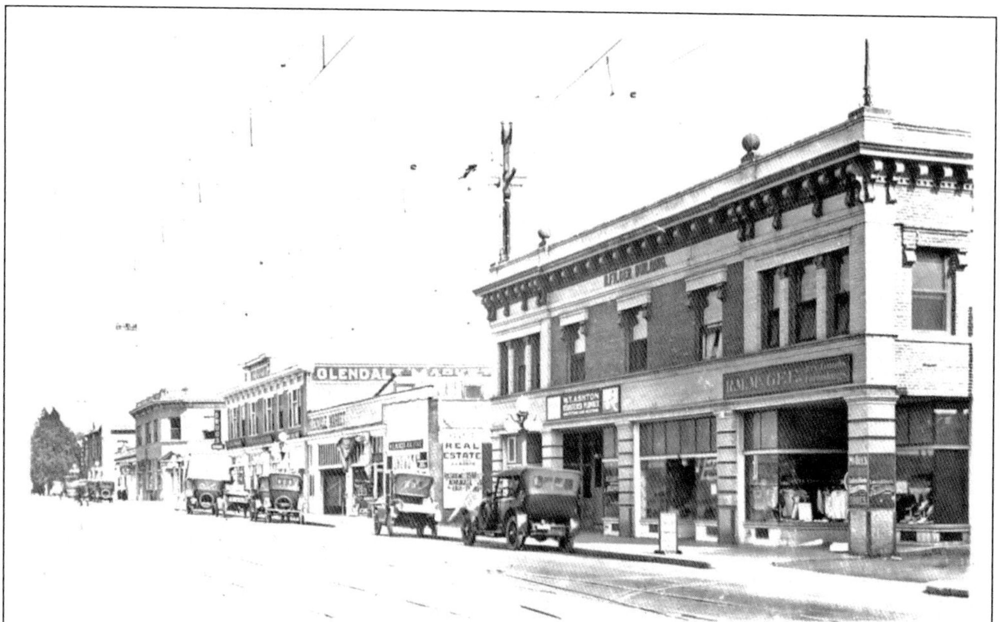

Looking east along the south side, this *c.* 1921 view of Broadway reveals that the street was home to a variety of businesses, including the substantial Filger Building. The Glendale Market was one of the few markets in town. (Courtesy of the Special Collections Room, Glendale Public Library.)

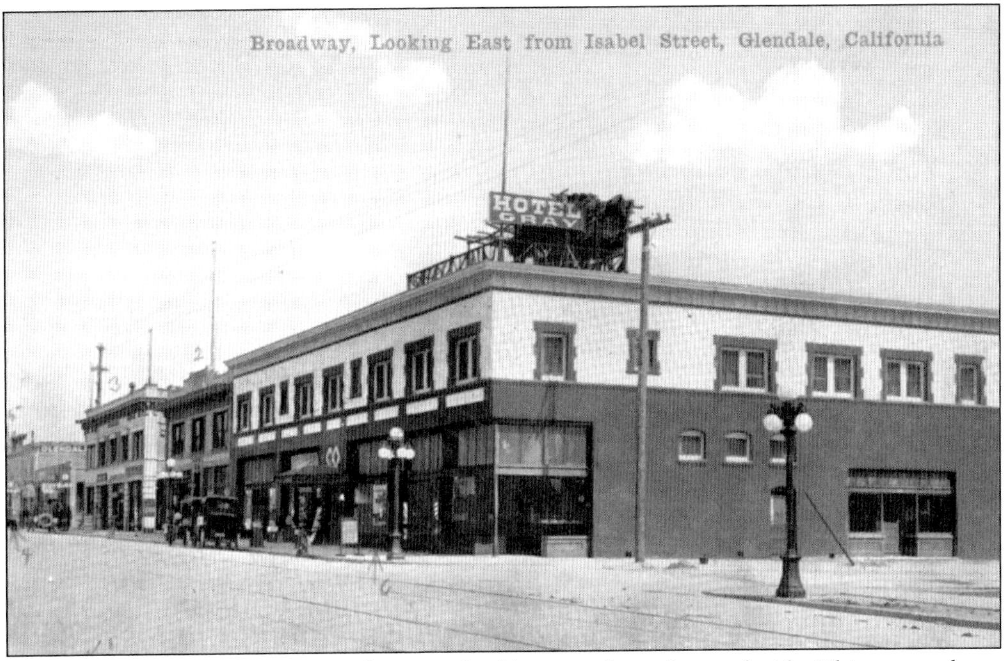

Streetcar tracks line Broadway in this view, looking east along the south side. This postcard was published by the Van Ornum Colorprint Company of Los Angeles around 1919. (Courtesy of the Special Collections Room, Glendale Public Library.)

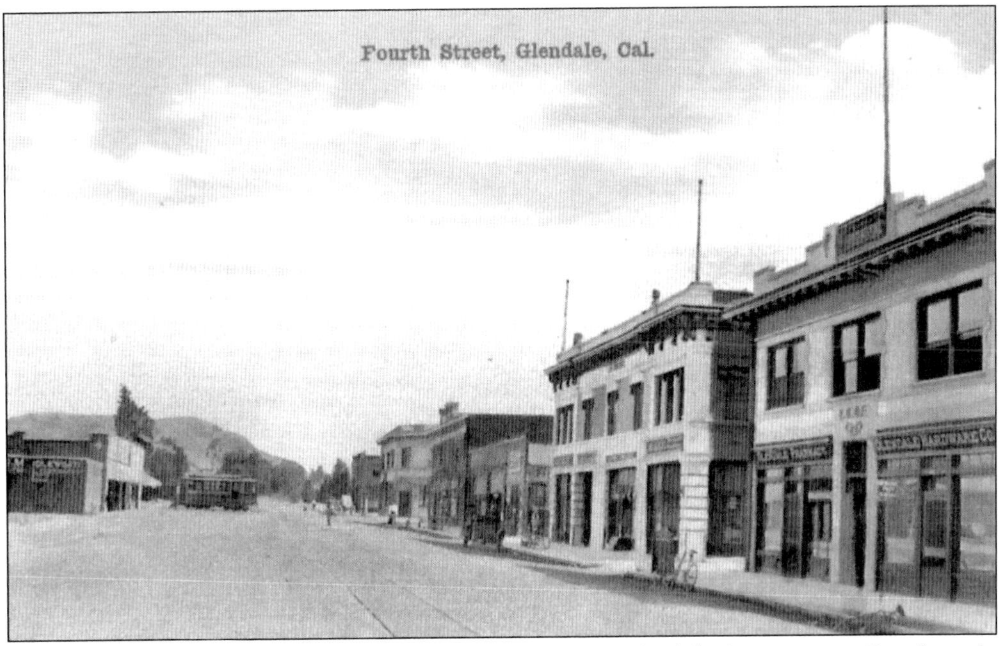

Glendale and Eagle Rock No. 1 rounds the corner from Glendale Avenue onto Broadway in this *c.* 1911 eastward view. Cars on that line traveled between the two cities via Colorado Street, Wilson and Glendale Avenues, and Broadway, terminating at Brand Boulevard. (Courtesy of the Glendale Historical Society.)

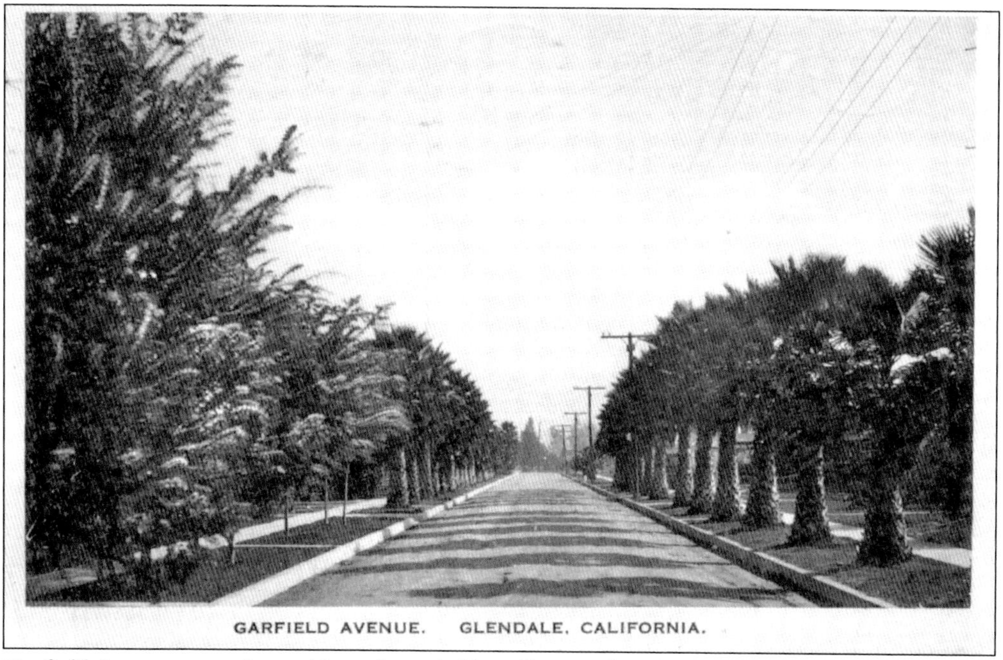

Garfield Avenue, complete with curbs and sidewalks, was lined with palms and other trees that nearly hid the homes. This postcard was published by the Western Publishing and Novelty Company of Los Angeles about 1920. (Courtesy of the Special Collections Room, Glendale Public Library.)

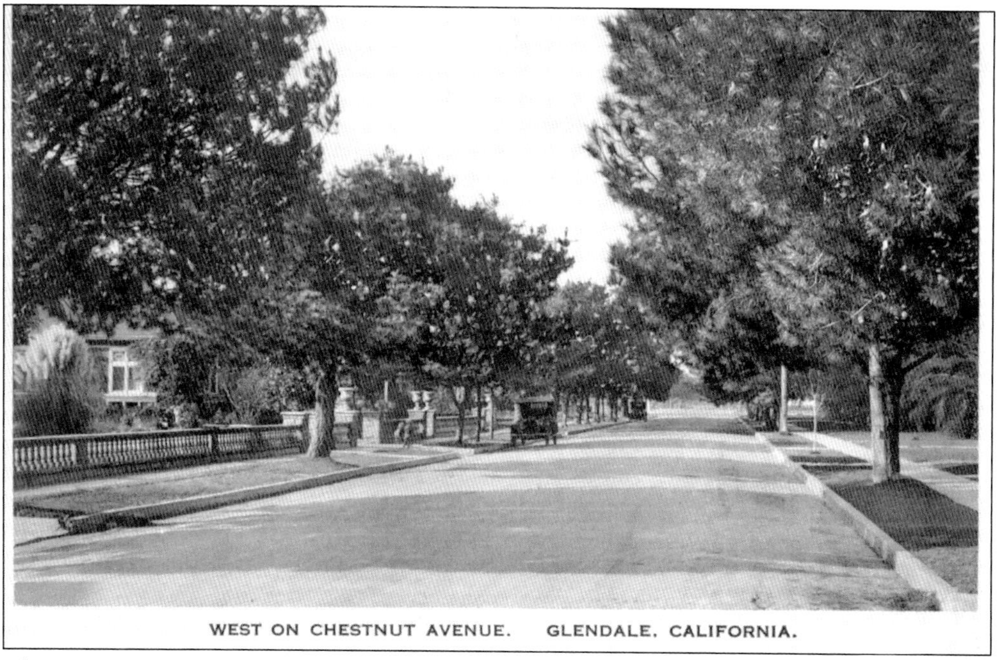

Chestnut Street, which ran east and west from South Brand Boulevard, was one of the many new streets being laid out around town that were named for trees or plants. This postcard was published by the Western Publishing and Novelty Company of Los Angeles around 1920. (Courtesy of the Special Collections Room, Glendale Public Library.)

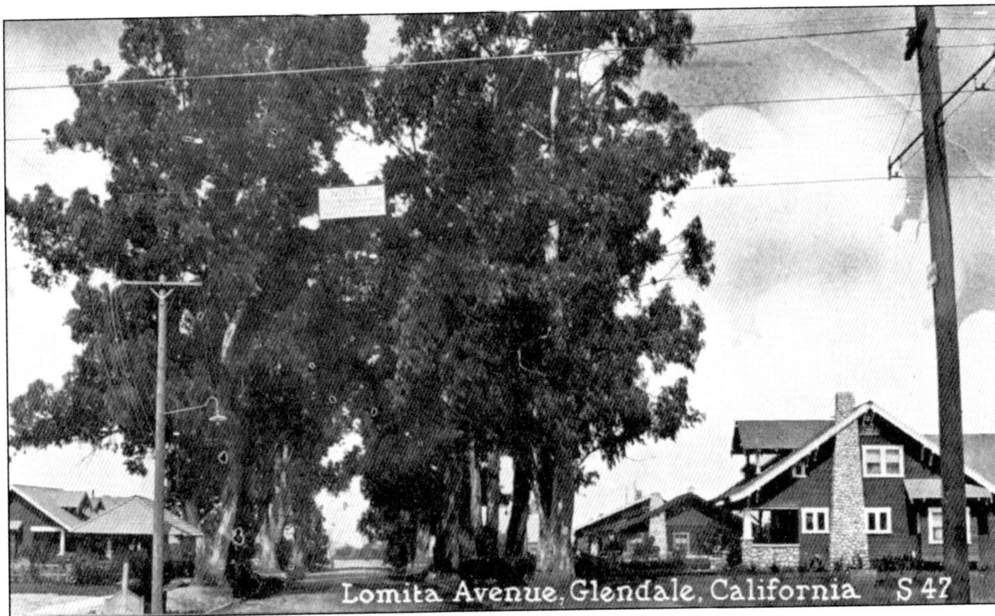

Lomita Avenue was lined with eucalyptus trees that had been planted by rancher Harry Crow in 1875. A severe windstorm in 1926 felled many of the trees. One of the city's oldest streets, Lomita appears on early regional survey maps. This postcard was published by the Souvenir Publishing Company around 1915. (Courtesy of the Special Collections Room, Glendale Public Library.)

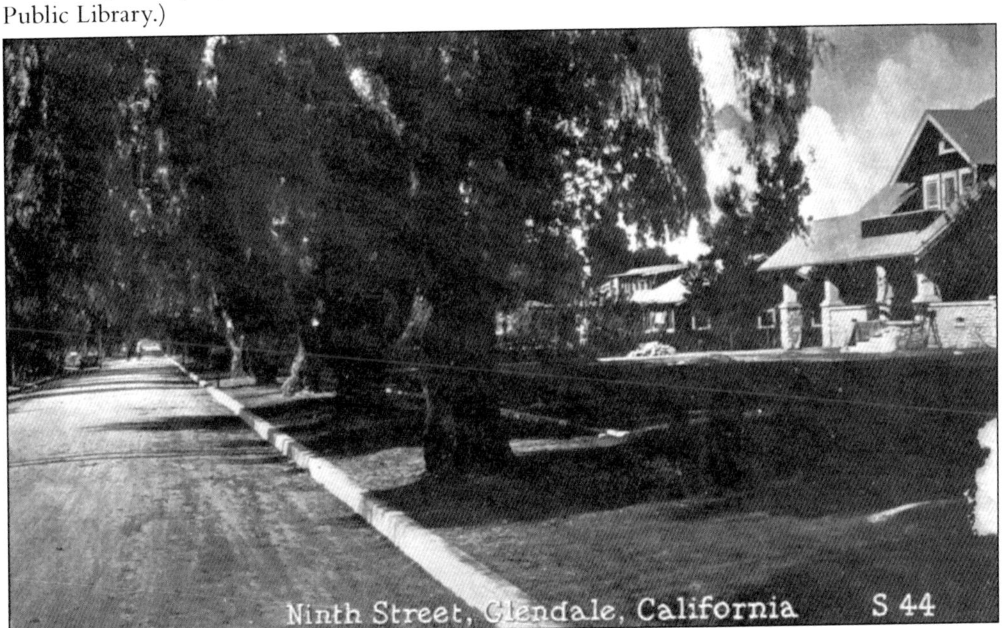

Ninth Street was renamed Windsor Road in 1918 during a movement to replace numbered streets with place names as the cities of Glendale and Tropico merged. An Englishwoman proposed that it be named for the Windsor family of England. Somerset Farms, the home of Glendale pioneer J. C. Sherer, was located on Windsor near Verdugo Road. This postcard was published by the Souvenir Publishing Company about 1915. (Courtesy of the Bruce B. Herman Collection.)

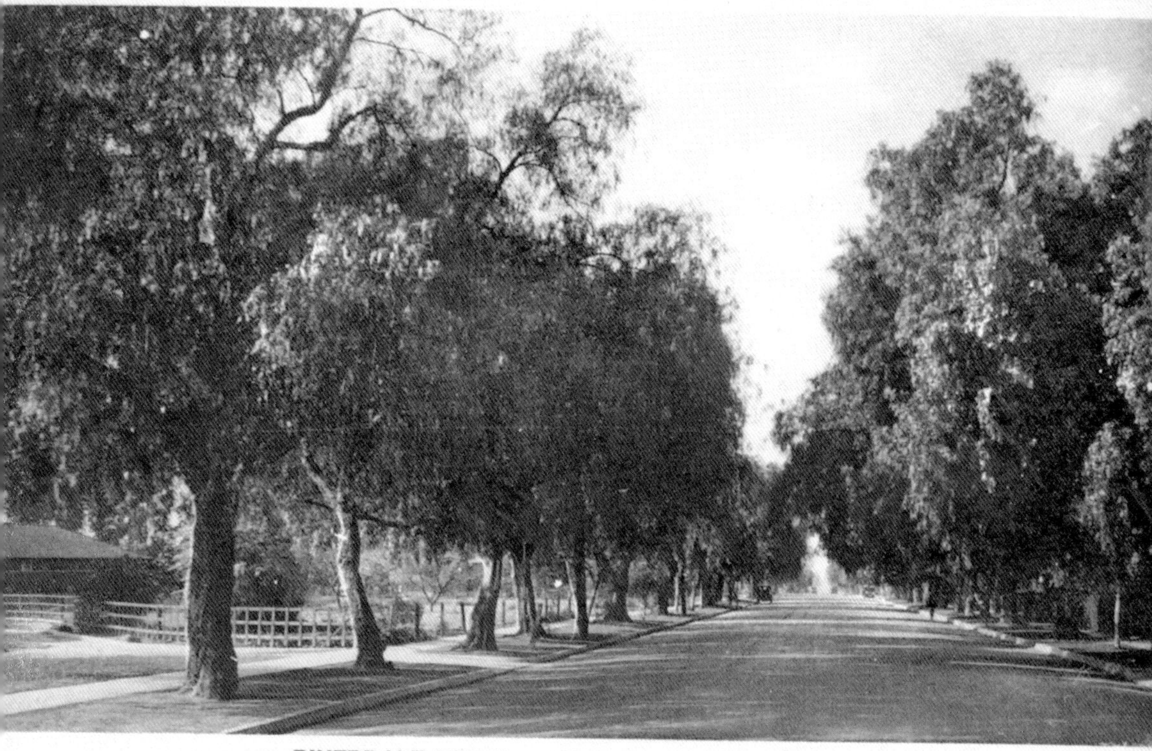

RIVERDALE DRIVE. GLENDALE, CALIFORNIA.

One of the city's earliest tracts was named Riverdale Heights, inspiring the naming of Riverdale Drive, which runs east and west and terminates at San Fernando Road, adjacent to the Los Angeles River. At the start of the 20th century, the Riverdale tract offered parcels from one to three acres priced from $700 to $1,500. The terms were one-third down, with the balance due monthly over a period of two years. The area's first school was also named Riverdale. Built in 1883, it was renamed the Cerritos Avenue School in 1913 to distinguish it from two new schools being constructed in the area. This postcard was published by the Western Publishing and Novelty Company of Los Angeles around 1920. (Courtesy of the Special Collections Room, Glendale Public Library.)

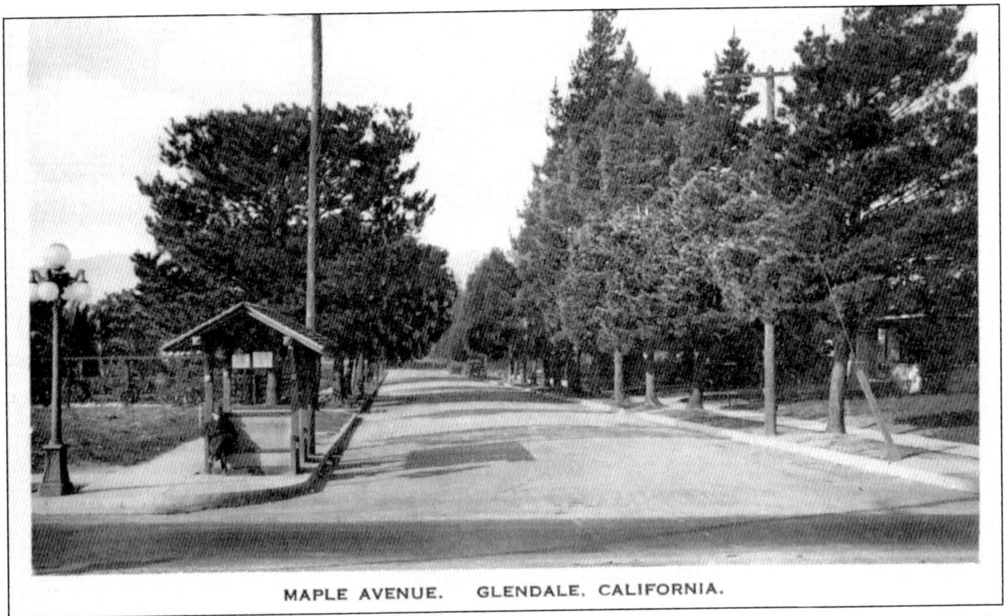

A passenger waits for the streetcar at the corner of Brand Boulevard and Maple Street. Maple was one of the southernmost streets in the new city of Glendale, which incorporated in 1906. The street runs from Pacific Avenue all the way to the city's eastern border (east of Verdugo Road). This postcard was published by the Western Publishing and Novelty Company of Los Angeles about 1920. (Courtesy of the Bruce B. Herman Collection.)

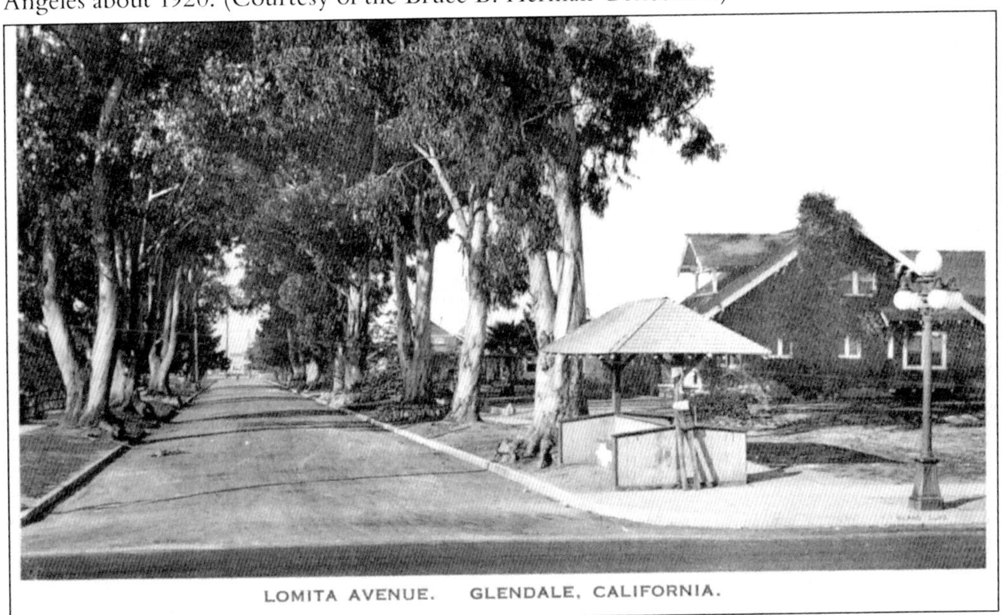

Lomita Avenue became known as an artists' colony due to the number of actors who lived there. Helen Holmes, the star of *The Hazards of Helen*, produced by the Kalem Company in 1914 and filmed in Glendale, lived in one of the street's many charming homes. For relaxation, Holmes often rode her palomino horse along the banks of the Los Angeles River. This postcard was published by the Western Publishing and Novelty Company of Los Angeles around 1920. (Courtesy of the Bruce B. Herman Collection.)

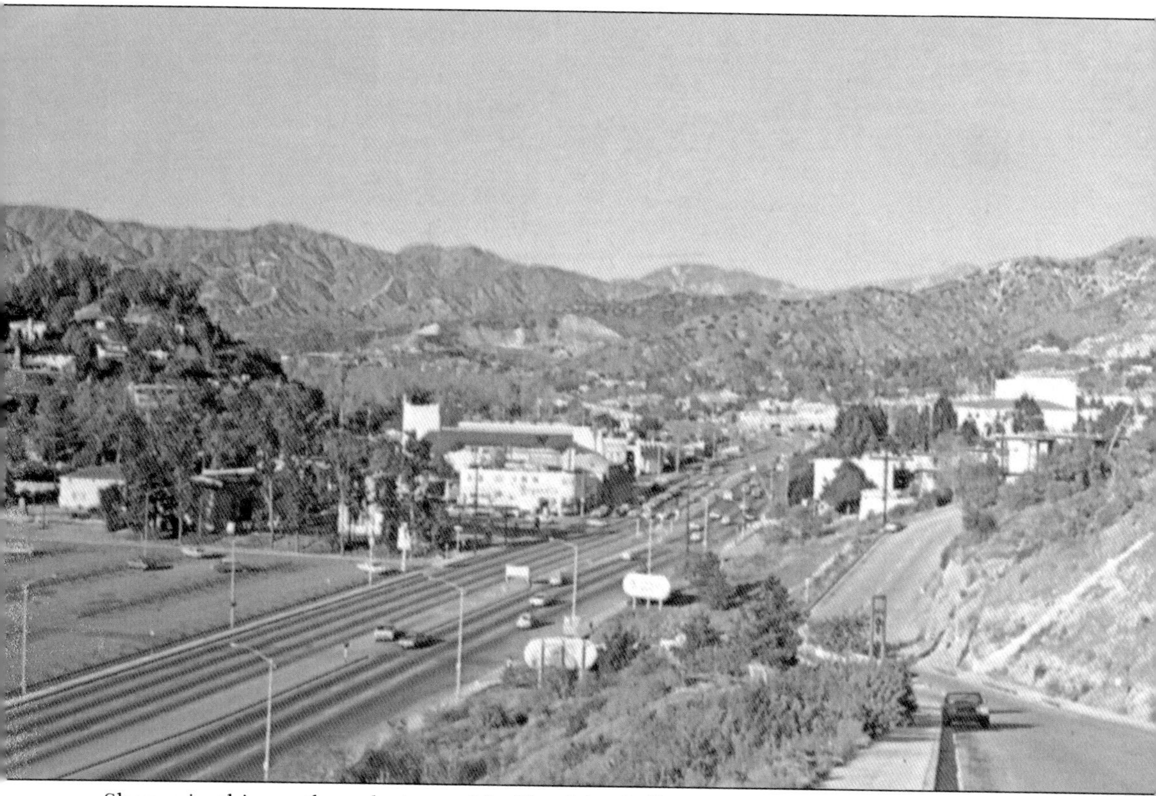

Shown in this northward view with Glendale College on the right, Verdugo Road is one of the city's oldest thoroughfares. It was named for Jose Maria Verdugo, a native son of the Mexican town of Loreto. Verdugo, a soldier in the service of the king of Spain and stationed at the San Gabriel Mission, applied for permission to graze his cattle and horses in this area. Permission was granted in 1784, and the Verdugos later built a series of adobes throughout their land grant, which included much of what is now Glendale, Burbank, Eagle Rock, Highland Park, and a portion of Pasadena. Verdugo cultivated grapes, made wine, and grew fruit trees and vegetables. The rancho was between the missions of San Gabriel and San Fernando, and travelers were often met by an armed guard headed by a member of the Verdugo family. The escort protected them from grizzly bears, wild horses, and other animals roaming the rancho's hills. This postcard was published by Columbia Wholesale Supply of North Hollywood. (Courtesy of the George Ellison Collection.)

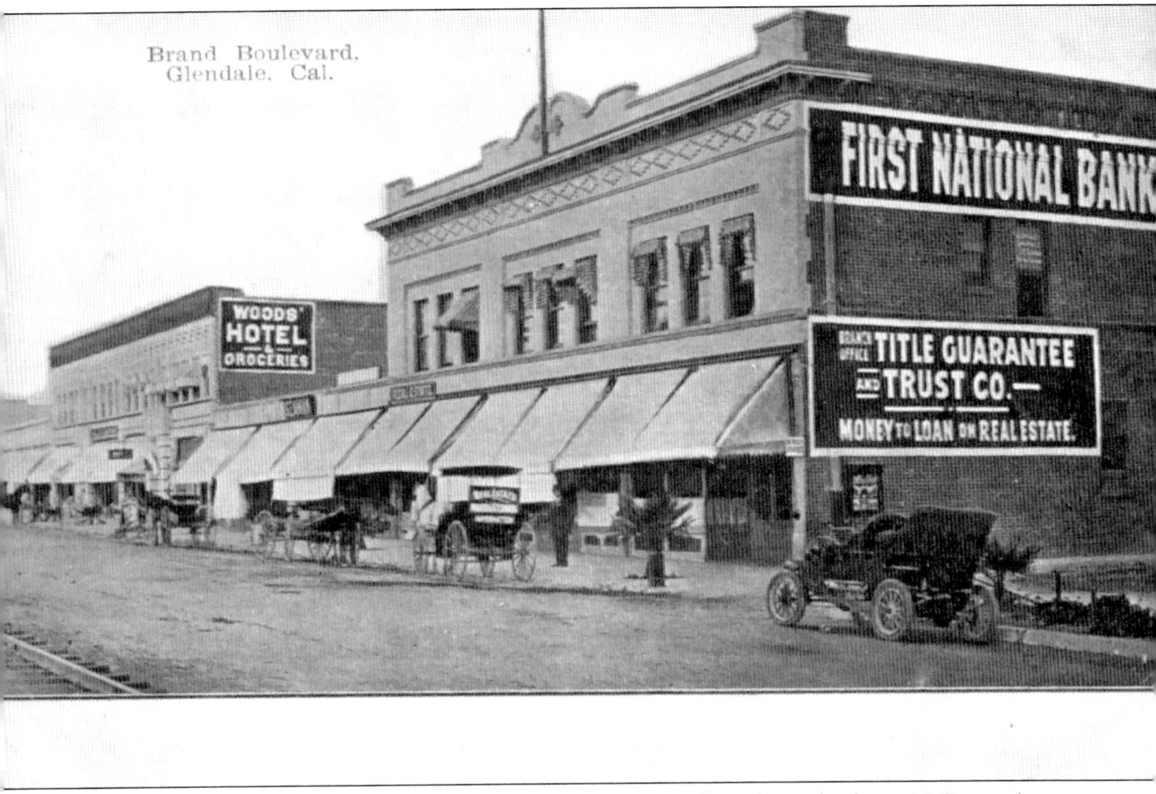

L. C. Brand owned a wide swath of land stretching north and south along N Street (now Brand Boulevard). After his electric railway line (tracks at lower left) was completed in 1904, he began selling various parcels but retained one portion of land bounded by Brand Boulevard, Broadway, and Maryland and Wilson Avenues. He built several structures on the east side of the block, seen here, including the First National Bank of Glendale, which opened in 1905 just north of Fourth Street (now Broadway). Many other businesses were constructed through financial help advanced by Brand's bank. The Woods Hotel building (pictured) housed the beginnings of the San Fernando Valley Home Telephone Company, founded in 1903 with L. C. Brand as president. Brand disposed of the entire block several years later. A successful businessman, he took out full-page advertisements in a Los Angeles paper every Sunday and Wednesday in 1903. At the top of the advertisement, a boldface caption asked, "Have You Been to Glendale?" This postcard was published by the Polycrome Company of San Francisco about 1910. (Courtesy of the Special Collections Room, Glendale Public Library.)

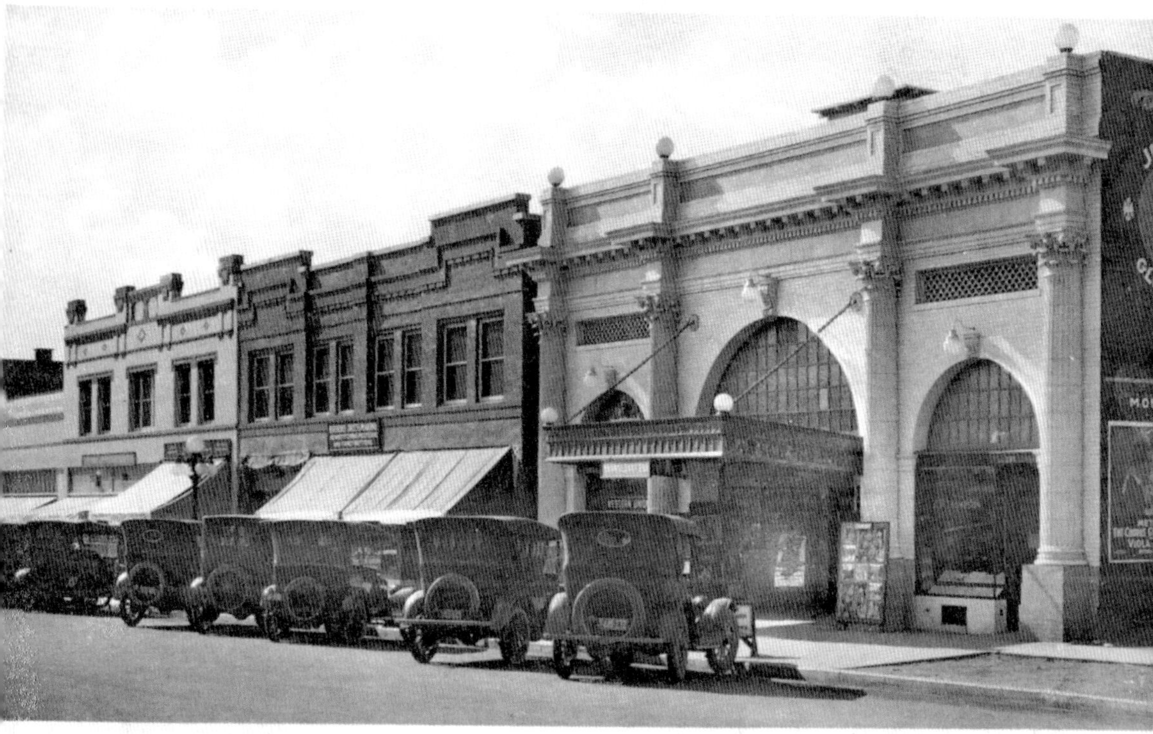

BUSINESS BLOCK, BRAND BOULEVARD. GLENDALE, CALIFORNIA.

The Palace Grand Theatre (right) opened on Brand Boulevard in November 1914 with the Mary Pickford movie *Tess of the Storm Country*, which had been filmed in the countryside around Chatsworth. Located in the heart of the downtown business area, the theater was built by Los Angeles businessman Henry C. Jensen at a cost of $30,000. It boasted dressing rooms, an orchestra pit, and a large auditorium. The two stores on either side had entrances in the lobby. Both vaudeville and motion pictures were shown in the theater, whose opulence created a stir in the community and caused two previous movie theaters, the Majestic and the Glendale, to go out of business. Jensen put his son Walter in charge. Weekly programs were printed, and youngsters were hired to distribute one to each home throughout the city. (Courtesy of the Bruce B. Herman Collection.)

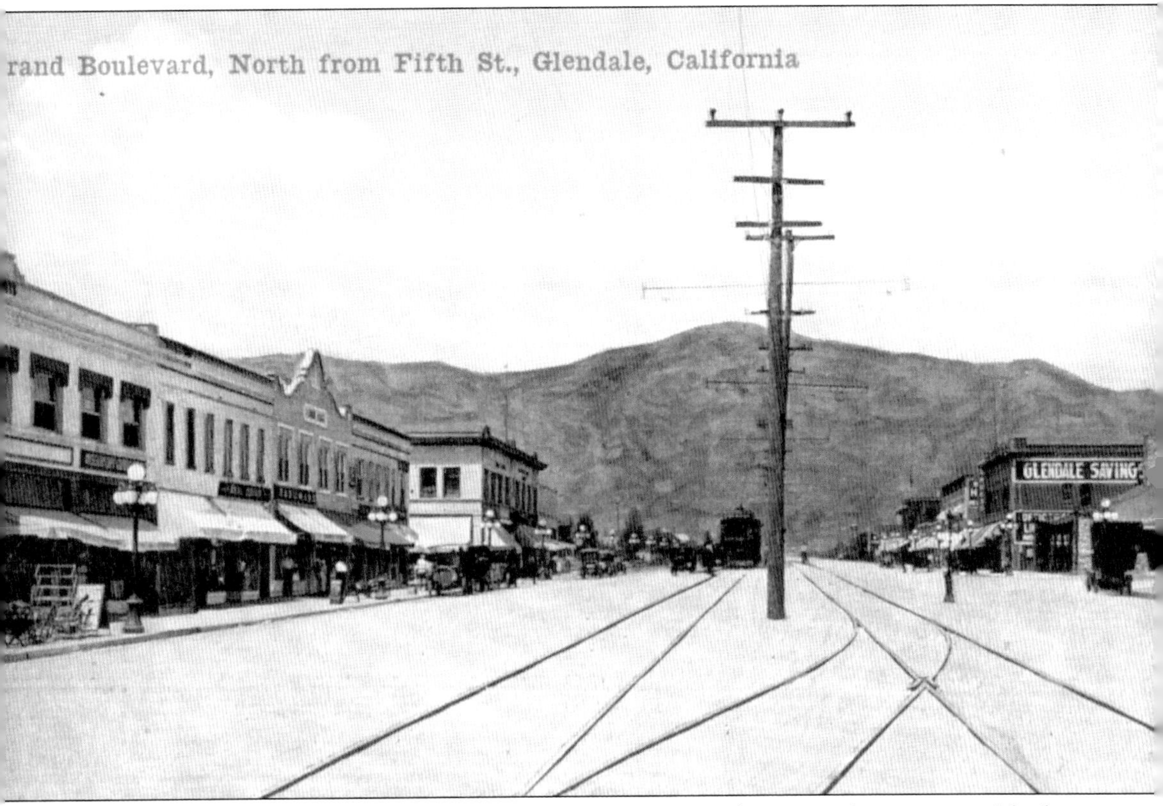

Brand Boulevard, depicted in this *c.* 1915 northward view, became a busy street with the advent of the Pacific Electric Railway line. L. C. Brand, in conjunction with both the Glendale Improvement Association and the Tropico Improvement Association, had sought for some time to bring a line to Glendale. Working in tandem with E. D. Goode, the secretary of the Glendale group, Brand was successful in getting the right-of-way needed to bring the line up N Street, at which point the Tropico Association suggested renaming that street for Brand. It was seconded some time later by the Glendale Association. Before the laying of track, Brand sold the railway project to the Los Angeles Interurban Railway Company, a Henry E. Huntington capital endeavor. It became part of the Pacific Electric Railway Company in December 1903. The first electric streetcars traveled through Tropico and then continued on to Glendale on Sunday, April 6, 1904. When the line was first built, it terminated at Broadway but was quickly extended to the top of Brand Boulevard. Later that same year, gala celebrations with barbecues were held in both towns. (Courtesy of the Bruce B. Herman Collection.)

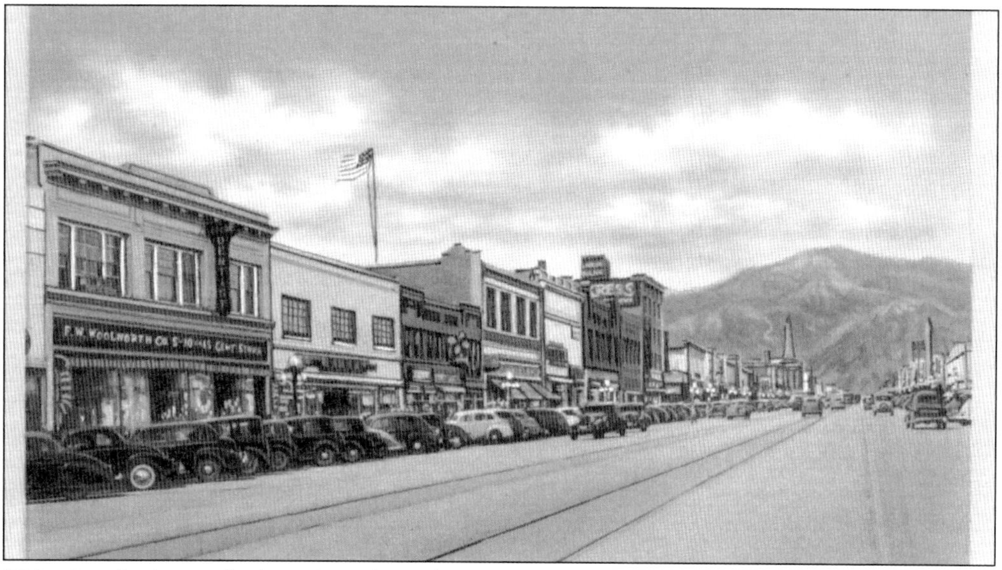

This view looks north along Brand Boulevard's west side. In the 1920s, the street had many popular stores, including Woolworth's and Kress. Woolworth's was founded in the late 1800s by F. W. Woolworth, a sales associate in a rural New York store who priced stock at a fixed amount, about 5¢ per item. Woolworth later expanded to a 10¢ line, and the five-and-dime store was born. Another popular store, Kress, is pictured here. Established in 1896, it sold a wide variety of durable and low-cost household items. (Courtesy of the Special Collections Room, Glendale Public Library.)

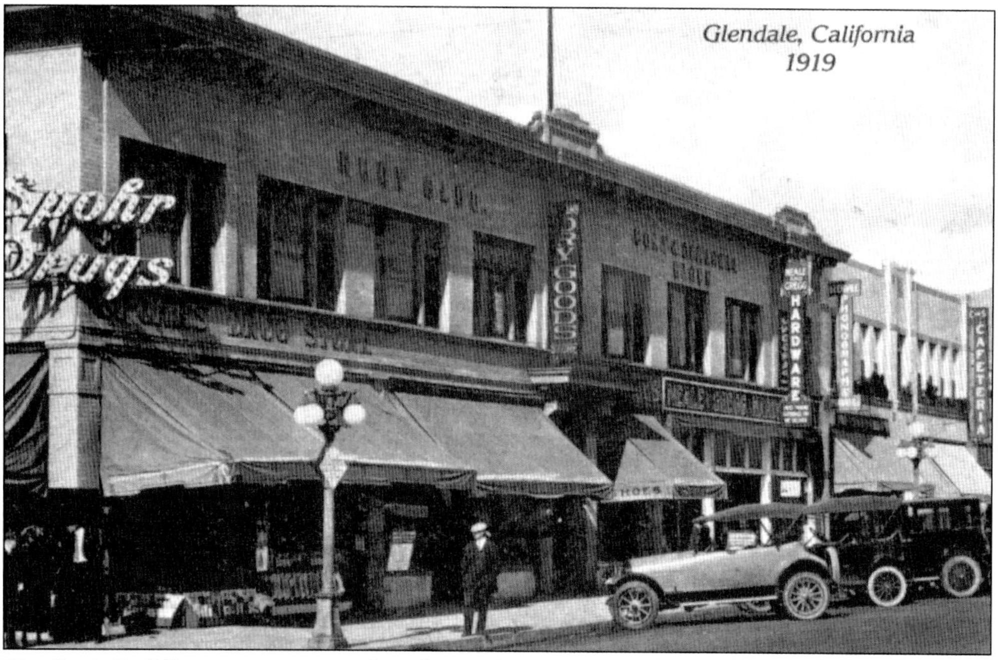

The Rudy Building was constructed on the northwest corner of Brand Boulevard and Broadway in 1911. Ahead of its time, the building featured a concrete foundation, pressed-brick facing, and skylights. Another innovation was the adjacent garage, with several stalls for use by owners of "machines." (Courtesy of the Special Collections Room, Glendale Public Library.)

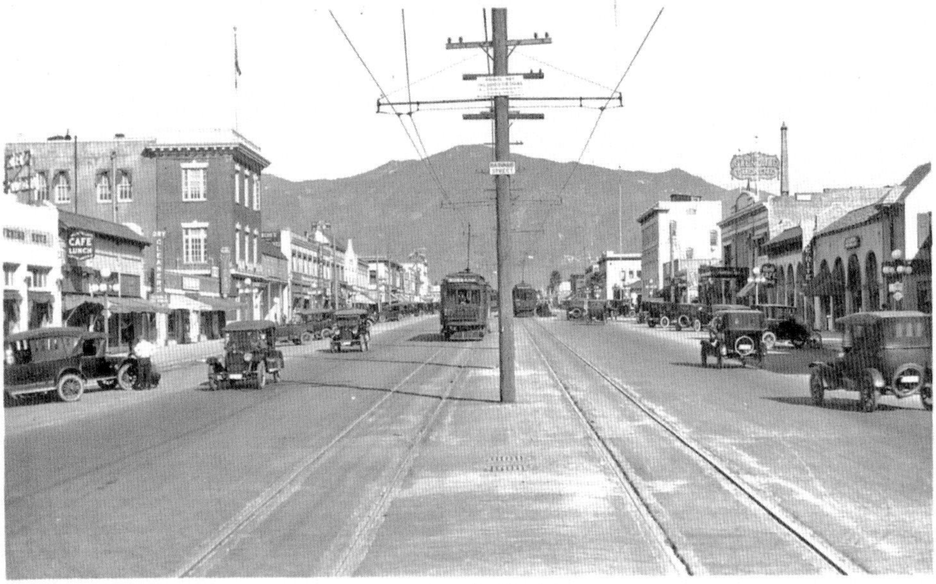

Brand Boulevard—Glendale

A Pacific Electric streetcar stops along busy Brand Boulevard. In 1911, the railway line was expanded to provide service from Glendale to Burbank. A line was cut through vineyards and peach orchards as far as Cypress Avenue in Burbank. The paralleling street later became Glenoaks Boulevard. This postcard dates to about 1922. (Courtesy of the Special Collections Room, Glendale Public Library.)

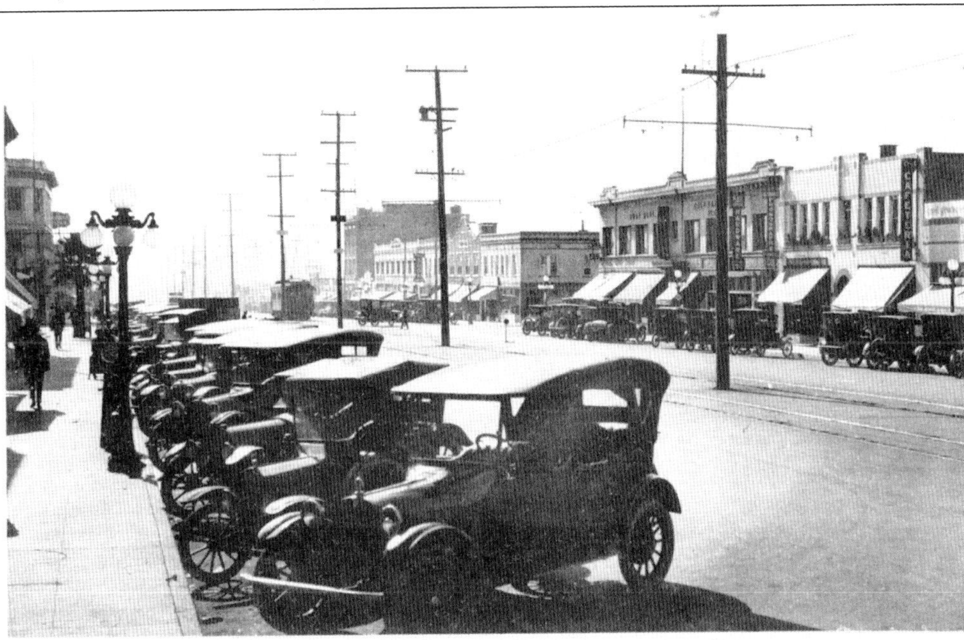

BRAND BOULEVARD. GLENDALE, CALIFORNIA.

Streetcars and automobiles share Brand Boulevard in this scene, looking south to the intersection with Broadway. This postcard was published by the Western Publishing and Novelty Company of Los Angeles. (Courtesy of the Special Collections Room, Glendale Public Library.)

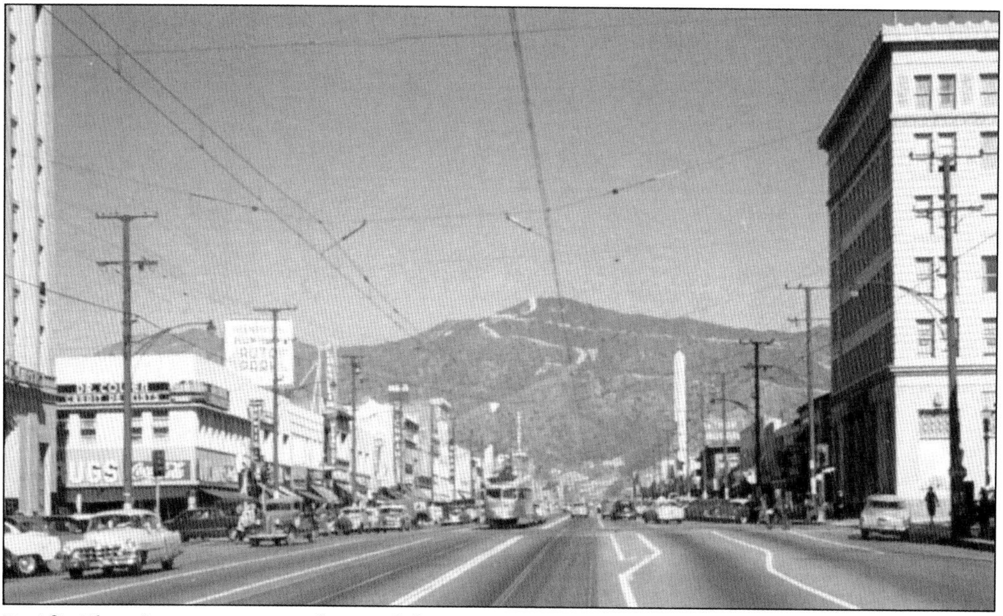

Pacific Electric streetcars travel up and down Brand Boulevard in this view, looking north from Broadway. In 1955, however, reduced revenues took the beloved "Red Cars" off the street. The rails were removed in 1956. Opposite the Security First National Bank, which dominates the intersection, is the remodeled Rudy Building, while the spire of the Alex Theatre stands in the distance. This postcard was published by Columbia Wholesale Supply of North Hollywood around 1953. (Courtesy of the George Ellison Collection.)

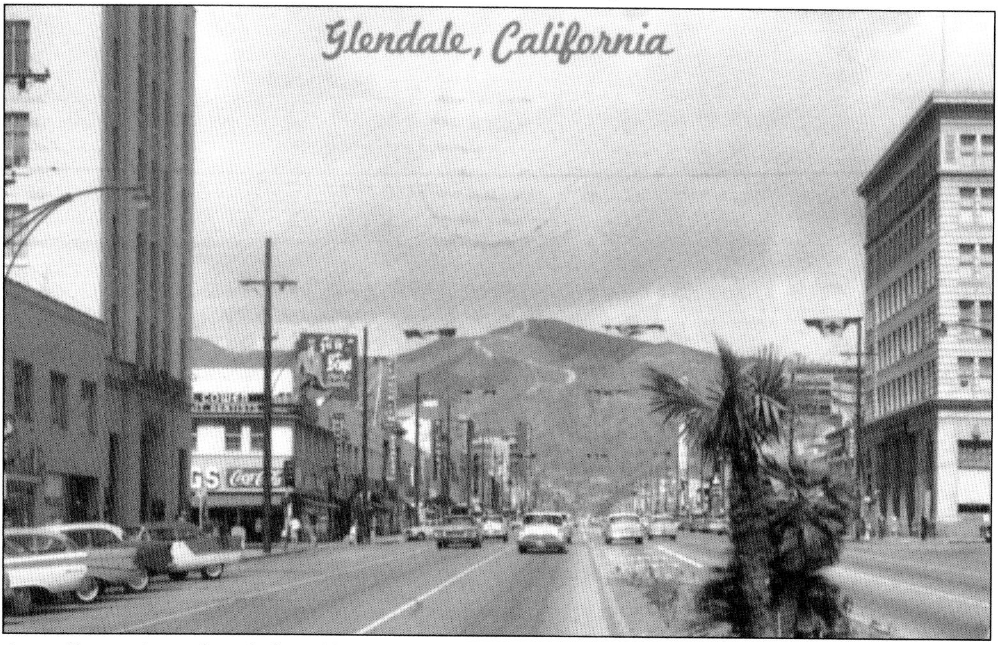

A median strip replaced the old streetcar tracks along Brand Boulevard, as evidenced in this northward view. The Glendale Federal Savings and Loan Association building (left) and the Alex Theatre spire (right) frame the beginnings of hillside development. This postcard was published by the H. S. Crocker Company about 1960. (Courtesy of the Bruce B. Herman Collection.)

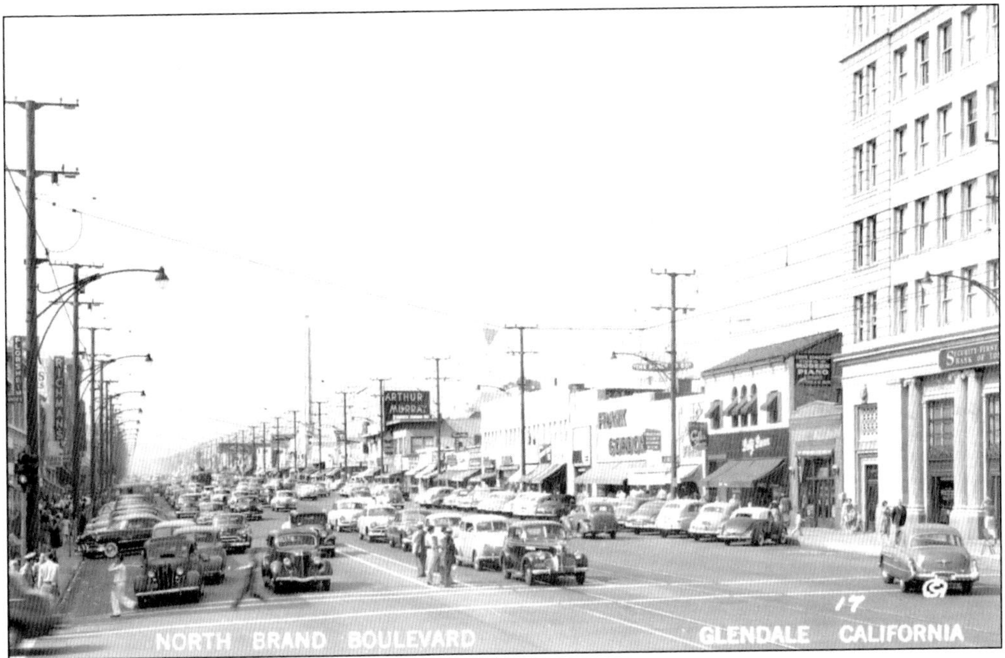

Streetcars and automobiles line Brand Boulevard in this *c.* 1950 view, looking north from Broadway. The main shopping street held a wide variety of stores and services that attracted shoppers from throughout the area. This postcard was published by the Angeleno Photo Service of Los Angeles. (Courtesy of the Special Collections Room, Glendale Public Library.)

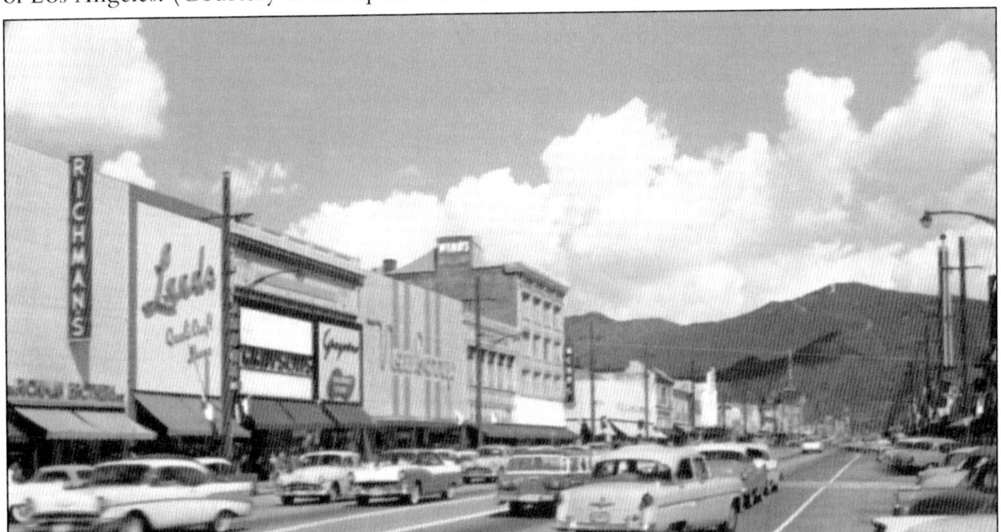

The 100 block of North Brand Boulevard was home to Webb's Department Store, a fixture on Brand since 1923. The building, designed by Alfred F. Priest, included a mezzanine and basement. Over the years, Webb's expanded into adjacent stores in the same block. By the time of the photograph, many of the other stores had modernized their facades. This postcard dates to about 1958. (Courtesy of the Bruce B. Herman Collection.)

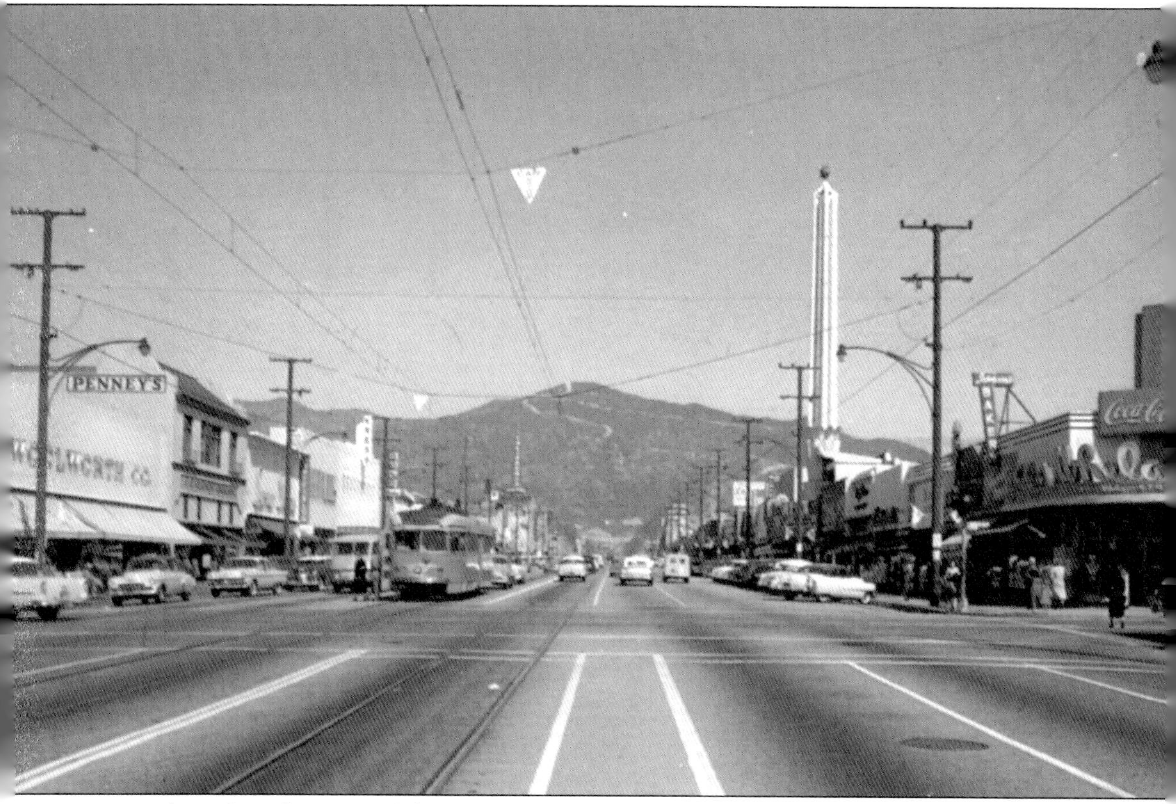

Brand Boulevard was noted for its new and modern stores serving the many shoppers arriving by streetcar. In the mid-1950s, the intersection with Wilson Avenue held F. W. Woolworth's, Penney's, and Kress (left). Whelan's dominated the northeast corner. Adjacent to it was the popular Johnson's Bakery. The large-capacity auditorium of the Alex Theatre (right) frequently hosted classes, fund-raisers, and fashion shows during the 1940s and 1950s. The last Pacific Electric streetcar left Glendale for Los Angeles in 1955. Although the streetcars had provided quick commutes between the cities since 1904, the company had been losing money. One factor was the numerous grade crossings, which cut the speed of the streetcars, reducing their competitive edge in the transportation field. This postcard was published by Colourpicture of Boston around 1955. (Courtesy of the George Ellison Collection.)

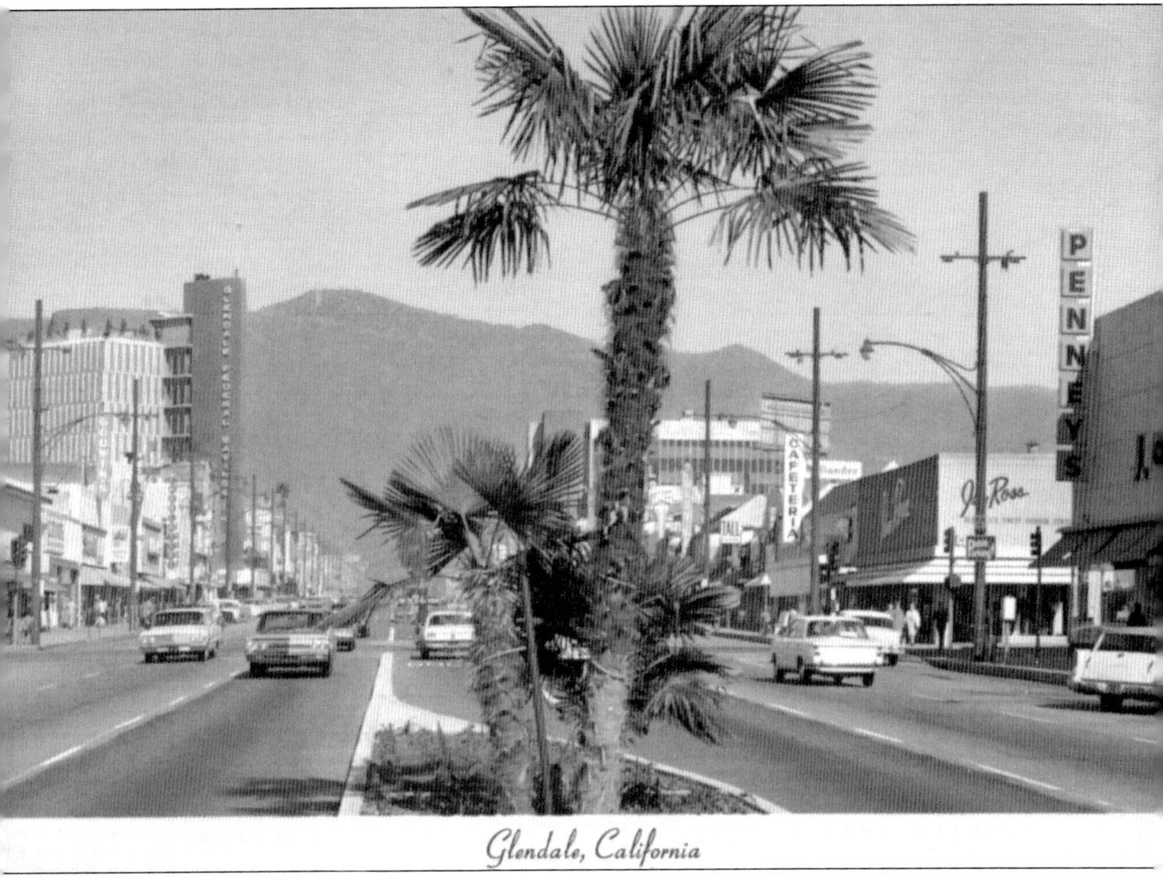

The Valley National Bank (right, partially obscured by a tree) attracted media attention when Casey Stengel of New York Yankees fame joined its board of directors. The bank was organized in 1957 as Glendale National, mainly through the efforts of former mayor John M. Lawson. Stock was sold to many Glendale residents, including Lawson's sister Edna and her husband, Casey Stengel. Named a vice president, Stengel brought great exposure to the bank. In 1966, after its name had changed to Valley National, the bank moved to a new six-story headquarters on Brand Boulevard, across from Glendale Federal (left). This postcard was published by the Western Publishing and Novelty Company of Los Angeles. (Courtesy of the George Ellison Collection.)

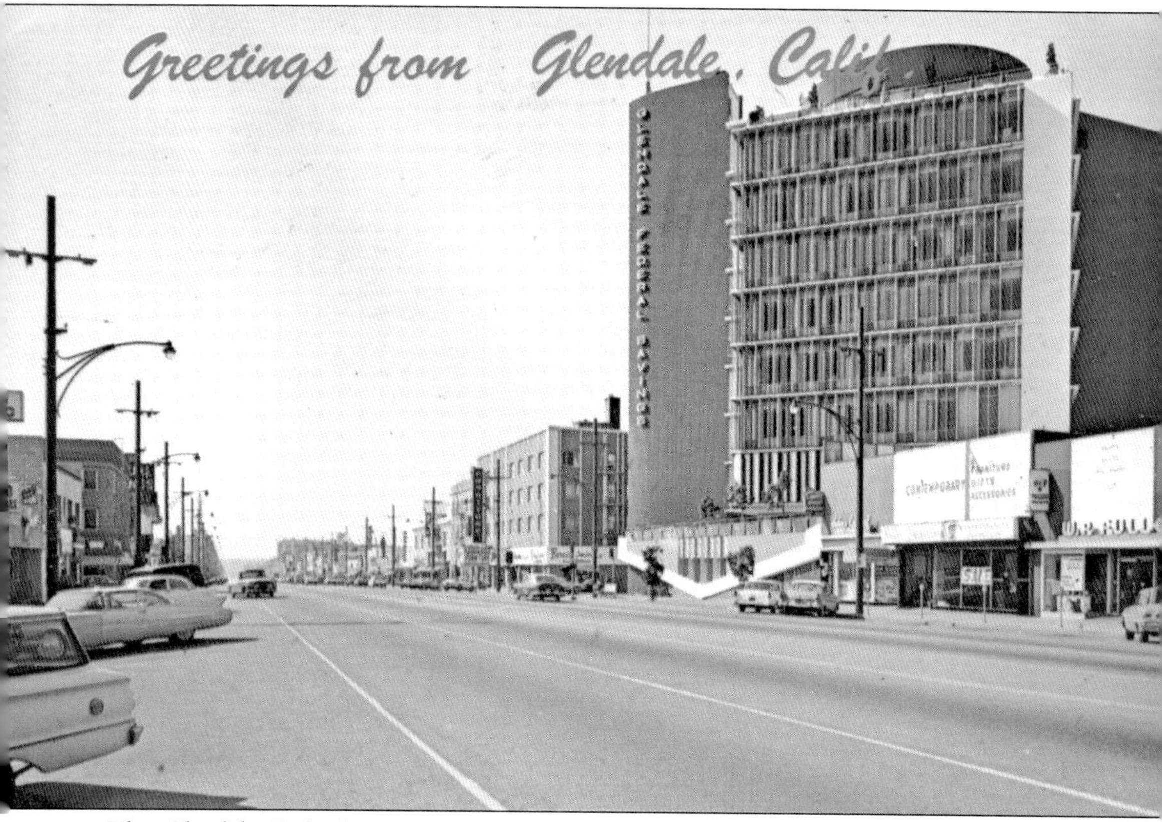

The Glendale Federal Savings and Loan Association building dominates the skyline in this view, looking south on Brand Boulevard. Joseph E. Hoeft established the First Federal Savings and Loan Association in 1934 on an investment of some $5,000 and grew it into a multimillion-dollar business that later became Glendale Federal. The bank's signature building opened in 1959 at 401 North Brand Boulevard, at the corner of Lexington Drive. Hoeft also focused his business acumen on the local community, becoming president of a newly formed advisory council for the Glendale Symphony Orchestra Association in 1957. He supported the symphony (the oldest continuing community orchestra in the country) for many years. In 1962, Glendale Federal sponsored a performance of the symphony on KNX-TV. The 1971–1972 concert season began with a tribute to Hoeft, who was by then president emeritus of the association. Hoeft died in 1972 and was succeeded at Glendale Federal by Raymond D. Edwards. Edwards had come to the savings and loan association as a teller in 1945. (Courtesy of the George Ellison Collection.)

Six

Landscapes and Views

The Tongva Indians were the first to appreciate the hills and valleys of what would become Glendale. Renamed the Gabrielenos by the Spanish missionaries, they were living in settlements along the lower slopes of the San Gabriels when Jose Maria Verdugo, a soldier stationed at the San Gabriel Mission, began scouting out the area. Even though he was only in his early 20s, Verdugo, like the others in his outfit, sought to acquire land. While out on patrol, he saw huge parcels seemingly free for the taking. Though the area appeared desert-like, the all-important water was plentiful, and Verdugo settled here, naming his new land San Rafael. One of the first and largest land grants, it was officially permitted in 1784, along with the San Pedro and Los Nietos land grants. Once water flowed, the land began producing vegetables, grapes for wine, a multitude of fruit trees, including peaches and pears, and some of the state's first citrus trees.

The landscape remained nearly unchanged for more than a century, but by the 1850s, the land-rich and cash-poor Verdugos had fallen victim to a huge mortgage and began selling portions of their land. An 1871 court ruling divided the property among claimants such as Andrew Glassell, Prudent Beaudry, Fernando Sepulveda, and David Burbank. This division opened the way for entrepreneurs from the East, who began buying large parcels from the original claimants and establishing themselves as ranchers. Among the first were Capt. Cameron Thom and Erskine M. Ross, who combined their acreage in the Rossmoyne area to grow olives trees, and W. C. B. Richardson, whose large Santa Eulalia ranch marked the original land grant's southernmost border, near the Los Angeles River.

The picturesque valleys and gently rolling hills have continued to attract waves of new people to Glendale to build homes and establish businesses.

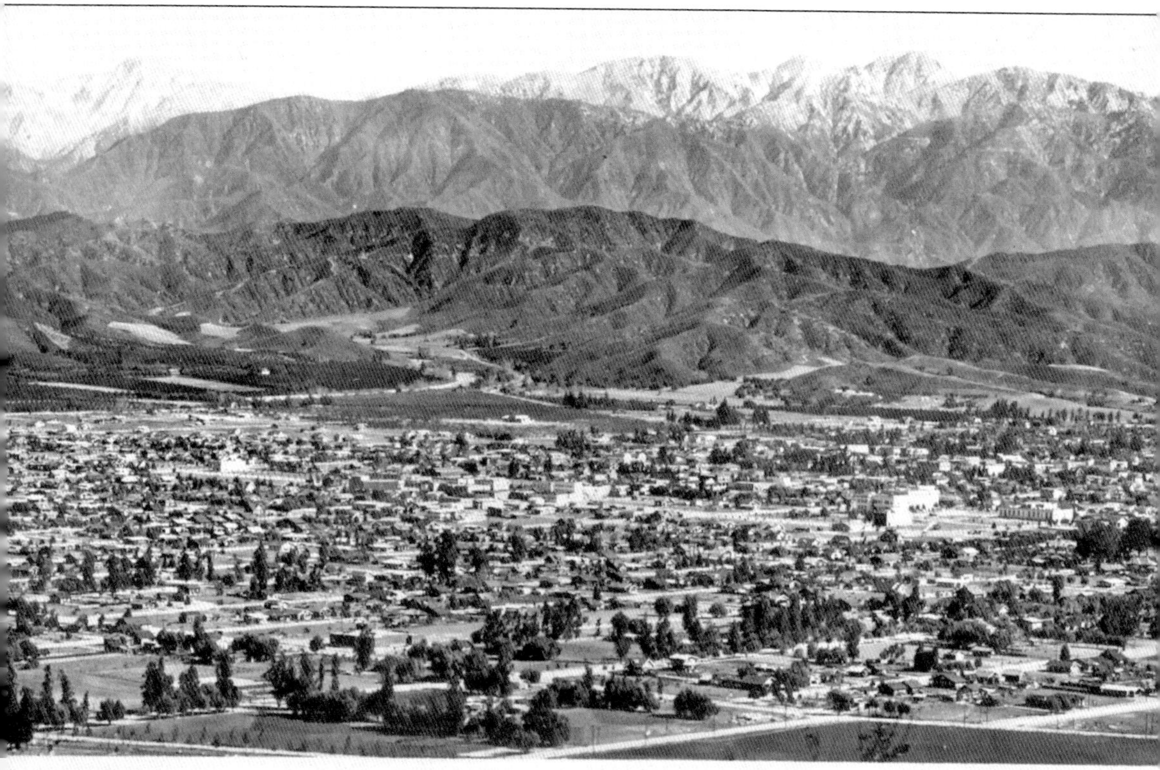

Glendale, Cal., "The Jewel City"

Glendale became known as the Jewel City in 1910, when a trend toward city nicknames, created by the chambers of commerce, spread throughout the many new communities in Southern California. Glendale's chamber was established in 1910, just four years after the city had incorporated. Edward Emery, a founding vice president of the chamber, soon became president and, in that capacity, came up with the moniker "Glendale, The Jewel City," noting that the city, surrounded by the Verdugo Hills, sparkled "like a jewel in the sun." His proposal was accepted by the city's governing agency, the board of trustees, with grateful thanks. Emery, who came to Glendale during its incorporation year, plunged enthusiastically into the young community. He was a charter director of the Glendale Savings Bank in 1913 and was involved in many other enterprises. (Courtesy of the George Ellison Collection.)

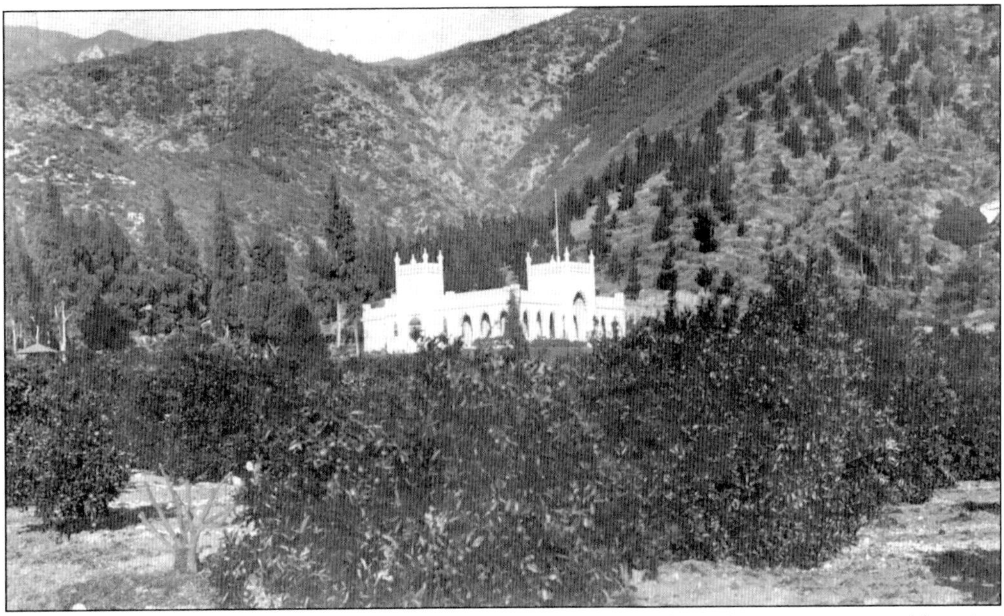

El Miradero, L. C. Brand's home, was surrounded by newly planted orange trees and by pine trees, which marched up the hill behind the dwelling. The first citrus trees were planted on Spanish missions in 1769. As more missions were established, more lemon and orange trees were grown throughout California. By the mid-1800s, orange groves were a commercial enterprise, and in 1867, the state had an estimated 17,000 trees. The transcontinental railroad spurred further growth as carloads of oranges were shipped East. This postcard dates to about 1908. (Courtesy of the Special Collections Room, Glendale Public Library.)

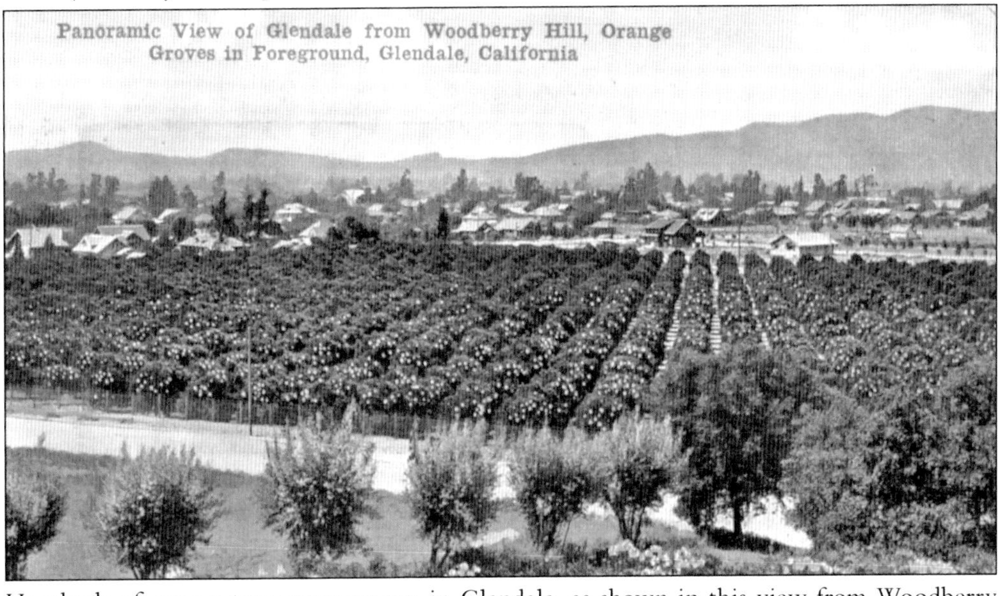

Hundreds of orange trees were grown in Glendale, as shown in this view from Woodberry Hill, the home of George B. Woodbury (also known as Woodberry), who owned 20 acres on Verdugo Road. Active in civic affairs, he was affiliated with the Verdugo Water Company when he developed and patented a successful irrigation device known as the Woodbury Sub-Irrigation System. (Courtesy of the Bruce B. Herman Collection.)

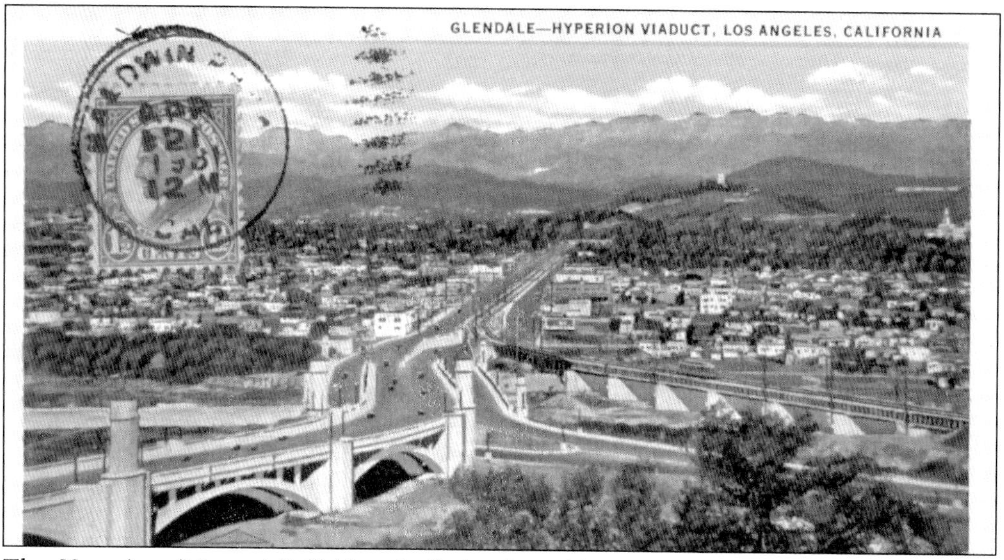

The Hyperion (Memorial) Bridge, built in the mid-1920s, connected Los Angeles with Glendale. The bridge over the Los Angeles River was one of several constructed during that time. The Hyperion, along with the other bridges that crossed the river at Broadway, Los Feliz Road, Glendale Boulevard, and Fletcher Drive, provided a fast commute from the city into the suburbs in the new automobile era. The spans were an important part of the rapid development of Glendale. This postcard was published by the Western Publishing and Novelty Company of Los Angeles about 1930. (Courtesy of the Bruce B. Herman Collection.)

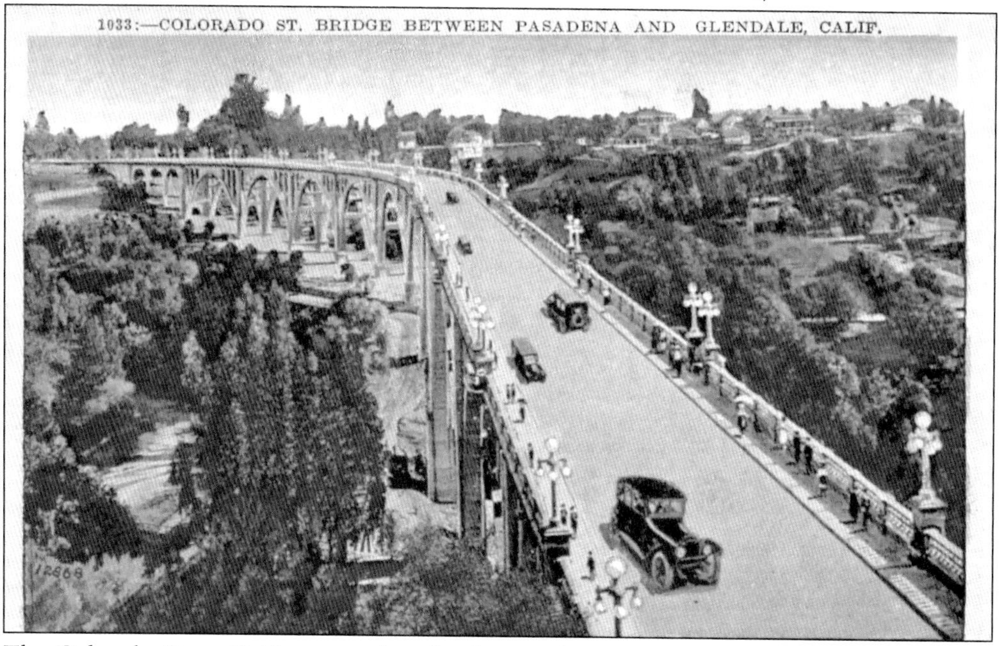

The Colorado Street Bridge, spanning the Arroyo Seco in Pasadena, was built in 1913 and was named for Colorado Boulevard, Pasadena's major east-west thoroughfare. The 1,486-foot span, created in the elegant Beaux Arts style, connected Pasadena with its western neighbors, Eagle Rock and Glendale. This postcard was published by the M. Kashower Company of Los Angeles around 1925. (Courtesy of the Bruce B. Herman Collection.)

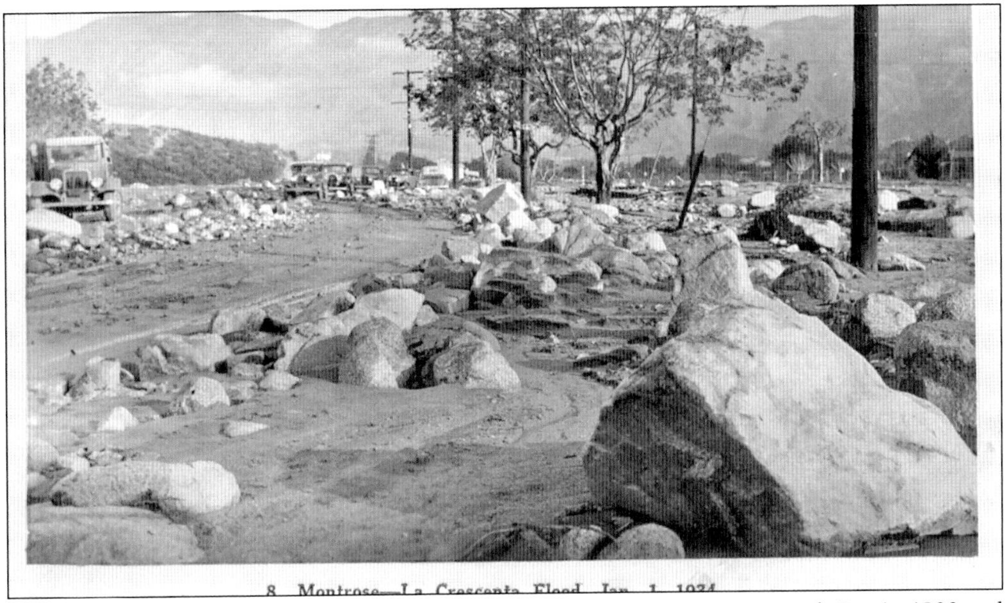

The most damaging flood to occur in the local foothills began on New Year's Eve in 1933 and continued into New Year's Day. A November fire in the hills had raged from the Arroyo Seco to Tujunga, burning vegetation and making the hills vulnerable to the days of heavy rain that later fell. Around midnight on December 31, major debris, water, and mud flowed down the slopes, destroying nearly everything in their path and killing more than 40 people. (Courtesy of the Special Collections Room, Glendale Public Library.)

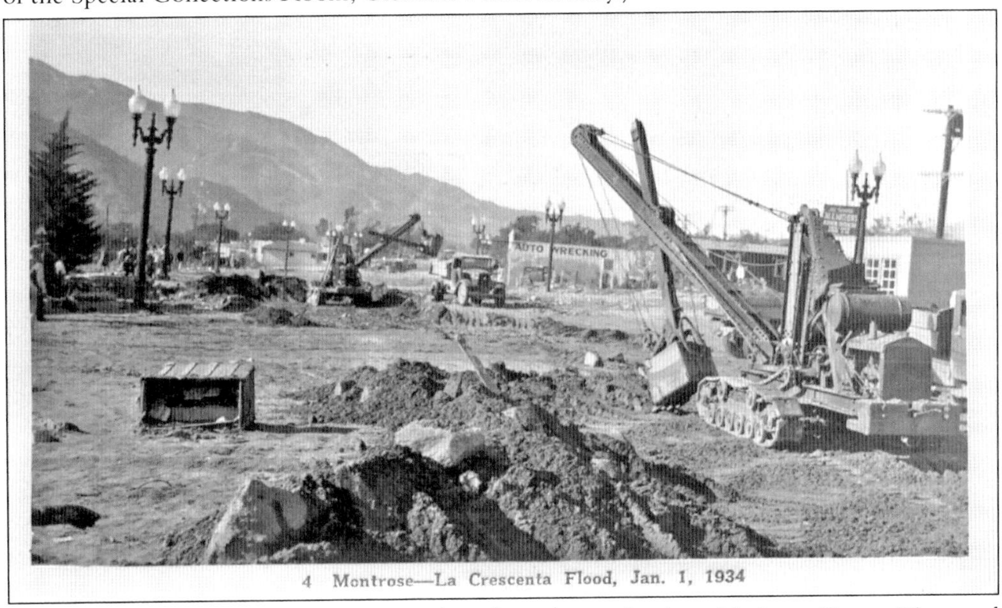

The 1933–1934 flood brought layers of mud, rocks, and other debris to Ocean View and Honolulu Avenues, the principal streets in Montrose. The nearby communities of Tujunga and Sunland were also affected, as was the area along the Verdugo Wash, which flowed into Glendale. Cleanup commenced immediately, with hundreds of WPA laborers attacking the debris with picks and shovels. Heavier equipment was later brought to the scene. (Courtesy of the Special Collections Room, Glendale Public Library.)

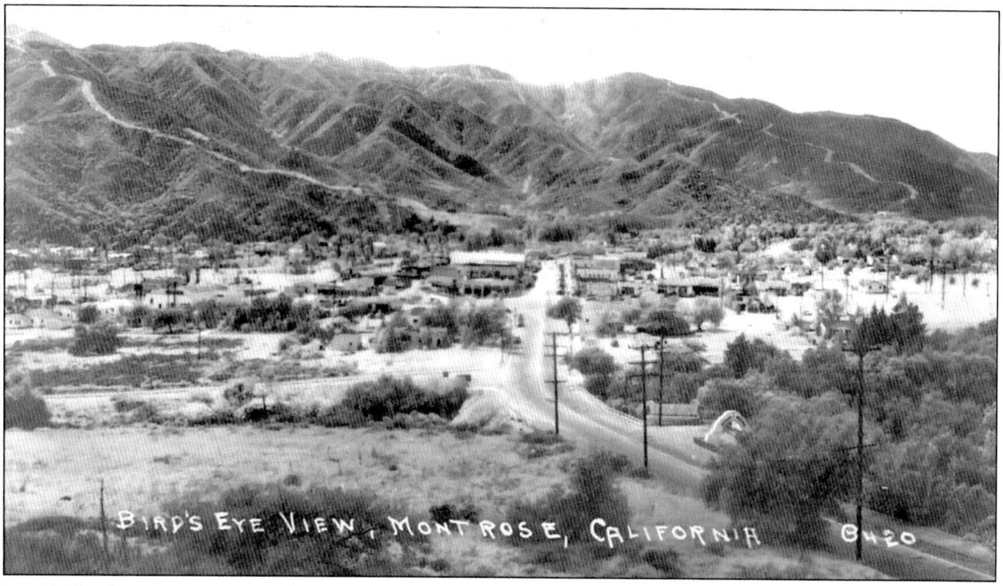

In 1913, the community of Montrose was established on a 300-acre tract north of Glendale by the real estate team of Holmes and Walton. More than 4,000 interested people came to the opening day barbecue, arriving on horseback or in horse-drawn vehicles. The community was laid out in the form of a rose, with circular streets leading from the main thoroughfare. (Courtesy of the Special Collections Room, Glendale Public Library.)

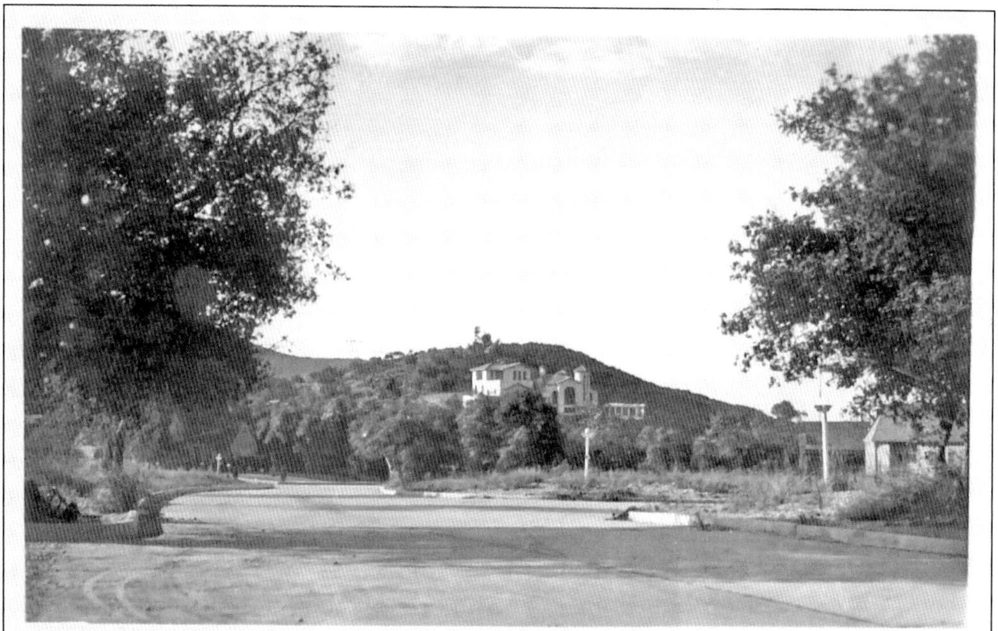

William Sparr purchased land in the countryside north of Glendale and started the Sparr Fruit Company there. In the early 1920s, the property was subdivided. One of the earliest homes was built by Melancton Walters. The 1923 Walters home, pictured around 1929, was a large, 6,000-square-foot version of the Spanish Colonial Revival style popular in the 1920s. (Courtesy of the Special Collections Room, Glendale Public Library.)

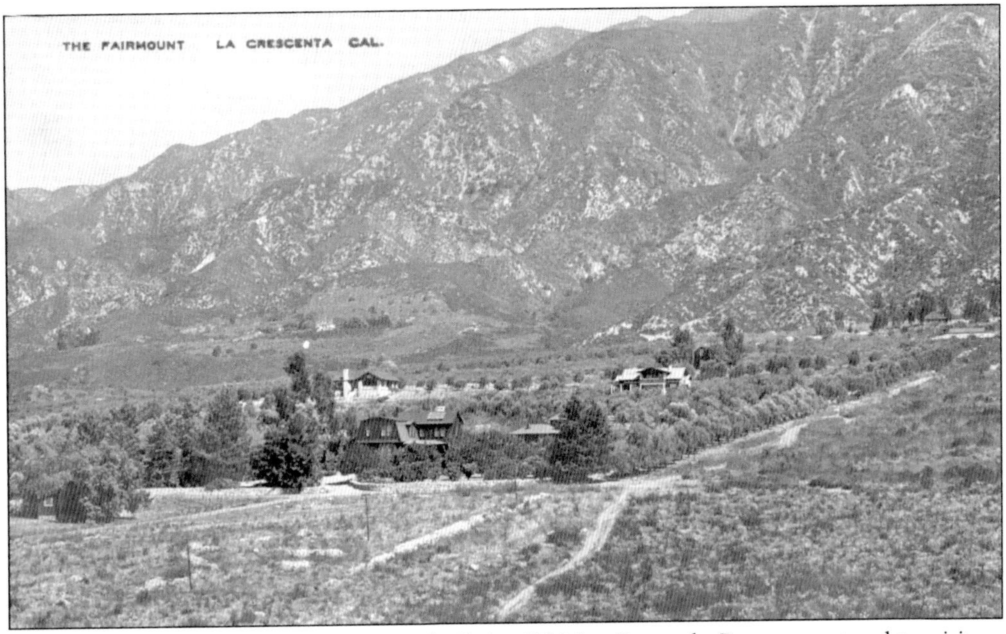

The Fairmount Hotel in La Crescenta, built in 1900 by Gertrude Bremen, catered to visitors who came to enjoy Crescenta Valley's fresh air and rural setting. Early settler Benjamin Briggs planted olive trees near the hotel. The wagon track running along the edge of the olive groves is now Briggs Avenue. The hotel later became a private home. (Courtesy of the Special Collections Room, Glendale Public Library.)

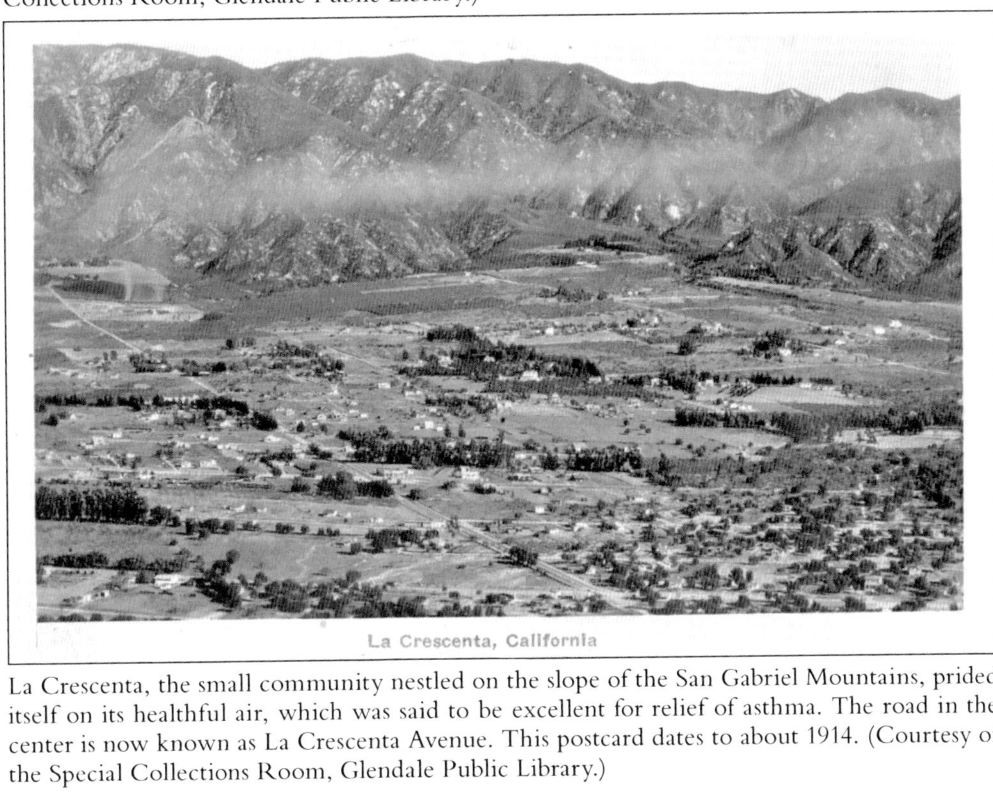

La Crescenta, the small community nestled on the slope of the San Gabriel Mountains, prided itself on its healthful air, which was said to be excellent for relief of asthma. The road in the center is now known as La Crescenta Avenue. This postcard dates to about 1914. (Courtesy of the Special Collections Room, Glendale Public Library.)

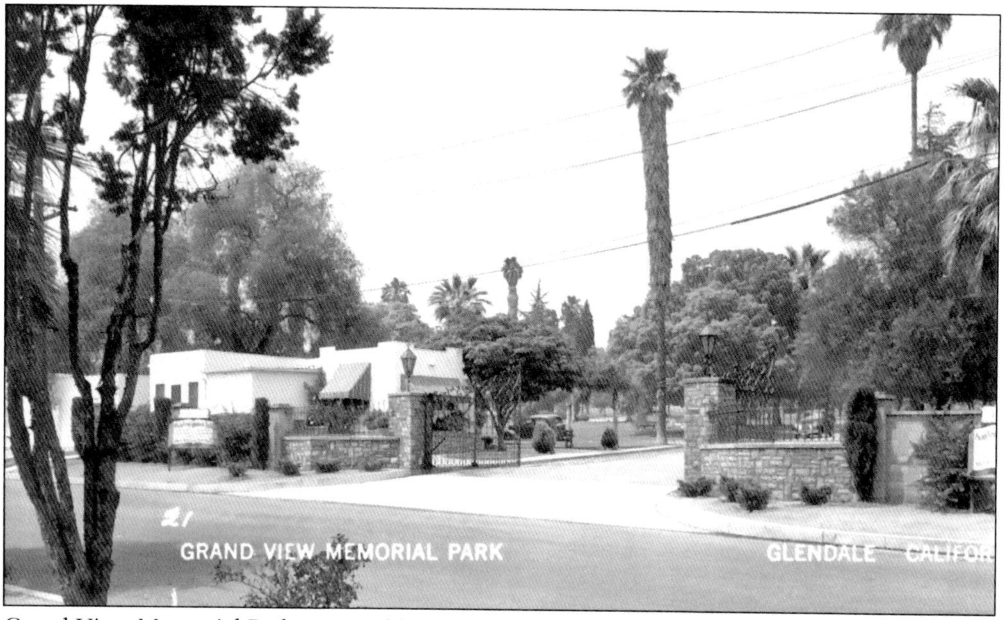

Grand View Memorial Park was established in the 1880s as Grand View Cemetery and was the only such facility in the vicinity until Forest Lawn was founded in 1906. All of Grand View's buildings, including a large mausoleum and crematory, were constructed in a Spanish style. Many of the city's earliest leaders are buried in the historic cemetery on Glenwood Road. This postcard was published by the Angeleno Photo Service of Los Angeles around 1950. (Courtesy of the Special Collections Room, Glendale Public Library.)

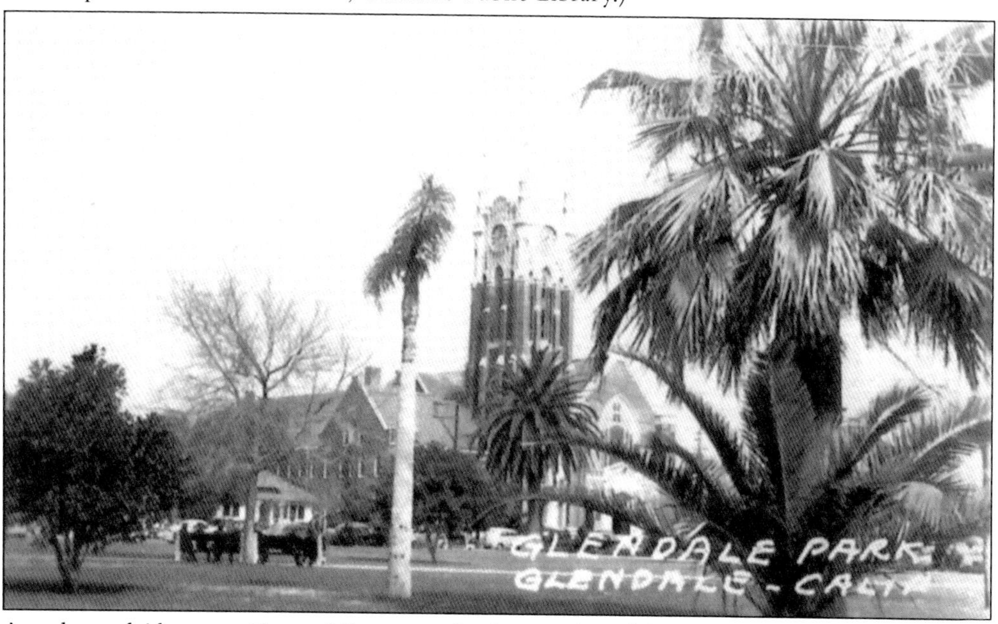

A park was laid out on Harvard Street on the former site of the Glendale Union High School building, which had been extensively damaged in the 1933 Long Beach earthquake and later condemned and demolished. At the corner of Harvard and Louise Streets stood the Glendale Presbyterian Church, constructed in 1922. This postcard dates to about 1945. (Courtesy of the Glendale Historical Society.)

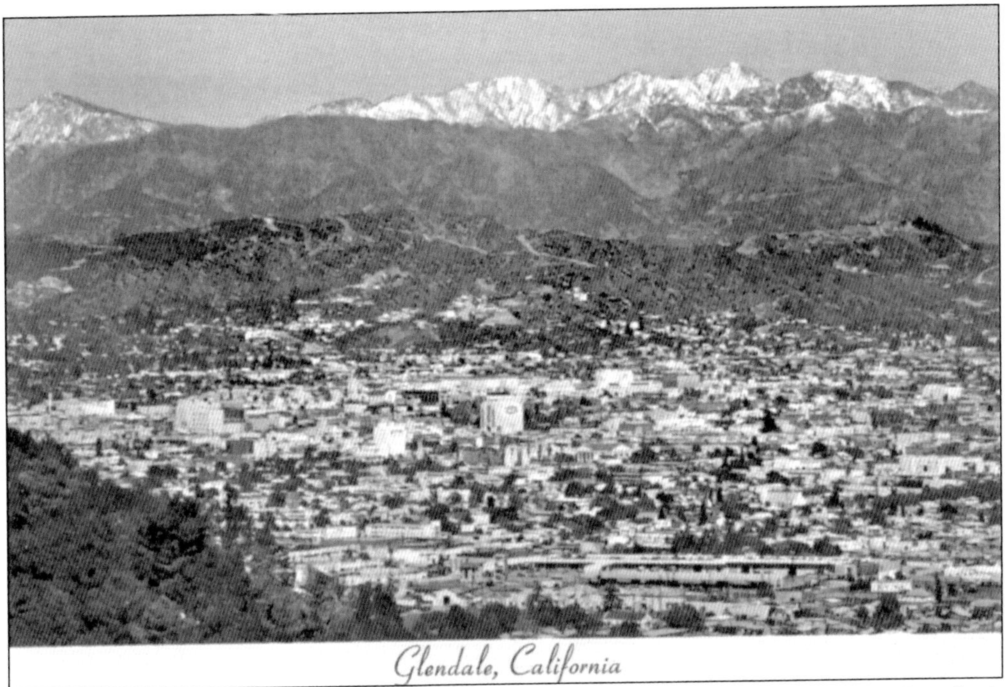

An aerial view of Glendale, taken from the world-famous Forest Lawn Memorial Park, is framed against the snow-capped San Gabriel Mountains. This postcard was published by the Western Publishing and Novelty Company of Los Angeles around 1966. (Courtesy of the George Ellison Collection.)

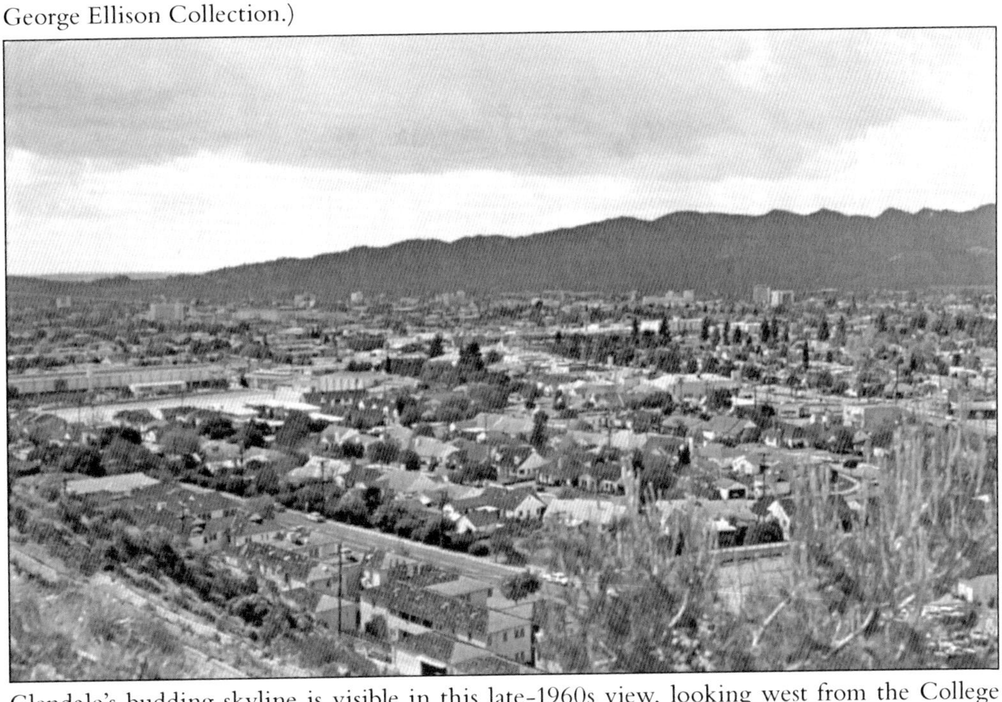

Glendale's budding skyline is visible in this late-1960s view, looking west from the College Hills area with Griffith Park in the background. This postcard was published by Columbia Wholesale Supply of North Hollywood. (Courtesy of the George Ellison Collection.)

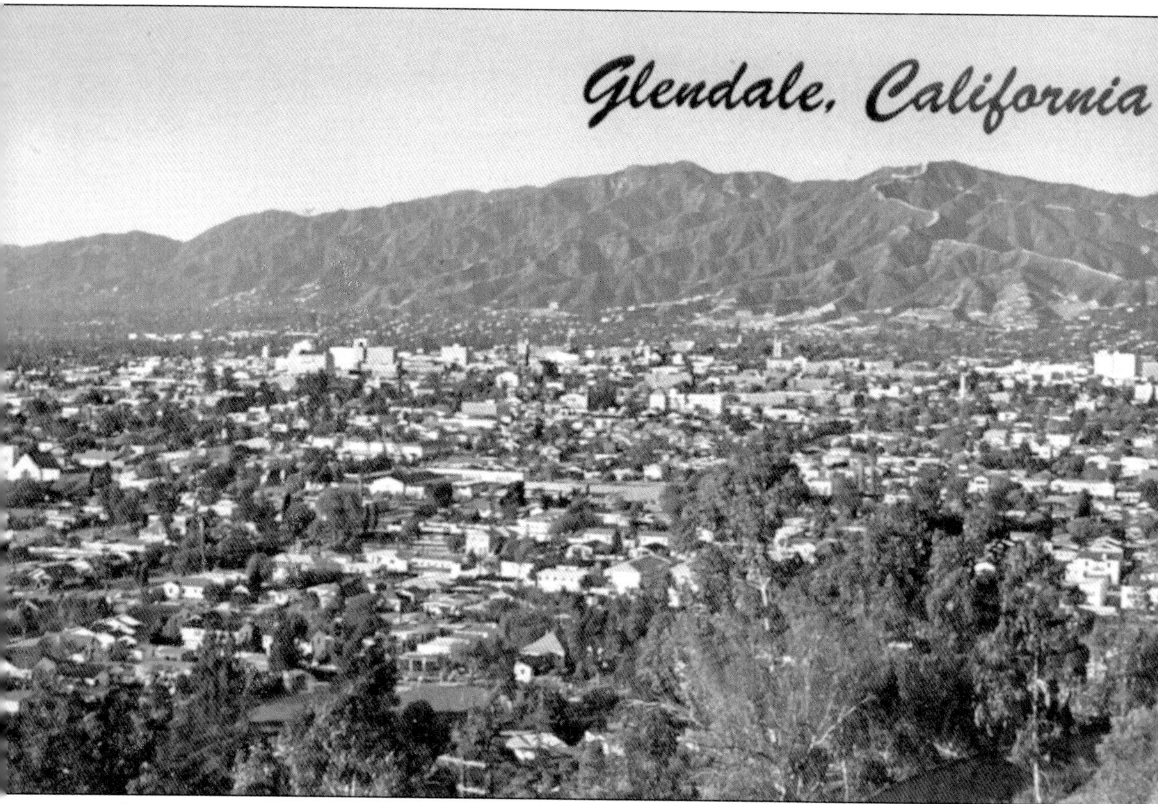

This view of Glendale, taken from Forest Lawn in the mid-1950s, reveals extensive hillside development stretching west toward Burbank. In the foreground, several churches are visible. Some of these churches would be damaged in the 1971 Sylmar earthquake. This postcard was published by Columbia Wholesale Supply of North Hollywood about 1954. (Courtesy of the George Ellison Collection.)

Seven

Forest Lawn

Forest Lawn has been a part of Glendale's history since 1906 but has largely remained a separate feature from city life. People know of Glendale as the home of Forest Lawn, where many famous figures have been laid to rest. Forest Lawn is a sanctuary and final resting place for loved ones. Its grand gates, lush hillside landscaping, statues, artwork, fountains, and English-inspired buildings make the place seem like a fairyland. Also a tourist destination, it contains a museum. There are more postcards of Forest Lawn than any other feature in Glendale.

The cemetery opened in Tropico, now a part of Glendale. A few eucalyptus trees were growing on the original 55 acres, which were covered with brush and, when Hubert Eaton took over, some granite monuments. Eaton, a man of strong convictions and religious principles, had a philosophy of "Perseverance conquers all." A college graduate, he already had several careers behind him and only took the sales job at the cemetery in order to repay a failed investment in a silver mine. Harkening back to his religious upbringing, Eaton sought to provide a place of burial that would bring comfort to the living. He brought with him an idea that was new in California—the concept of "before need," which he had heard about in his home state of Missouri.

Hubert Eaton found his vision for the cemetery while hiking the grounds on New Year's Day in 1917 and went home to write down his ideas. His vision included park-like sweeping green lawns, towering trees, and plentiful open spaces. He achieved this by planting hundreds of trees and plants and by discontinuing the use of tombstones, opting instead for uniform, engraved bronze tables set flush with the ground. Customers balked at first, but when Eaton came up with a 10-percent-off deal for forgoing "monument privileges," his idea took hold.

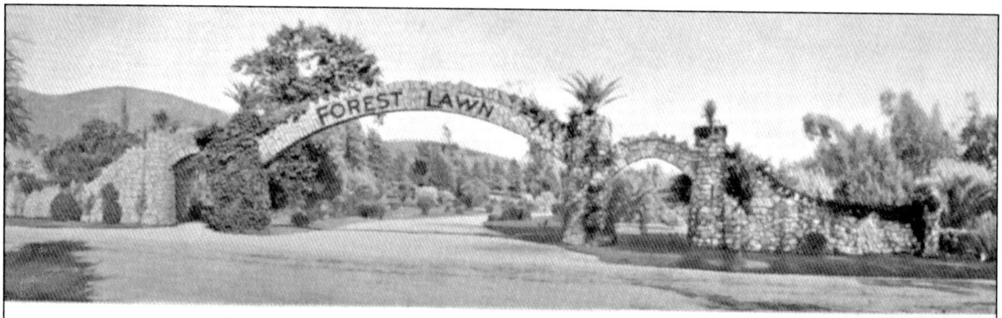

ENTRANCE TO FOREST LAWN MEMORIAL-PARK

Unlike any similar project in the United States, Forest Lawn combines in a memorial-park of great natural beauty, provision for every mortuary need—earth burial, cremation, mausoleum crypt, columbarium niche or private vault—all under the direct administration and supervision of one management.

The unity of purpose thus secured assures the purchaser of many benefits; one ideal in the work of developing and beautifying the property; a marked reduction in the overhead expense and the conservation of the maintenance or perpetual care fund.

Decay and neglect can never encroach upon Forest Lawn Memorial-Park. Its perpetual care fund is so guarded by the laws of California that the principal can never be dissipated, while the interest thus derived will perpetually care for Forest Lawn without taxation or assessment upon the lot owner.

Forest Lawn began as a small cemetery in Tropico in 1906. Under the guidance of Dr. Hubert Eaton, who joined the staff as a salesman in 1912, it became a burial place known for its ground-level gravestones and for its perpetual care program. (Courtesy of the Special Collections Room, Glendale Public Library.)

1051A:—ENTRANCE TO FOREST LAWN MEMORIAL PARK, GLEN DALE, CALIF.

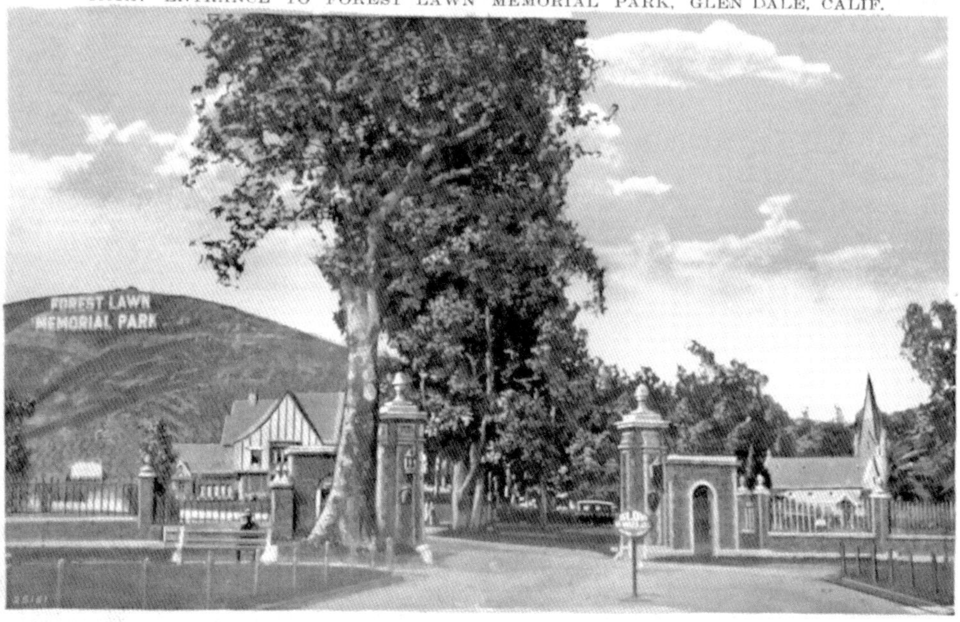

Eaton wrote a "Builder's Creed," setting out his goals and aims, on New Year's Day in 1917 and renamed the cemetery Forest Lawn Memorial Park that same year. As the park grew, a new gate and reception building welcomed visitors. The sycamore tree near the gate was one of the oldest landmarks in the San Fernando Valley and, at one time, the central point for survey lines throughout the area. This postcard was published by the M. Kashower Company of Los Angeles around 1927. (Courtesy of the Special Collections Room, Glendale Public Library.)

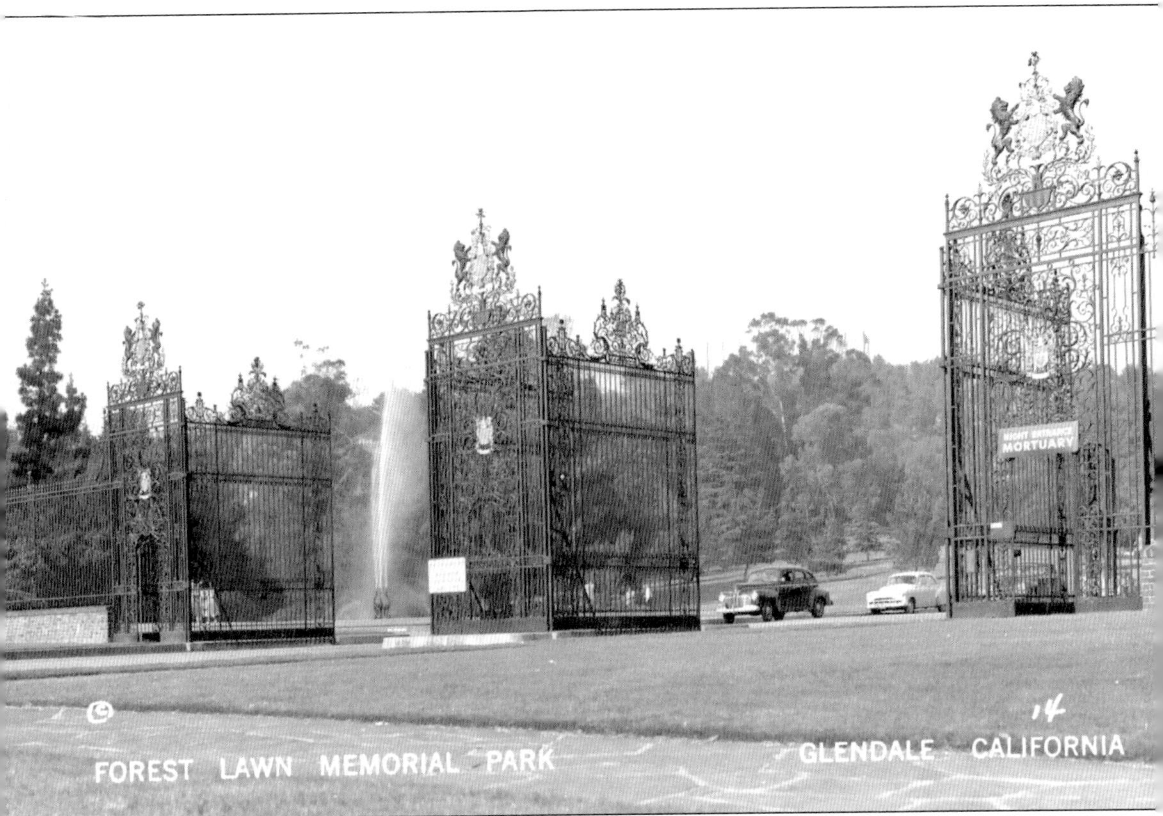

The 25-foot-high iron gates, said to be the largest in the world when they were installed in 1932, provide a dramatic entrance to Forest Lawn. Sweeping lawns and tree-lined streets set a quiet tone for the park, which sought to provide all needed services in one place, eliminating lengthy funeral processions and providing a quiet haven for the bereaved. Eaton's "Builder's Creed," which called for a "great park, devoid of misshapen monuments and other customary signs of earthly death," established goals for the future. This postcard was published by the Angeleno Photo Service of Los Angeles about 1950. (Courtesy of the Special Collections Room, Glendale Public Library.)

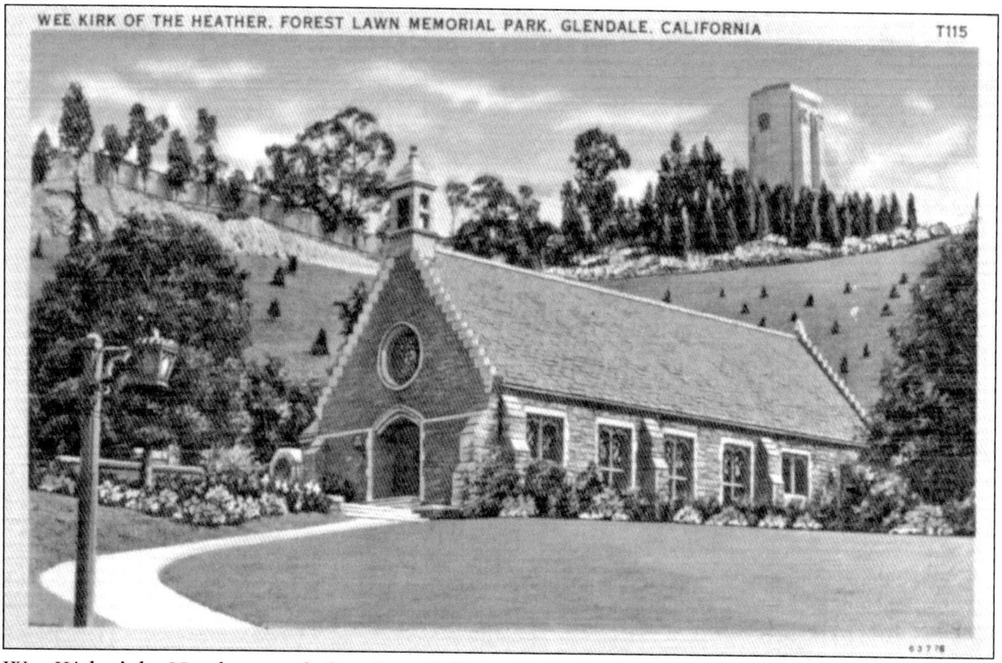

Wee Kirk o' the Heather, nestled against a hill, is a reproduction of the small church in Glencairn, Scotland, where Annie Laurie worshiped. The church has become a favorite wedding chapel for many of the couples married at Forest Lawn. This postcard was published by the Trichnor Art Company of Los Angeles around 1930. (Courtesy of the George Ellison Collection.)

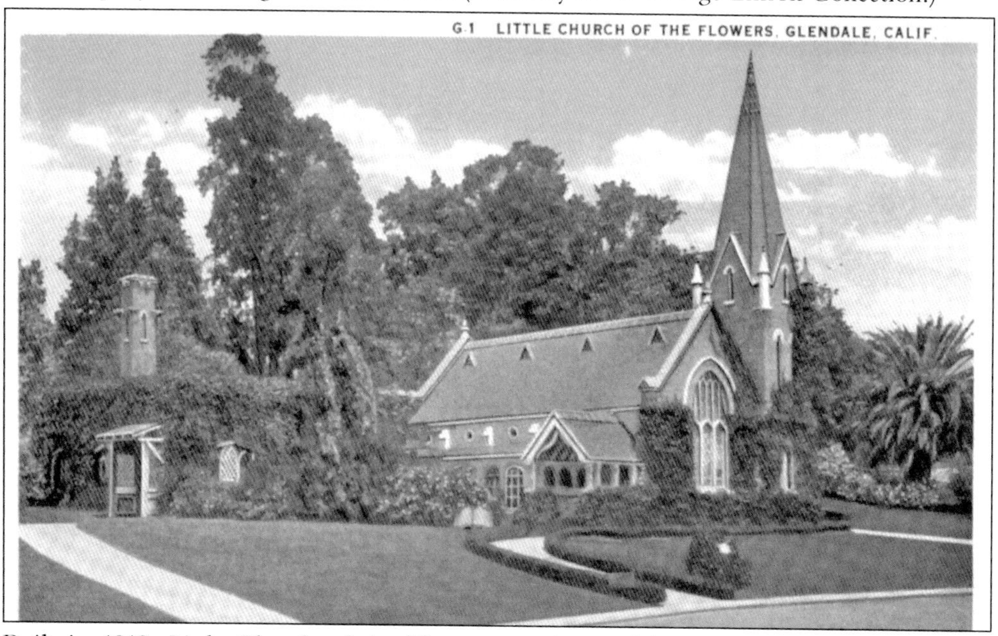

Built in 1918, Little Church of the Flowers was inspired by the 14th-century church at Stoke Poges, England, where Thomas Gray wrote the famous poem "Elegy Written in a Country Churchyard." This postcard was published by the Western Publishing and Novelty Company of Los Angeles about 1927. (Courtesy of the Special Collections Room, Glendale Public Library.)

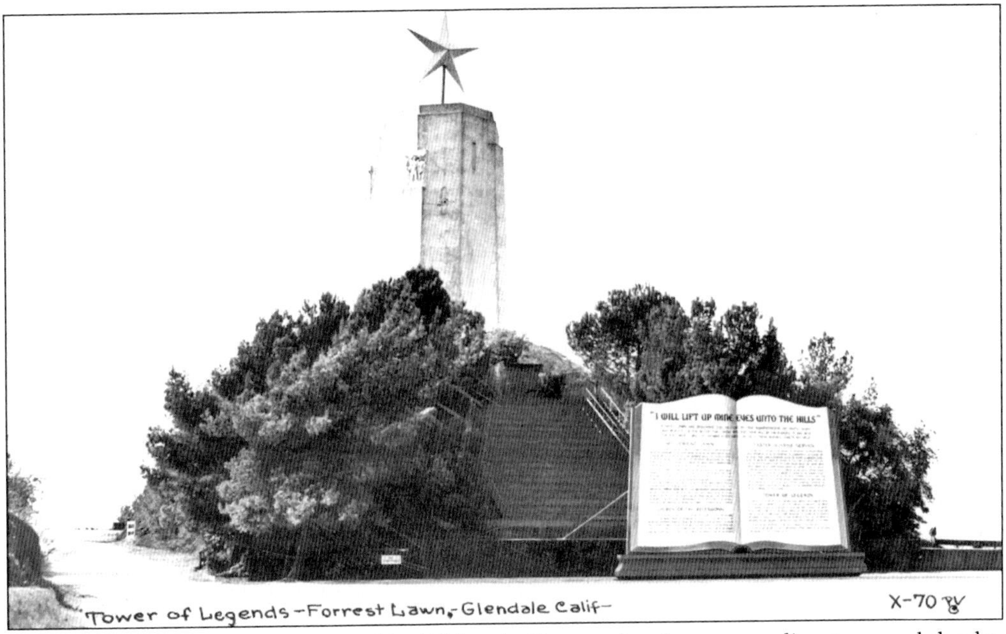

The Tower of Legends, constructed in 1925 to hold water for the surrounding trees and shrubs, depicted the allegorical life cycle of the Norse gods. Illuminated at night, it rose to 87 feet on the highest point in the park and was at one time the highest landmark north of Los Angeles. It served as the site of Easter sunrise services for many years and was torn down in 1948. This postcard dates to around 1926. (Courtesy of the Special Collections Room, Glendale Public Library.)

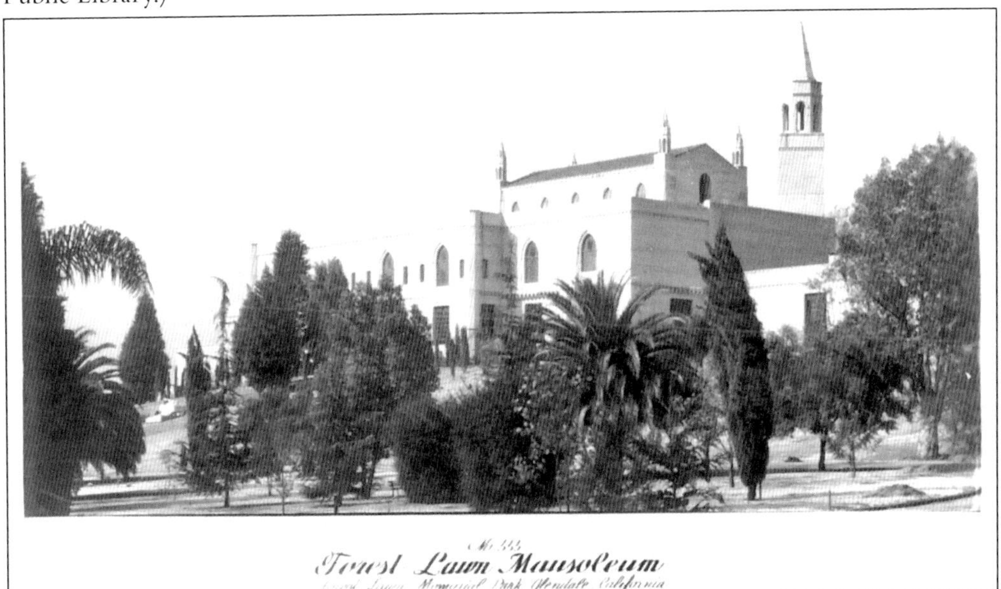

The Great Mausoleum holds an extensive collection of stained glass and sculpture. The Last Supper Window dominates the Memorial Court of Honor, which also includes reproductions of Michelangelo's works and crypts reserved for men and women who have performed an outstanding service to humanity. This postcard dates to about 1930. (Courtesy of the Special Collections Room, Glendale Public Library.)

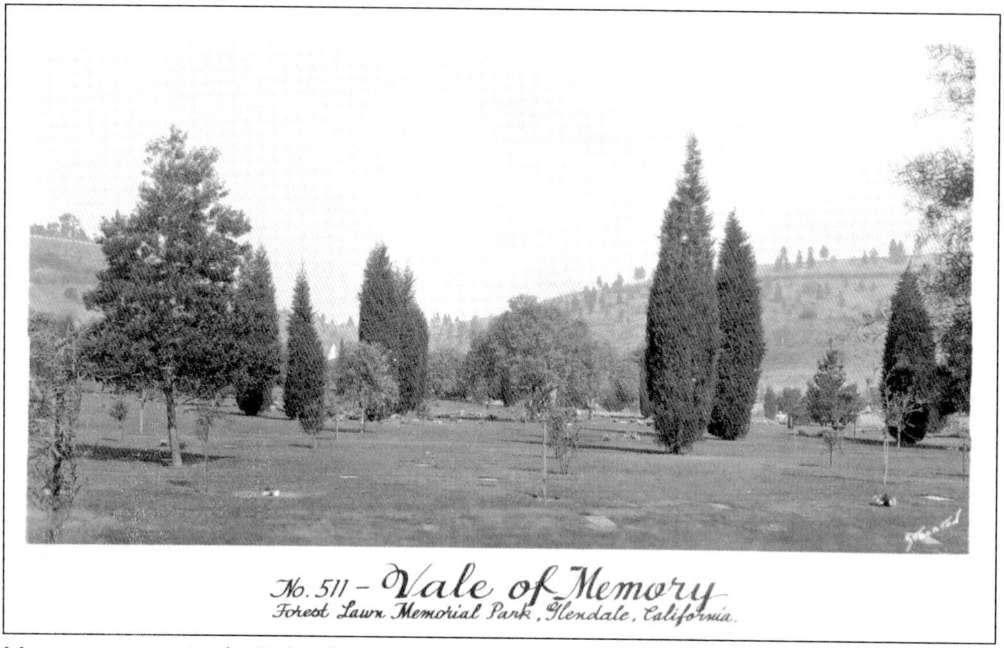

Many trees grew in the Vale of Memory, meeting Eaton's goal of providing a place of eternal rest among towering trees, great lawns, singing birds, and beautiful statuary. More than 20,000 trees and some 100,000 shrubs were planted in Forest Lawn. (Courtesy of the Special Collections Room, Glendale Public Library.)

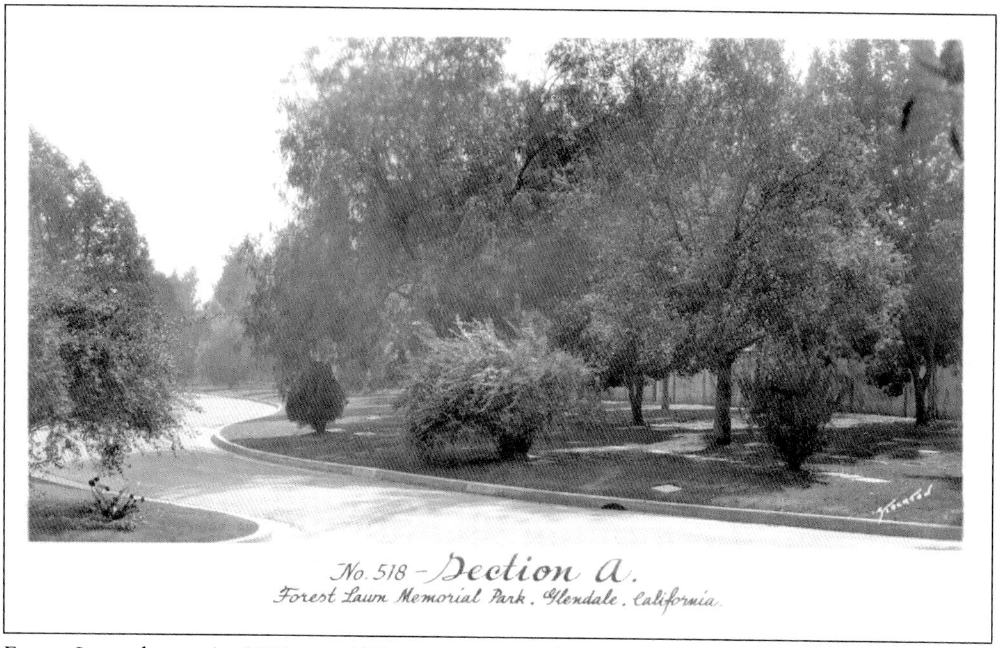

Forest Lawn began in 1906 as a 100-acre cemetery in Tropico, and many of Glendale's early settlers are buried in the oldest section, seen here. The land was once the residence of Andrew Glassell's daughter, Susan Glassell Mitchell. Glassell was one of the participants in the 1871 partition of the Spanish land grant received by Jose Maria Verdugo. (Courtesy of the Special Collections Room, Glendale Public Library.)

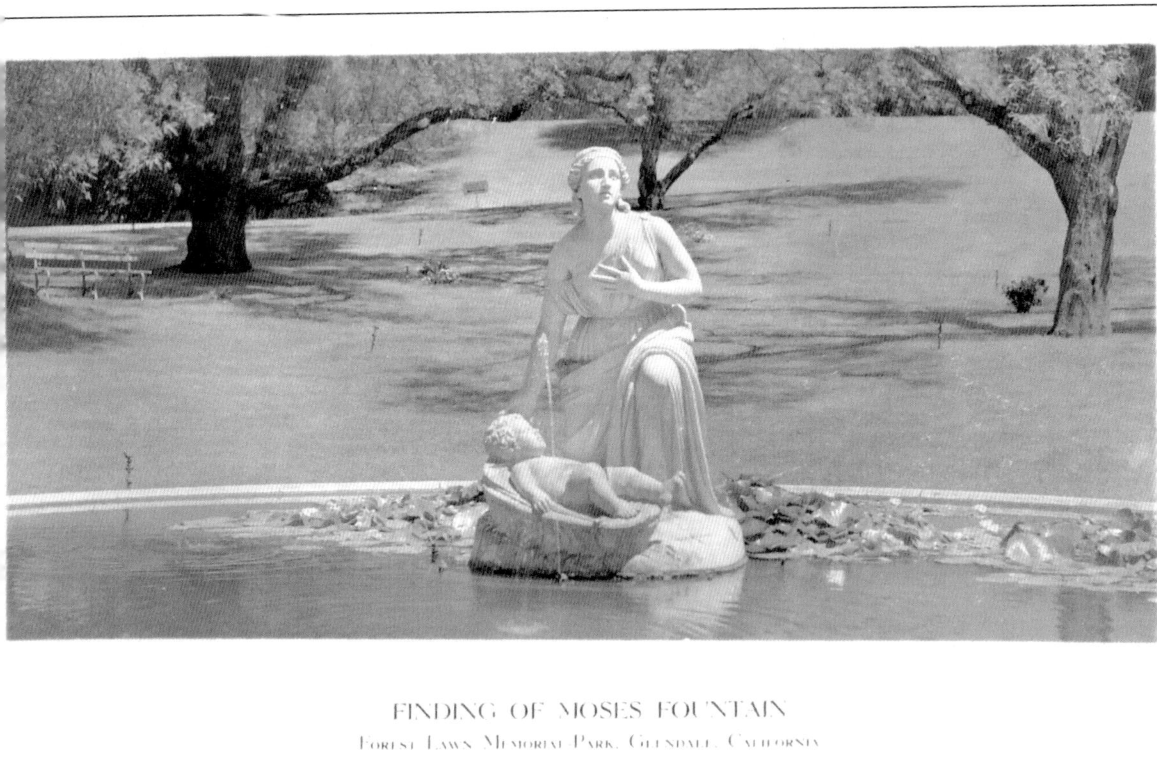

The *Finding of Moses* fountain pool, placed within the first curve of Cathedral Drive, was just one of many fountains dotting the landscape within the park. Hubert Eaton sought to provide a place where lovers could stroll, artists could sketch, and teachers could educate their students. In his "Builder's Creed," he also resolved to make Forest Lawn a place where loved ones could be memorialized in sculptured marble and pictorial glass. All was to be protected by the proceeds from an immense Endowment Care Fund. (Courtesy of the Special Collections Room, Glendale Public Library.)

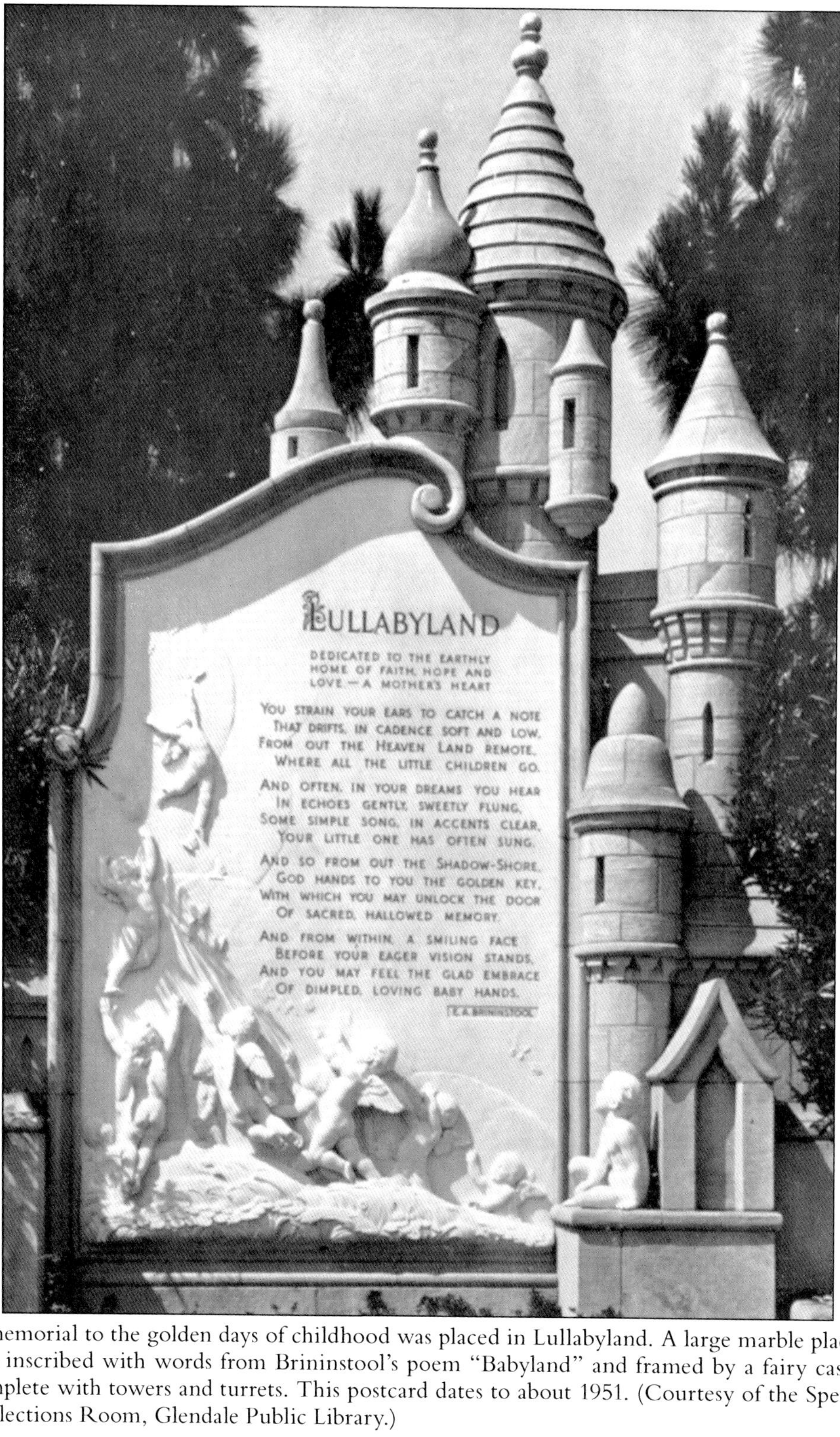

A memorial to the golden days of childhood was placed in Lullabyland. A large marble plaque was inscribed with words from Brininstool's poem "Babyland" and framed by a fairy castle, complete with towers and turrets. This postcard dates to about 1951. (Courtesy of the Special Collections Room, Glendale Public Library.)

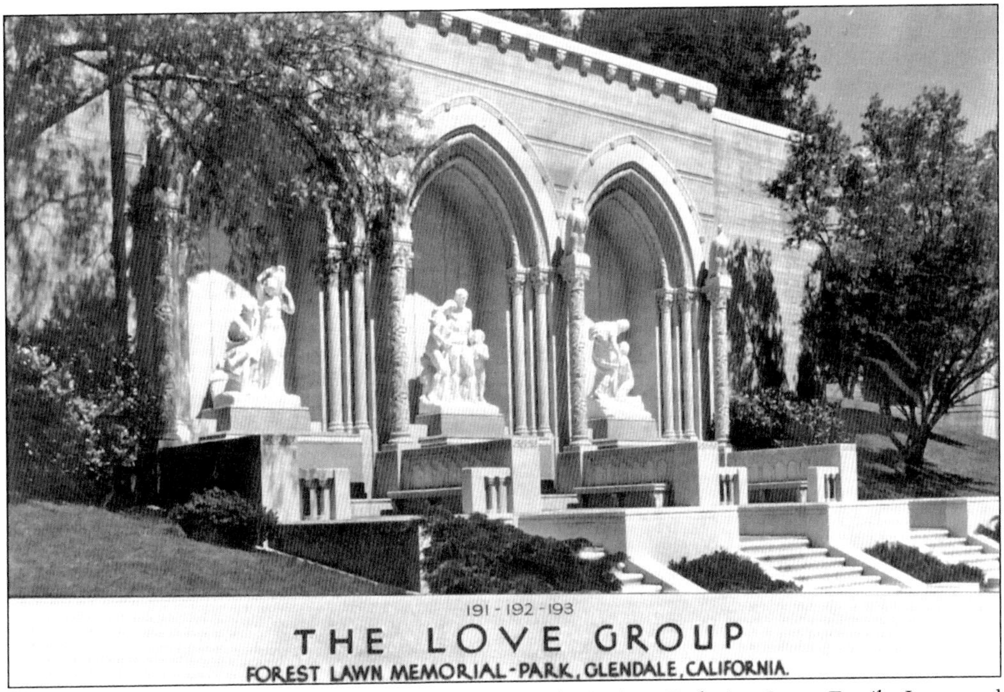

Three alcoves in the Shrine of Love hold statues depicting *Enduring Love*, *Family Love*, and *Father Love*, sculpted by Ernesto Gazzeri. The shrine was placed near the Great Mausoleum. This postcard dates to around 1929. (Courtesy of the Special Collections Room, Glendale Public Library.)

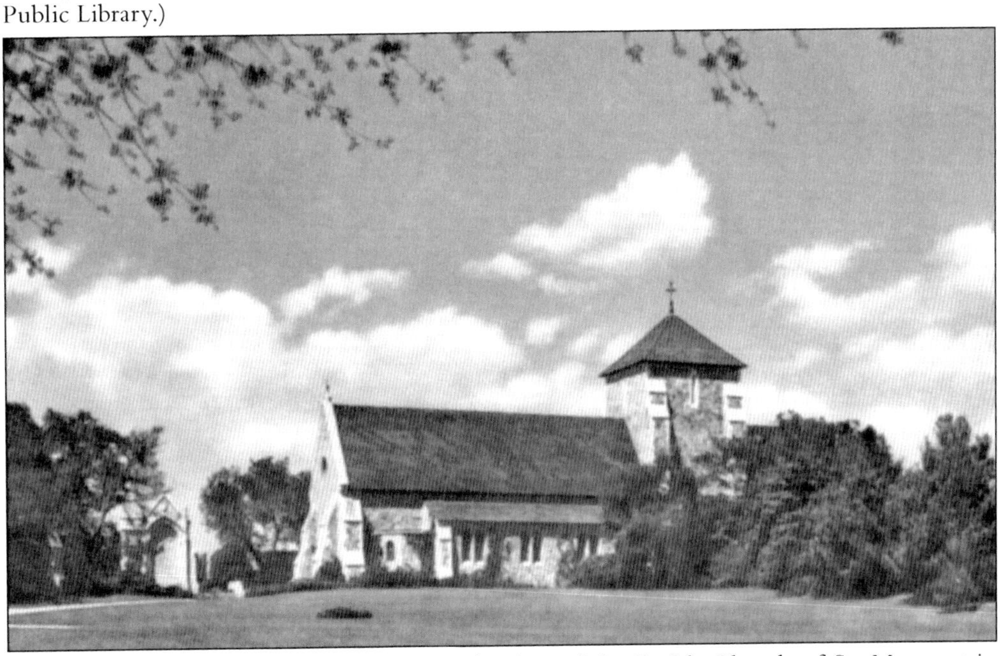

The Church of the Recessional is a reproduction of the Parish Church of St. Margaret in Rottingdean, England. Rudyard Kipling attended the church, which was the inspiration for his immortal poem "Recessional." This postcard was published by Adcraft Press of Los Angeles about 1945. (Courtesy of the Special Collections Room, Glendale Public Library.)

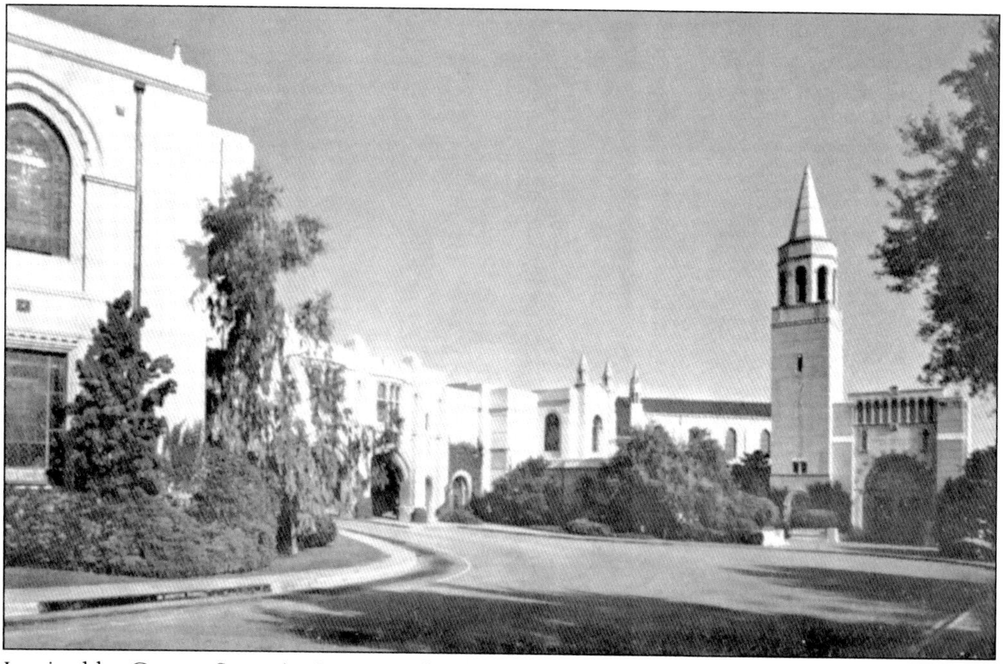

Inspired by Campo Santo in Genoa, Italy, the Great Mausoleum was built on a commanding spot, providing a sweeping view of the area. Eaton's creed is carved in stone near the entrance to the mausoleum. This postcard was published by the Forest Lawn Memorial Park Association around 1949. (Courtesy of the Special Collections Room, Glendale Public Library.)

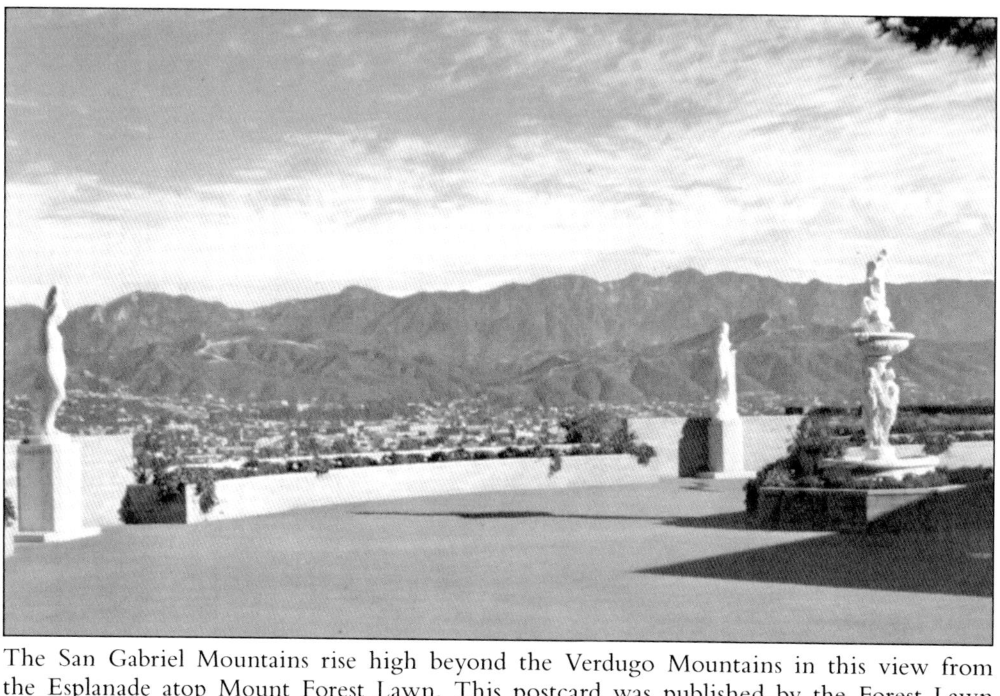

The San Gabriel Mountains rise high beyond the Verdugo Mountains in this view from the Esplanade atop Mount Forest Lawn. This postcard was published by the Forest Lawn Memorial Park Association about 1960. (Courtesy of the Special Collections Room, Glendale Public Library.)

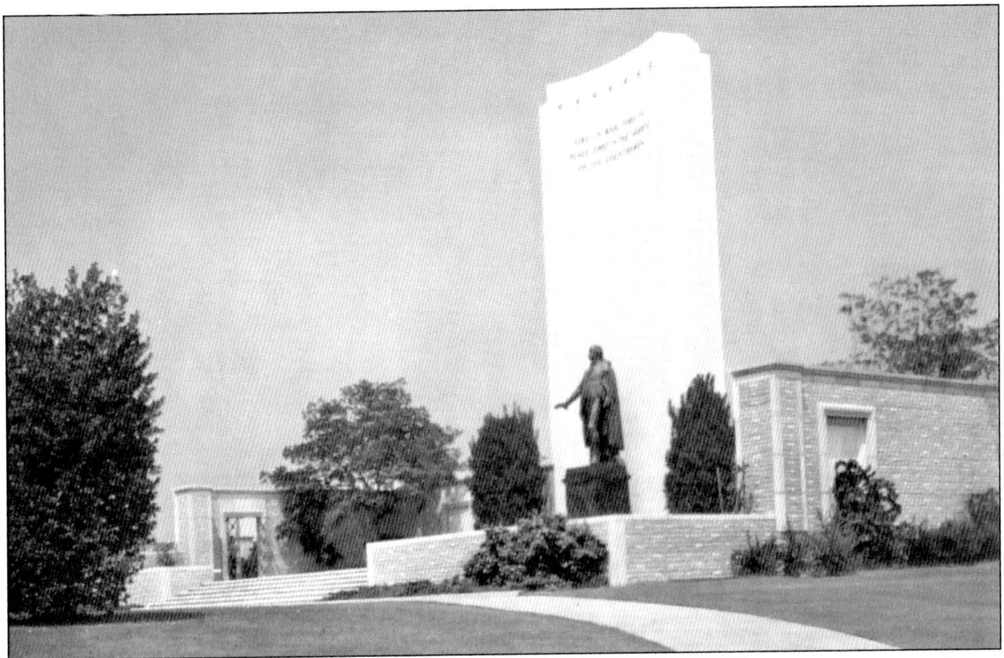

This bronze statue of George Washington, created by sculptor John Quincy Adams Ward, stands in the great Court of Freedom. It was commissioned for the Capitol in Washington, D.C. Due to an oversight, however, funds were never appropriated, and it came to Forest Lawn. (Courtesy of the Special Collections Room, Glendale Public Library.)

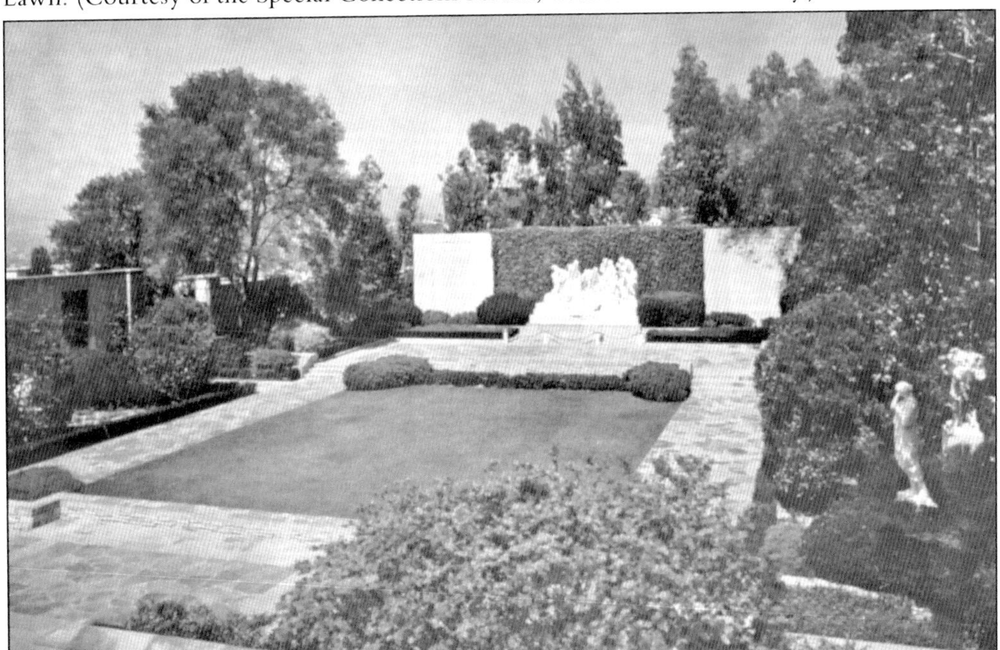

The Mystery of Life Garden combines sculpture and landscaping. Dominating the scene is *The Mystery of Life* statuary group, the largest piece of sculpture in the park when it was installed. Each of the 18 life-size figures symbolizes a different type of person, each with his own answer to the mystery of life. (Courtesy of the Special Collections Room, Glendale Public Library.)

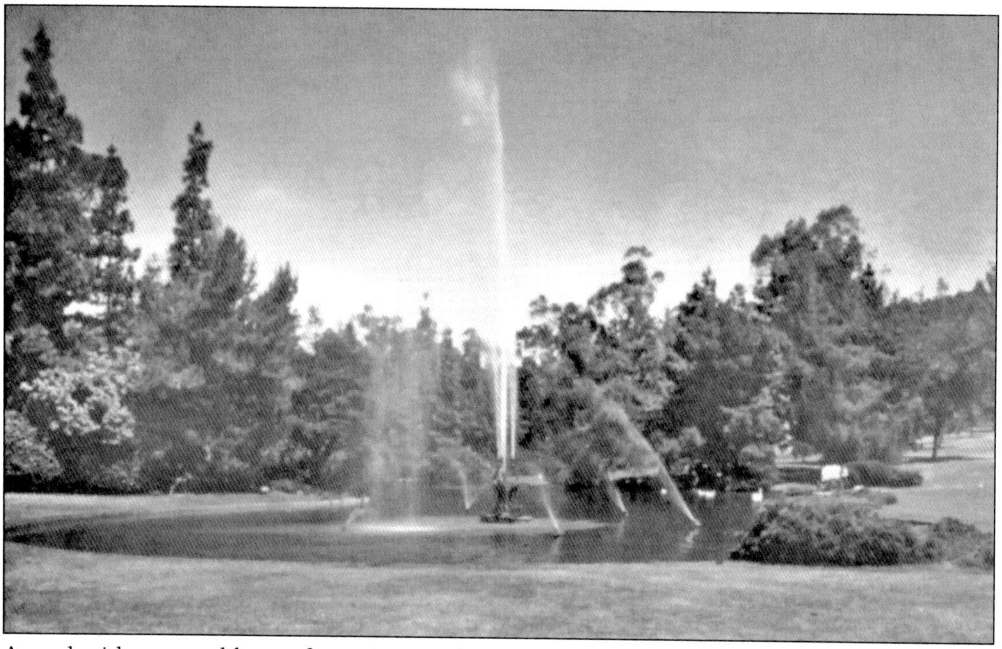

A pool with a central heron fountain was placed just within the entrance gates. By the side of the pool are *The Frog Baby* and *The Duck Baby*, created by Edith B. Parsons for the San Francisco Exposition of 1915. *The Duck Baby* was the first statue purchased by Eaton. (Courtesy of the Special Collections Room, Glendale Public Library.)

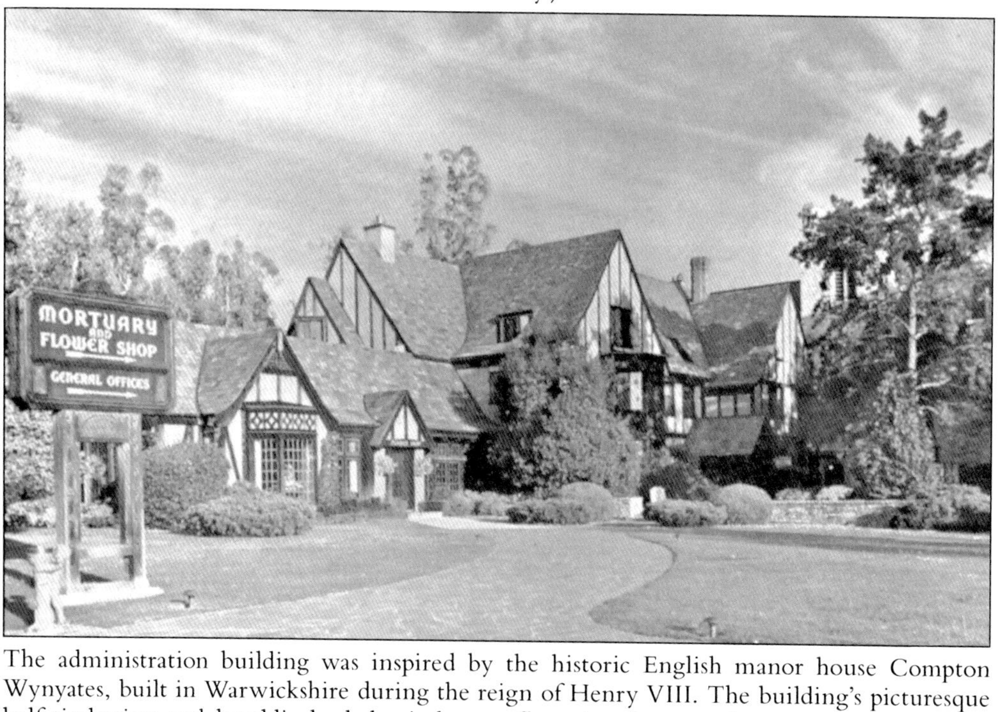

The administration building was inspired by the historic English manor house Compton Wynyates, built in Warwickshire during the reign of Henry VIII. The building's picturesque half-timbering and heraldic leaded windows reflect the charm and peace of 16th-century England. This postcard was published by the Forest Lawn Memorial Park Association around 1948. (Courtesy of the Special Collections Room, Glendale Public Library.)

Eight

Casa Verdugo

The romance of California's Spanish period was packaged up into a destination in northern Glendale and given the name Casa Verdugo. Its objective was to attract tourists and potential land buyers from all over the country. Railroad men and wealthy landowners like Leslie C. Brand schemed to create a tranquil yet exciting place to take the Glendale electric streetcar during a time when nothing but a few farmhouses populated the landscape. Glendale needed a destination to make it popular; hence the idea of a Spanish restaurant with costumed entertainers, alcoholic beverages, and a park-like setting with fabulous views of the mountains and valleys.

The restaurant was housed in the former adobe home of Rafael Verdugo and her husband, Fernando Sepulveda, both having left the Glendale area before the start of the 20th century. The name, meaning "the house of the Verdugo," fit well. Leslie C. Brand convinced a businesswoman from Los Angeles, who had already established a successful Spanish-style restaurant there, to become the operator of the new Casa Verdugo. Disputes between Pacific Electric owners and the restaurant operator caused a separation and establishment of a new Casa Verdugo in a new location a few blocks to the east.

Meanwhile, the Pacific Electric ran the Casa Verdugo as the Ramada for a short time until development pressures brought the demise of the old Spanish adobe, which was demolished in 1911. After the second Casa Verdugo closed, new owners established a third Casa Verdugo in a large home at the terminus of Brand Boulevard at Mountain Street, near the original home site. Over time, as development sprouted up around the Casa Verdugo Restaurant, the unincorporated community became commonly known as Casa Verdugo, and a post office by the same name was established. In 1926, much of the area was annexed to Glendale.

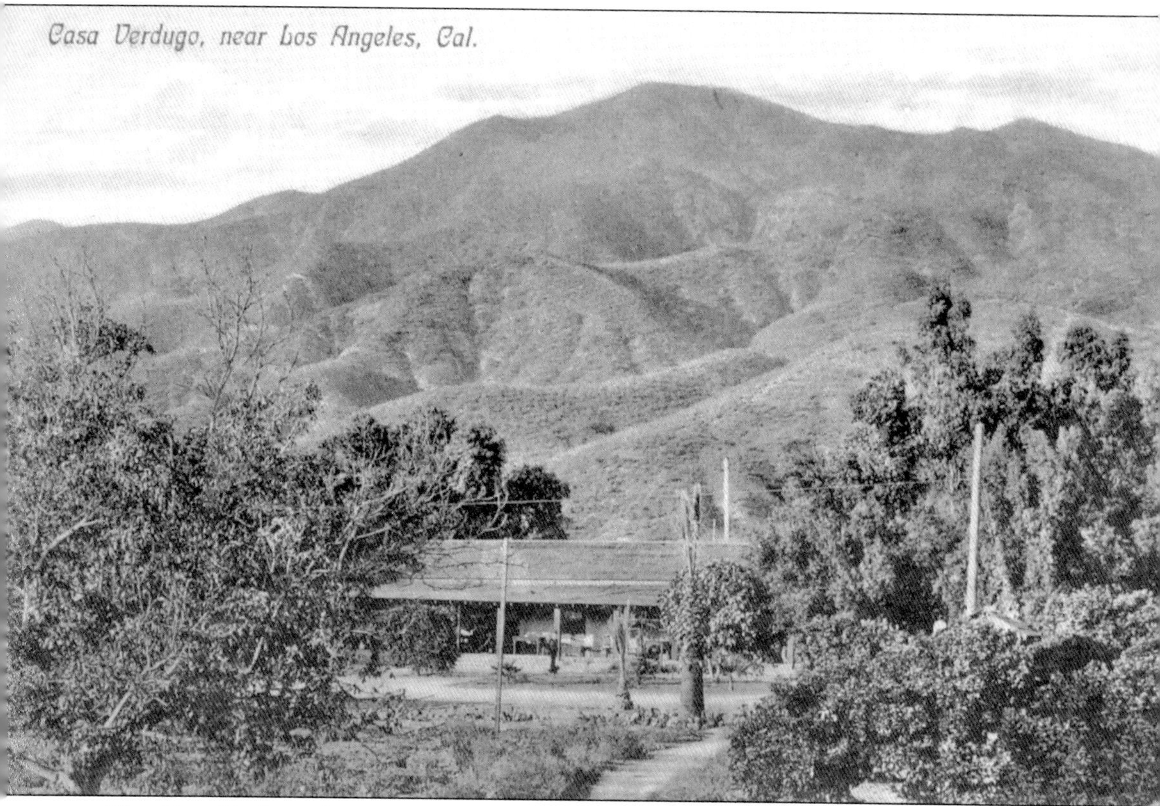

The Casa Verdugo Restaurant opened in an old adobe dwelling in 1904, after the Pacific Electric line was extended all the way up Brand Boulevard to Mountain Street. The adobe, one of many dwellings built by the extended members of the Verdugo family, was surrounded by pepper and olive trees and stood on the east side of the street. Piedad Yorba de Sowl and her husband, Charles, opened the restaurant, serving Spanish-style food. (Courtesy of the Special Collections Room, Glendale Public Library.)

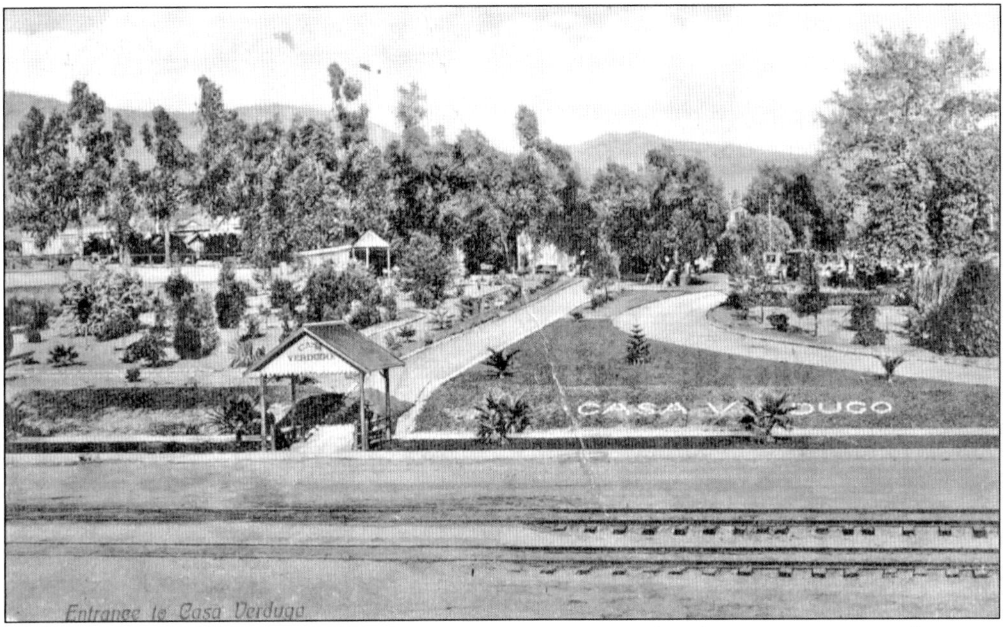

Casa Verdugo quickly became a popular destination for Pacific Electric passengers. The route from Los Angeles, only eight miles away, offered scenic views of the bluffs along the Los Angeles River and the orchards and strawberry fields surrounding the village of Glendale. This postcard was published by M. Rieder Publications of Los Angeles. (Courtesy of the Special Collections Room, Glendale Public Library.)

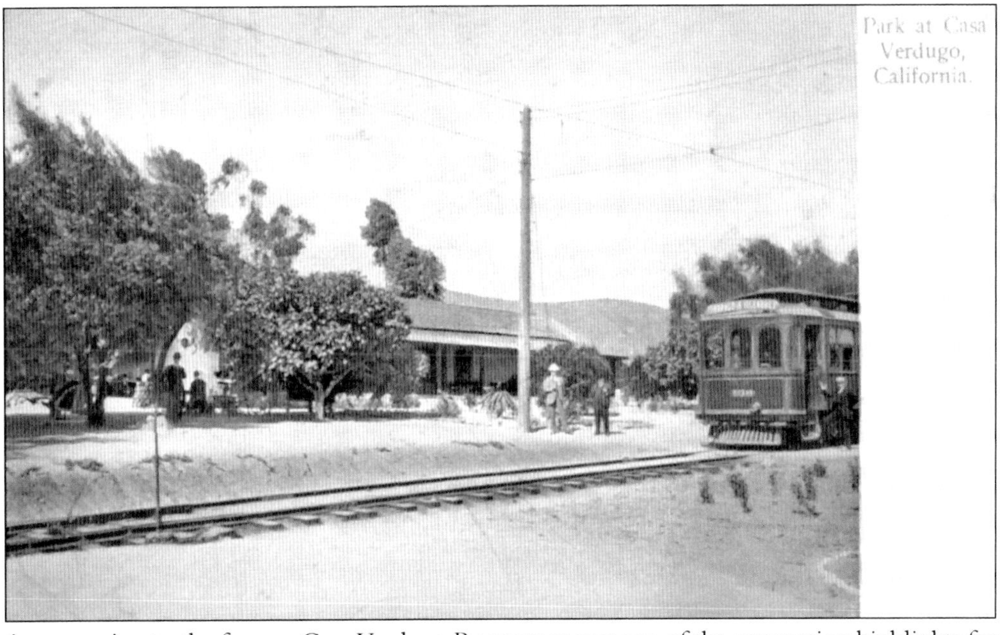

An excursion to the famous Casa Verdugo Restaurant was one of the convention highlights for Shriners when they gathered in Los Angeles in 1907. Delegates came from all over the country. In preparation for the event, residents hung bunting and flags to welcome the estimated 5,000 Shriners. Railroad officials said that more than half visited Casa Verdugo. (Courtesy of the Special Collections Room, Glendale Public Library.)

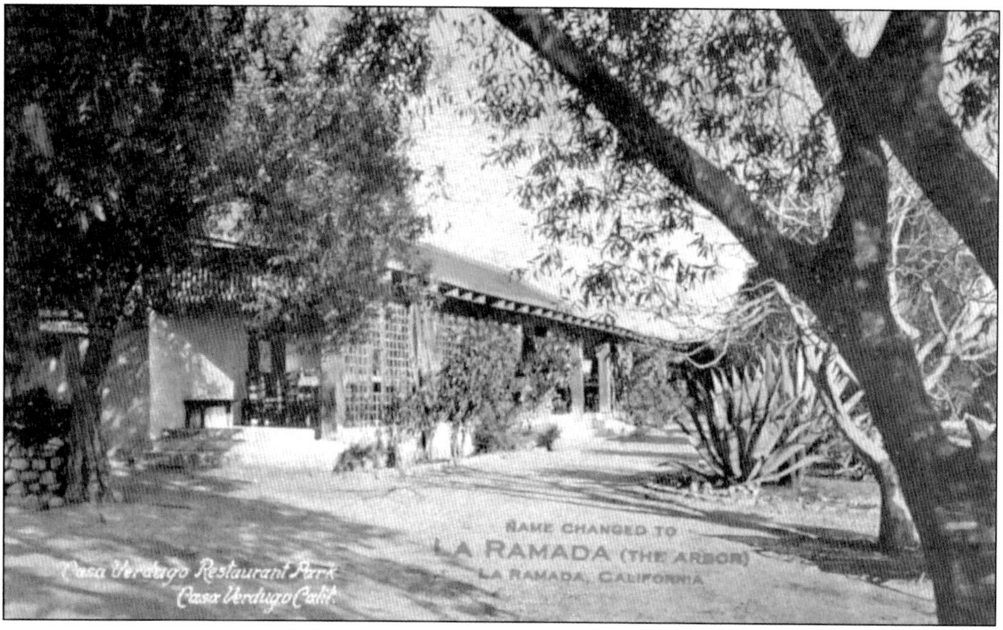

After a few years, railroad directors tried to persuade the proprietors of Casa Verdugo to stay open late, but Piedad Yorba de Sowl refused to do so. She left, taking the name of Casa Verdugo to another location nearby. The adobe restaurant, renamed La Ramada, stayed in business for a few more years. (Courtesy of the Special Collections Room, Glendale Public Library.)

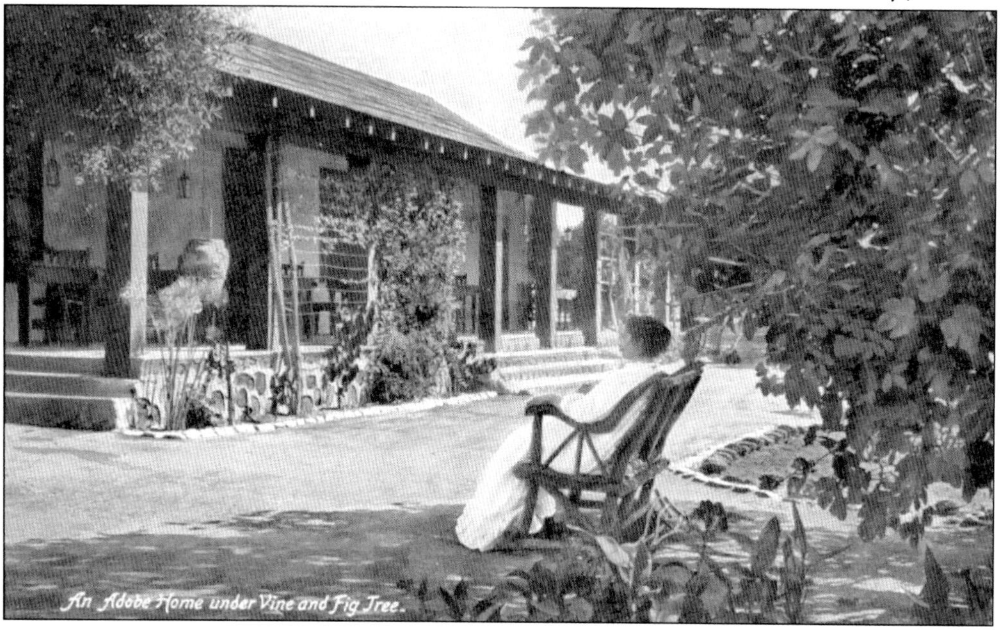

Proprietress Piedad Yorba de Sowl sits in a chair at the original Casa Verdugo, which was built in the same style as the other Verdugo adobes. Diners were seated on the long narrow porch, and a large outdoor dining area covered with palm leaves accommodated larger groups. Indoor rooms provided seating in colder weather. This postcard was published by M. Rieder Publications of Los Angeles around 1905. (Courtesy of the Special Collections Room, Glendale Public Library.)

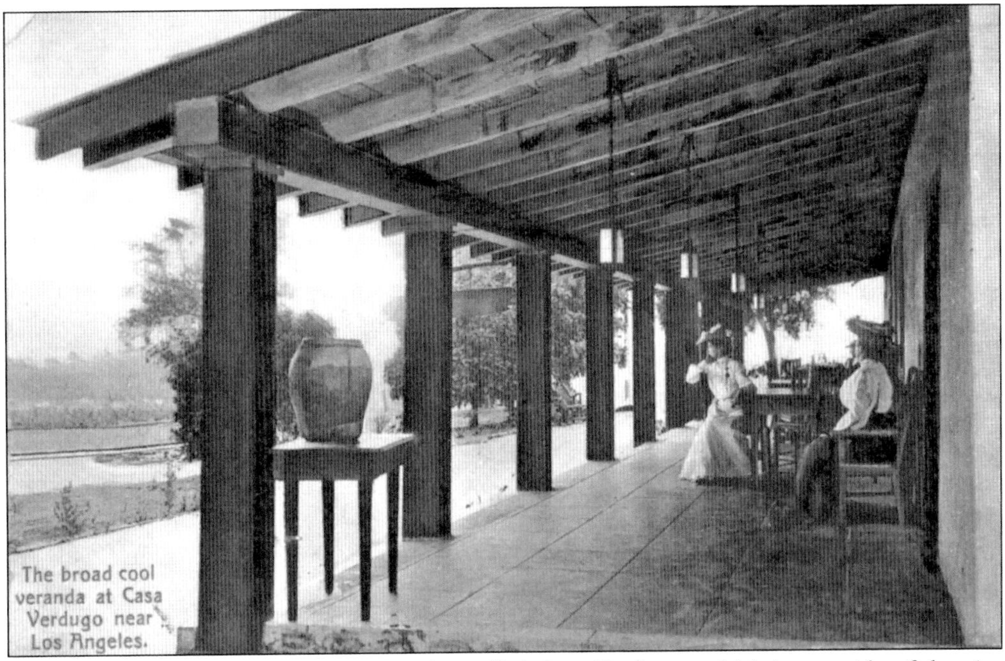

The restaurant was situated in an area also called Casa Verdugo, which lay outside of the city limits. The restaurant could therefore serve wine, which was prohibited in dry Glendale. This hand-colored postcard was made in Germany about 1907. (Courtesy of the Special Collections Room, Glendale Public Library.)

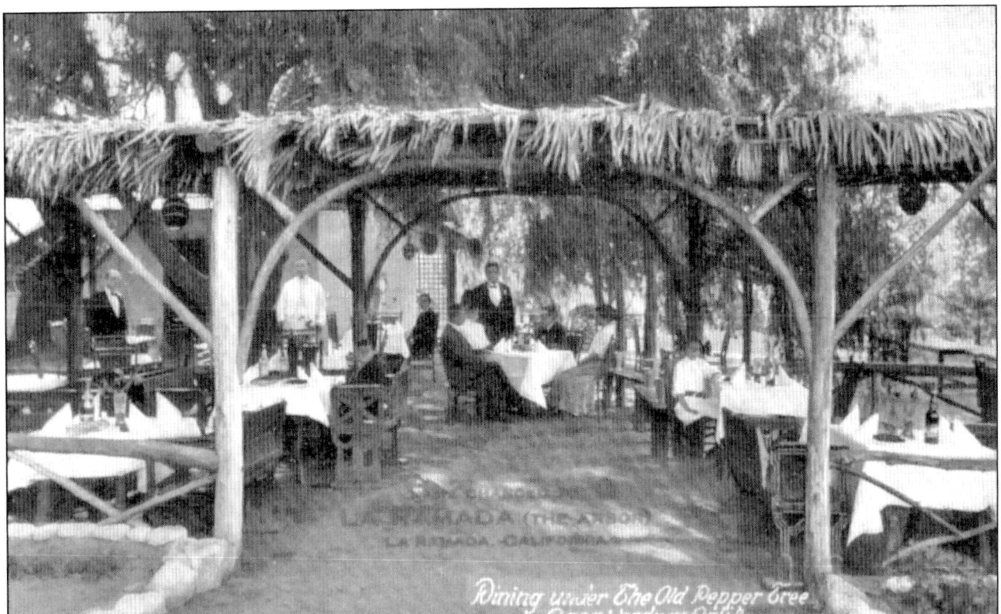

La Ramada remained in business until Prohibition began in 1920 and the wine service, which had been a prominent part of its menu, was no longer available. This postcard was published by Pacific Electric. (Courtesy of the Special Collections Room, Glendale Public Library.)

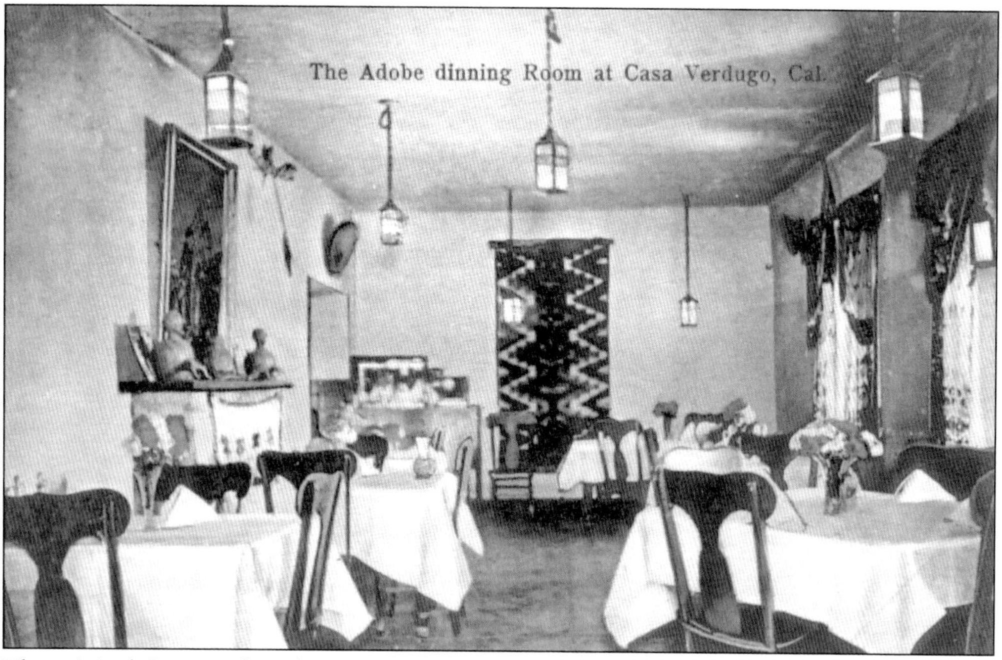

The original Casa Verdugo had several dining rooms furnished in an eclectic mix of Spanish, Mexican, and American styles. This postcard was published by the Newman Post Card Company of Los Angeles. (Courtesy of the Special Collections Room, Glendale Public Library.)

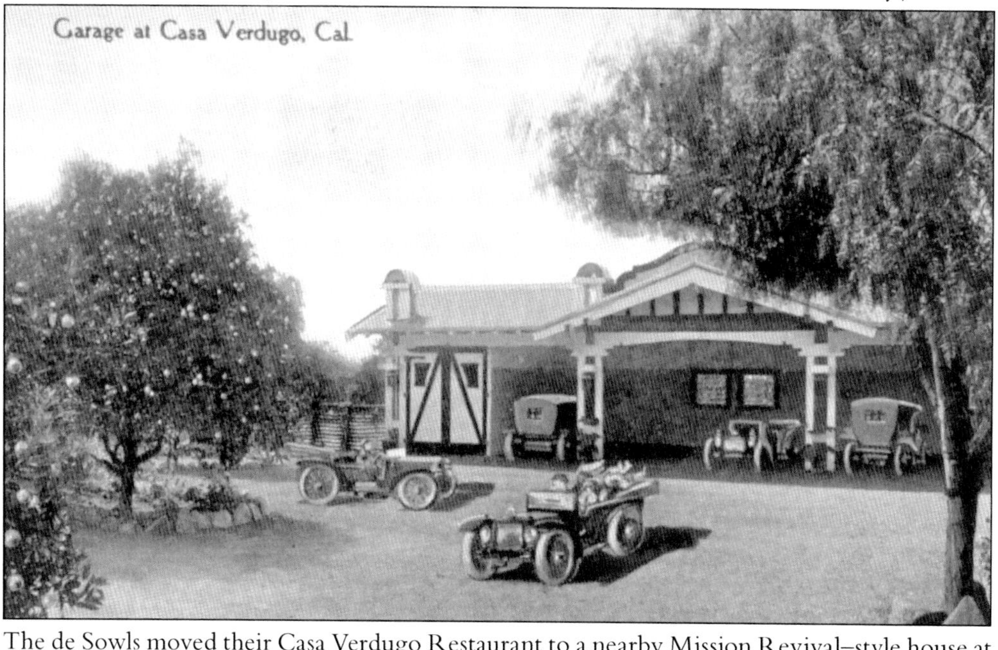

The de Sowls moved their Casa Verdugo Restaurant to a nearby Mission Revival–style house at the corner of Louise and Randolph Streets and converted the garage (pictured) into a kitchen. The new location was "Not the Railroad Place—The Original Casa Verdugo." The de Sowls proclaimed it a high-class Spanish restaurant with dinners specially prepared by Señora de Sowl. This coppergraph was made by the Phillips Printing Company of Los Angeles. (Courtesy of the Special Collections Room, Glendale Public Library.)

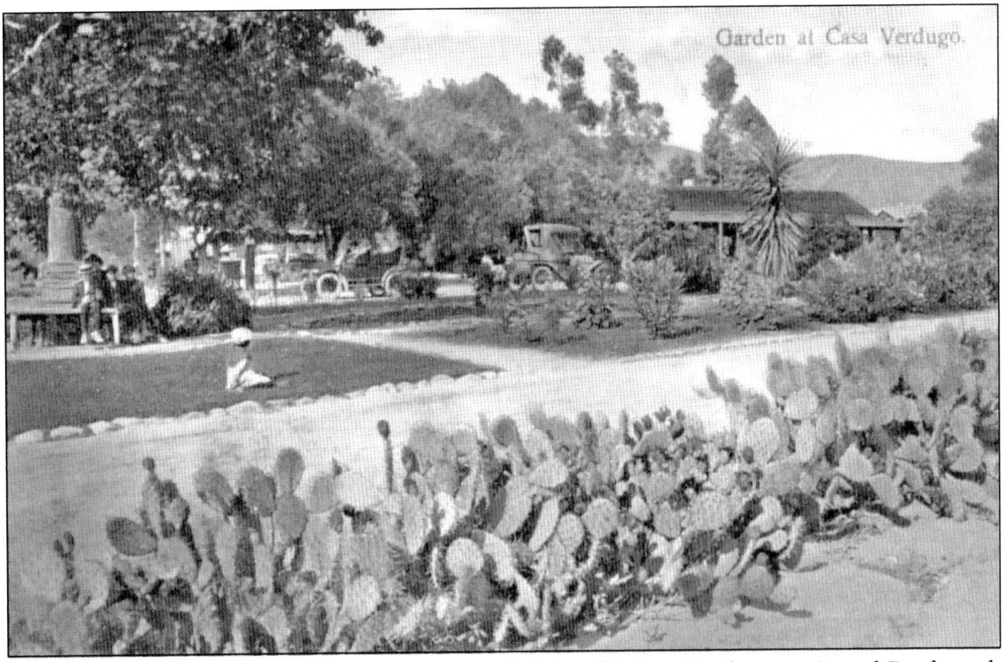

Cactus plants, palms, and pepper trees surrounded the old Casa Verdugo on Brand Boulevard. Waitresses dressed as señoritas serenaded the diners as they enjoyed their meals, evoking the atmosphere of Alta California. (Courtesy of the Special Collections Room, Glendale Public Library.)

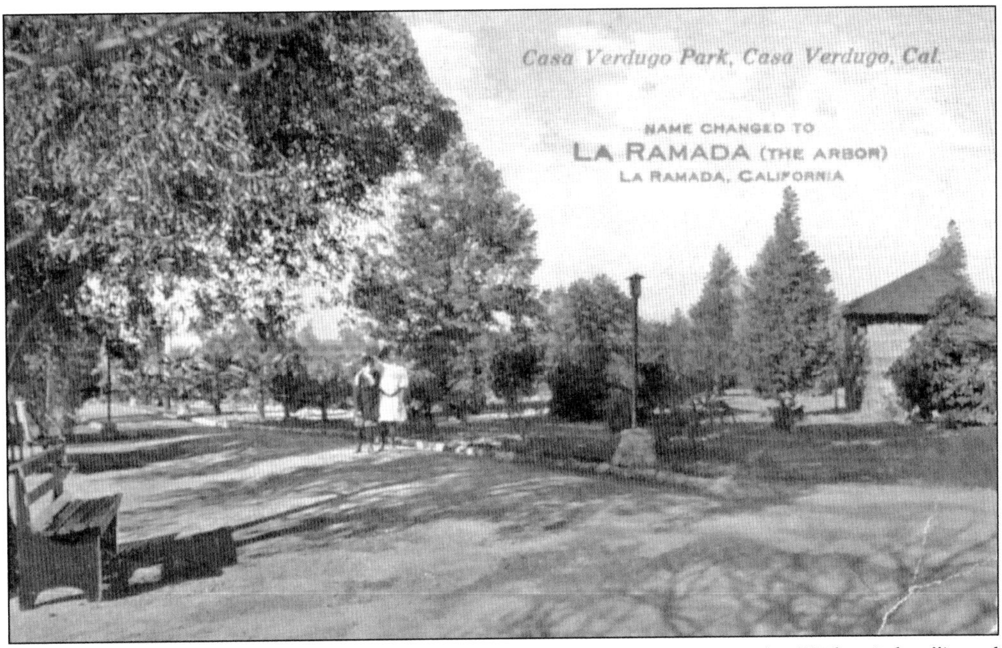

The Pacific Electric renamed the original adobe restaurant La Ramada ("The Arbor") and posted a sign at the end of the trolley line indicating that Casa Verdugo was closed for repairs. The de Sowls sued for $10,000 in damages, and the court backed their claim. This postcard dates to around 1911. (Courtesy of the Special Collections Room, Glendale Public Library.)

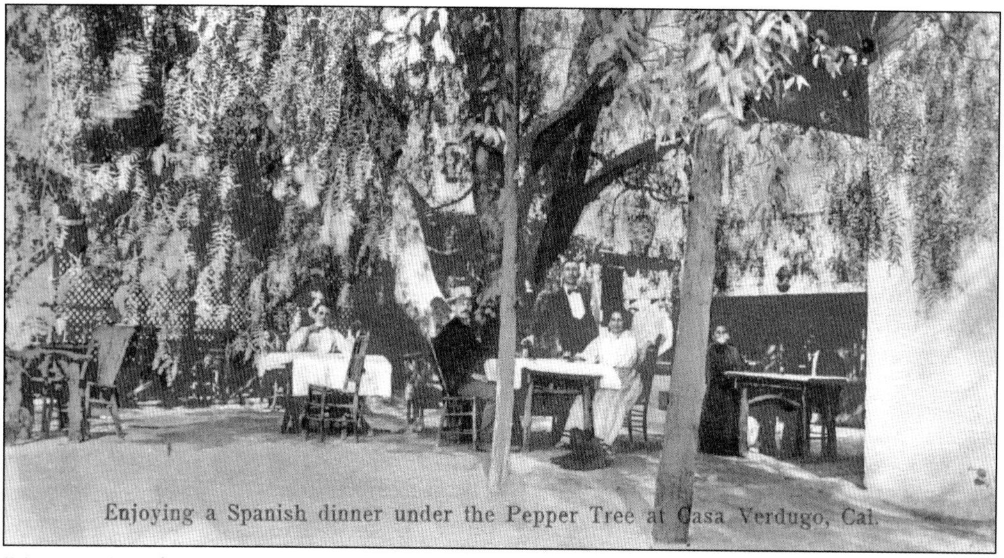

Diners enjoy their Spanish dinners under the pepper trees at Casa Verdugo. This postcard was published by the Newman Post Card Company of Los Angeles. (Courtesy of the Special Collections Room, Glendale Public Library.)

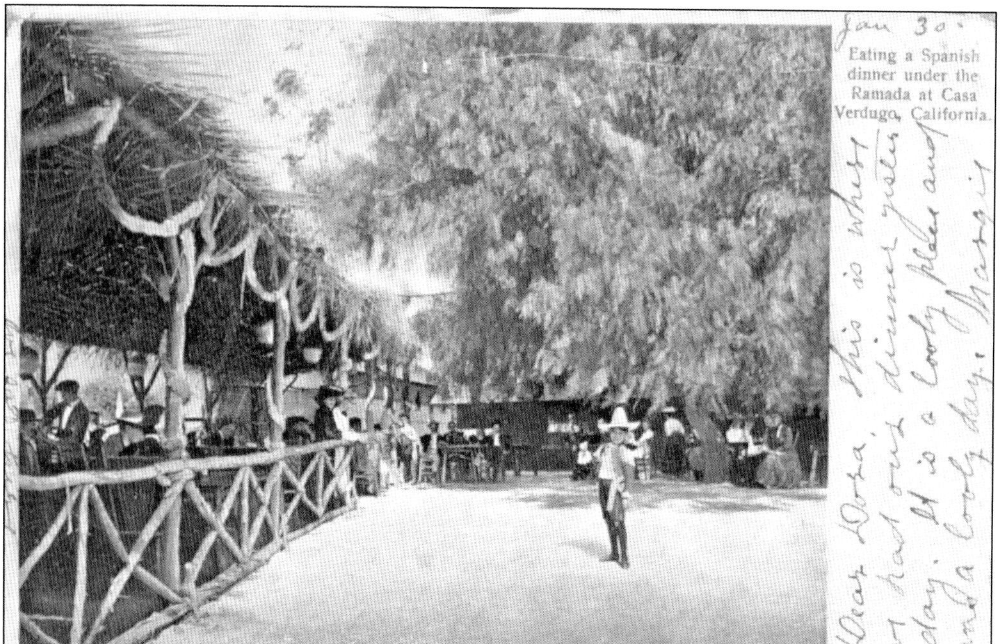

In 1915, Casa Verdugo was the scene of a "near riot" when a group of Los Angeles police detectives boarded a streetcar bound for a picnic in Verdugo Park but instead found themselves at the restaurant. At first the detectives treated it as a joke, but as time passed, they demanded that the conductor take them back toward the park. When he refused, they became agitated and the police were called. Eventually, officials remedied the situation, and the detectives were deposited in the cooling shade of Verdugo Park. This postcard was published by M. Rieder Publications of Los Angeles. (Courtesy of the Special Collections Room, Glendale Public Library.)

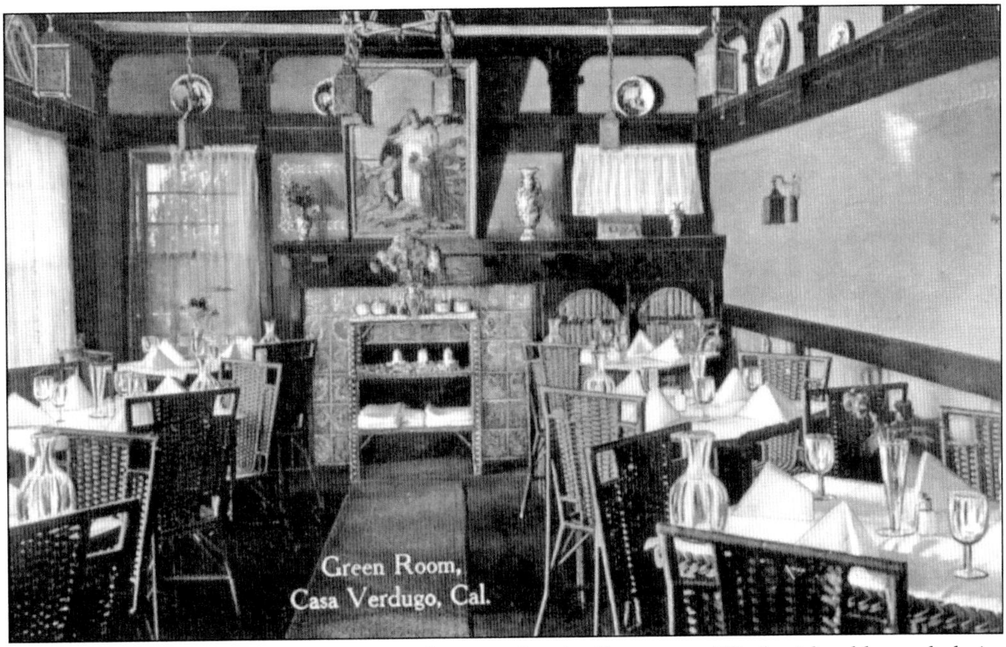

The Green Room at the new Casa Verdugo on Louise Street was filled with tables and chairs clustered around the Batchelder tile fireplace. (Courtesy of the Special Collections Room, Glendale Public Library.)

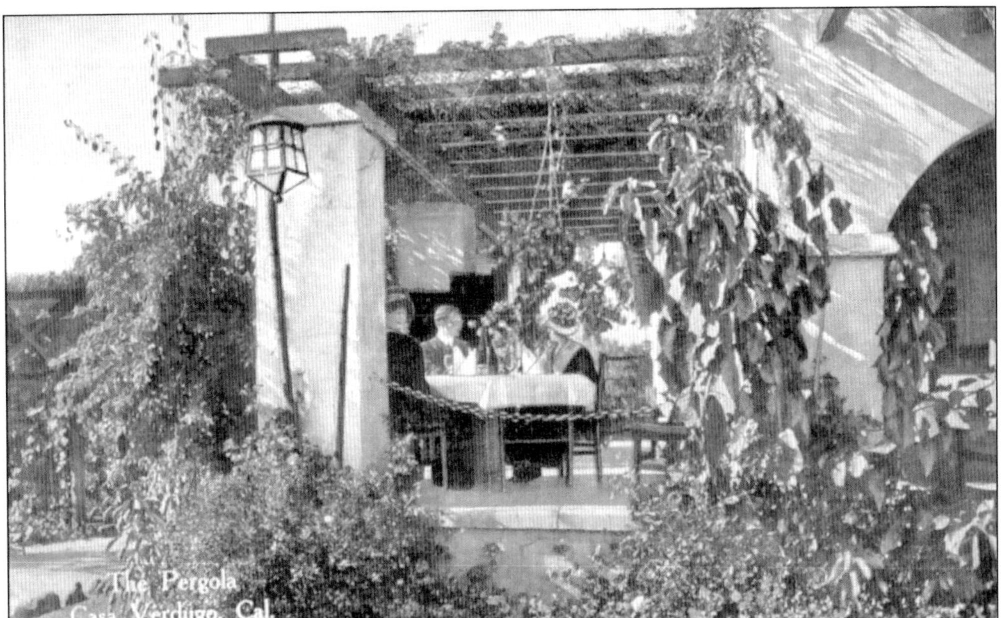

A pergola on the side of the Casa Verdugo on Louise Street provided shade for outdoor dining. The menu still offered the same Spanish-style dishes as at the previous location. (Courtesy of the Special Collections Room, Glendale Public Library.)

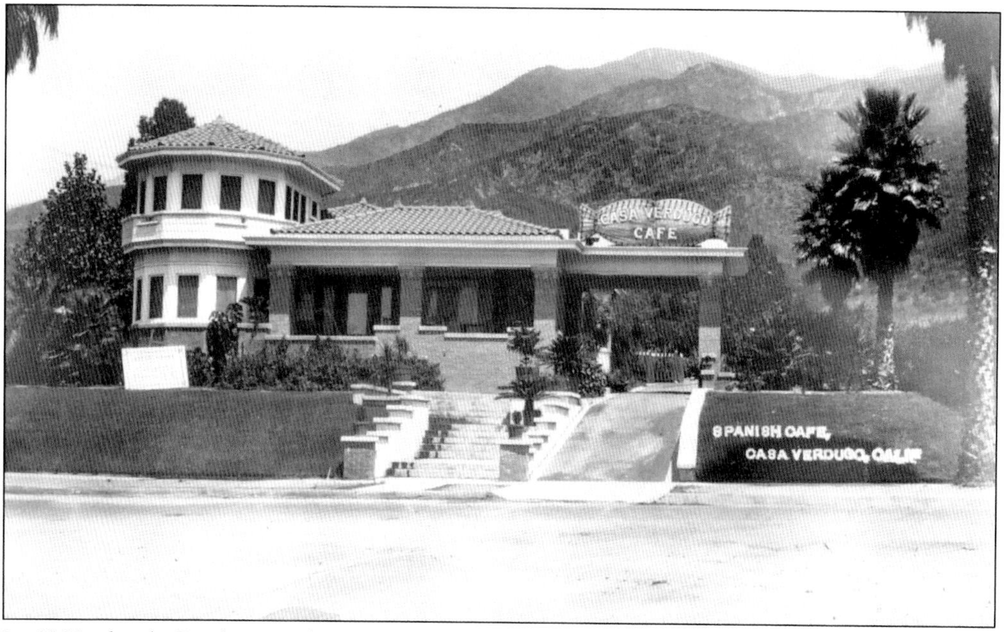

In 1920, the de Sowls moved again. This time, they chose to put their café in a large house on Mountain Street, on the northwest corner with Brand Boulevard and close to both of their previous locations. As before, they offered the atmosphere of old Spain and provided catering for large events. (Courtesy of the Special Collections Room, Glendale Public Library.)

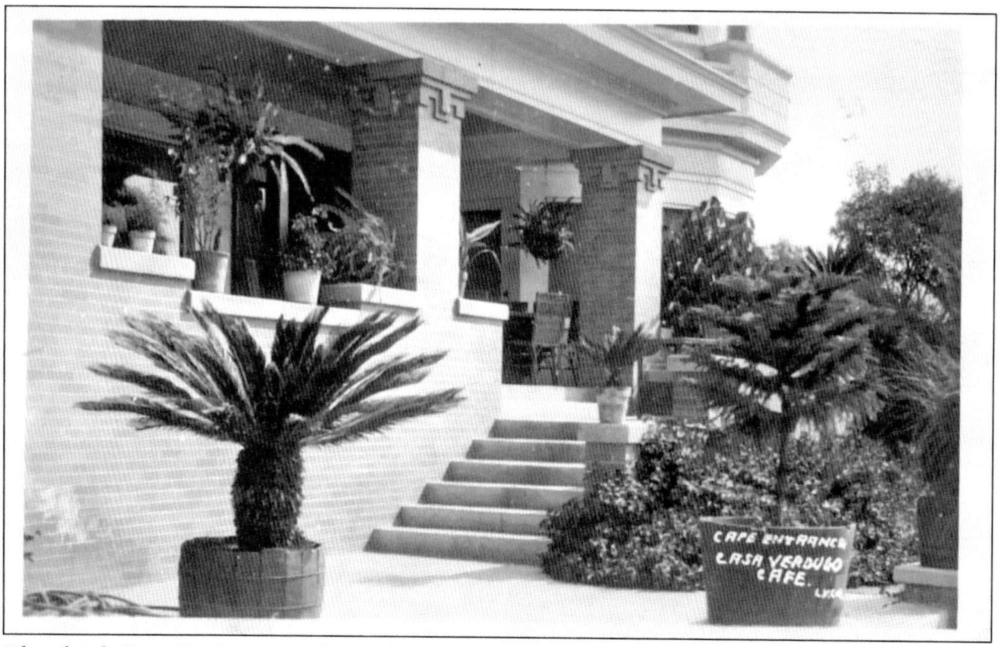

The third Casa Verdugo was located in a home built by Charles F. L. Richter, formerly of Chicago. He lived in the house for several years, returning to Chicago around the time World War I began. (Courtesy of the Special Collections Room, Glendale Public Library.)

Nine

The Glendale Sanitarium

As pneumonia and other respiratory illnesses were sweeping across the country, California was seen as the land of healthful air and a place to cure ailments. Treatment institutions offering clean mountain air sprouted up in locations like Glendale. The most famous was the Seventh Day Adventist Sanitarium, which opened in 1905 in the old Glendale Hotel, a Victorian-style edifice built as a luxury hotel during the 1885 and 1886 boom years. Soon out of business, the hotel housed a girls' school and later Glendale's first public high school before L. C. Brand bought it at auction. The Adventists had been seeking a place for a sanitarium, and when they approached Brand, he resold it to them at an affordable price. Tranquil, peaceful grounds were created around the old hotel where patients could stroll and absorb the healthful rays of the California sun. The Glendale Sanitarium became known across the country as a treatment home for many health problems.

Seventh Day Adventists had been represented in Southern California before the 1900s, but no church existed in Glendale until 1906, the year after the sanitarium opened. All but four of the charter members were employed by the sanitarium, and services were first held in the hotel's parlor and then in the dining room. In 1911, the Adventists purchased the Baptists' old sanctuary and moved it to Wilson Avenue and Isabel Street, near the sanitarium.

The Glendale Sanitarium grew and outlived the usefulness of the old hotel building, moving into a planned modern medical facility on the hills above Glendale in 1924. An assembly room on the first floor of the nurse's dormitory sufficed as a sanctuary until a church building was erected on sanitarium grounds. Today the Glendale Adventist Medical Center has replaced the old Glendale Sanitarium with a highly modern medical complex.

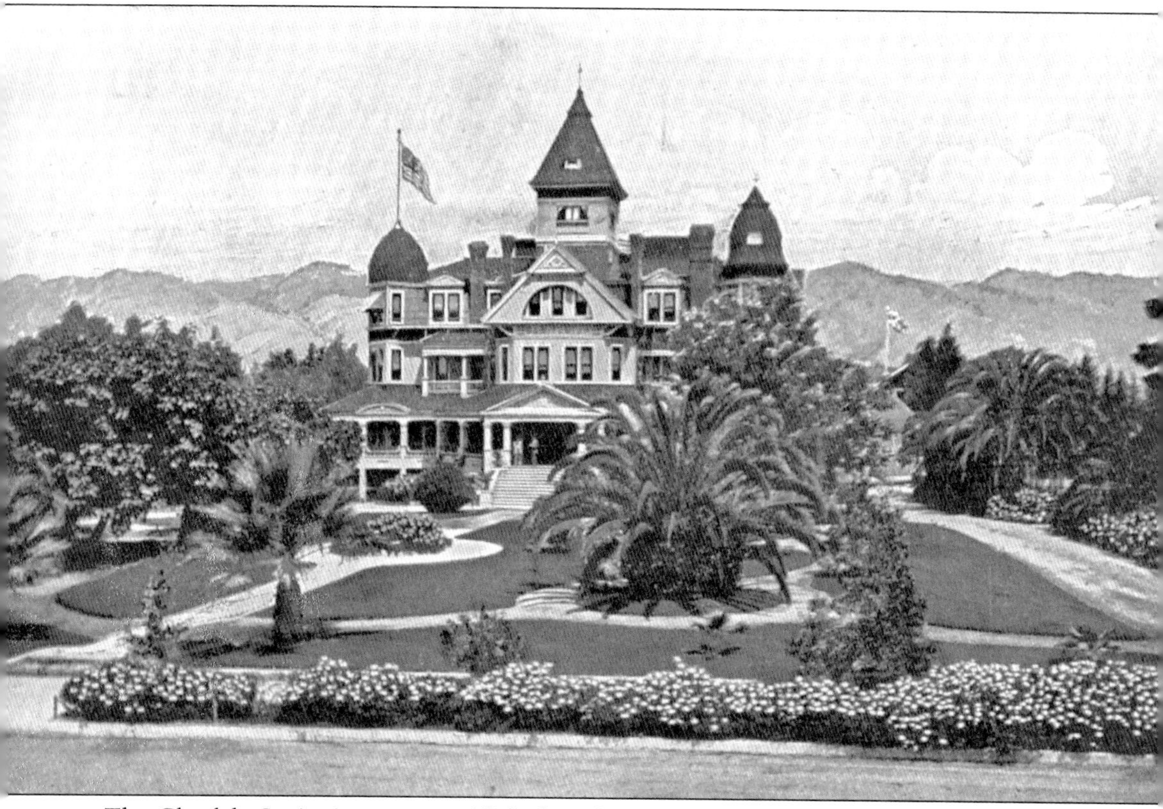

The Glendale Sanitarium was established in the Victorian-style Glendale Hotel, which had opened with great fanfare in 1887 and closed almost immediately due to financial difficulties. It became an Episcopal girl's school and then served as the site of the city's first high school. L. C. Brand purchased it for $10,000 and then put it back on the market for $20,000. The Seventh Day Adventist Church could only afford $15,000. When Brand heard this, he lowered the price to $12,000 due to the philanthropic nature of the church's project. Volunteers cleaned out the debris left by the previous occupants, and two bedrooms on the second floor were remodeled into an operating room. By the time the sanitarium opened in August 1905, all of the rooms were fully booked. (Courtesy of the Special Collections Room, Glendale Public Library.)

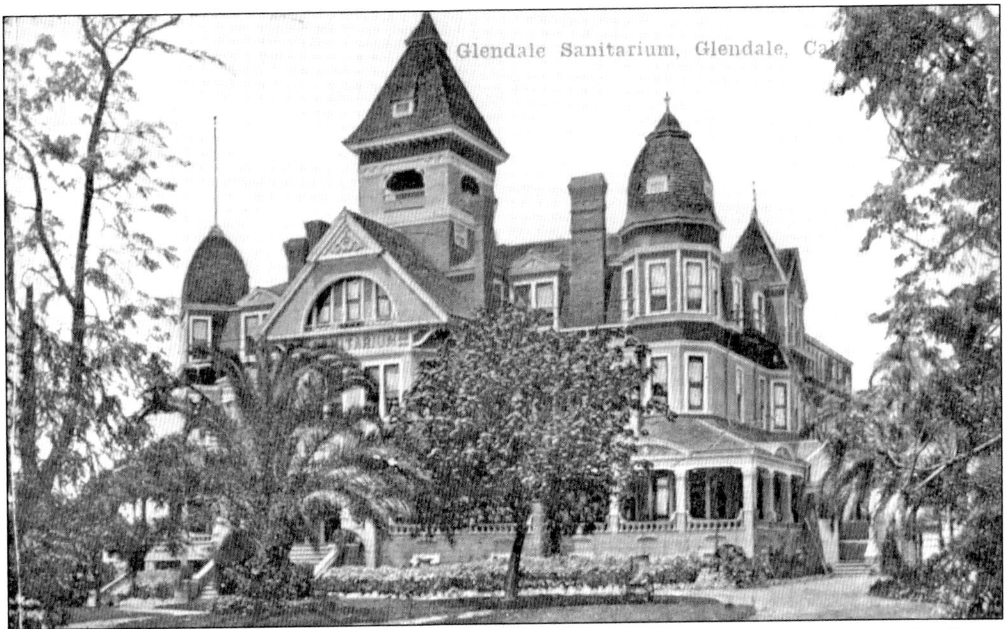

The sanitarium opened with 75 beds in a town with a population of just 1,100 people. "Few beds were needed by local residents," according to sanitarium publicity. Advertisements touted Glendale's "beautiful, hometown climate." This postcard was published by the Van Ornum Colorprint Company of Los Angeles. (Courtesy of the Special Collections Room, Glendale Public Library.)

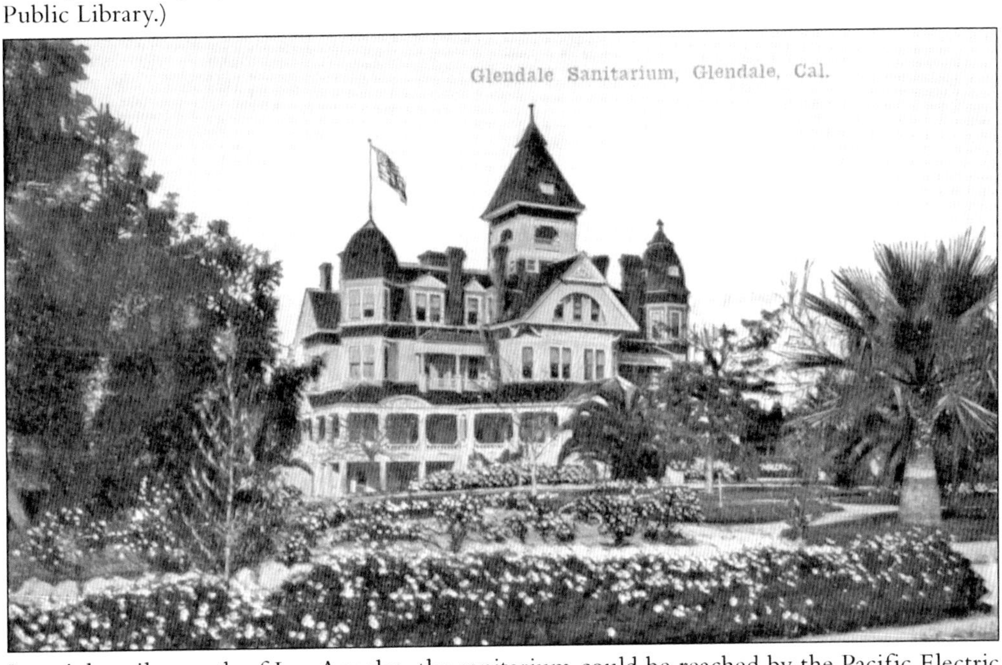

Just eight miles north of Los Angeles, the sanitarium could be reached by the Pacific Electric Railway. It featured Battle Creek methods of treatment and diet, providing convalescents and those needing rest and recuperation with a place suitable to their needs. This postcard was published by the Van Ornum Colorprint Company of Los Angeles. (Courtesy of the Special Collections Room, Glendale Public Library.)

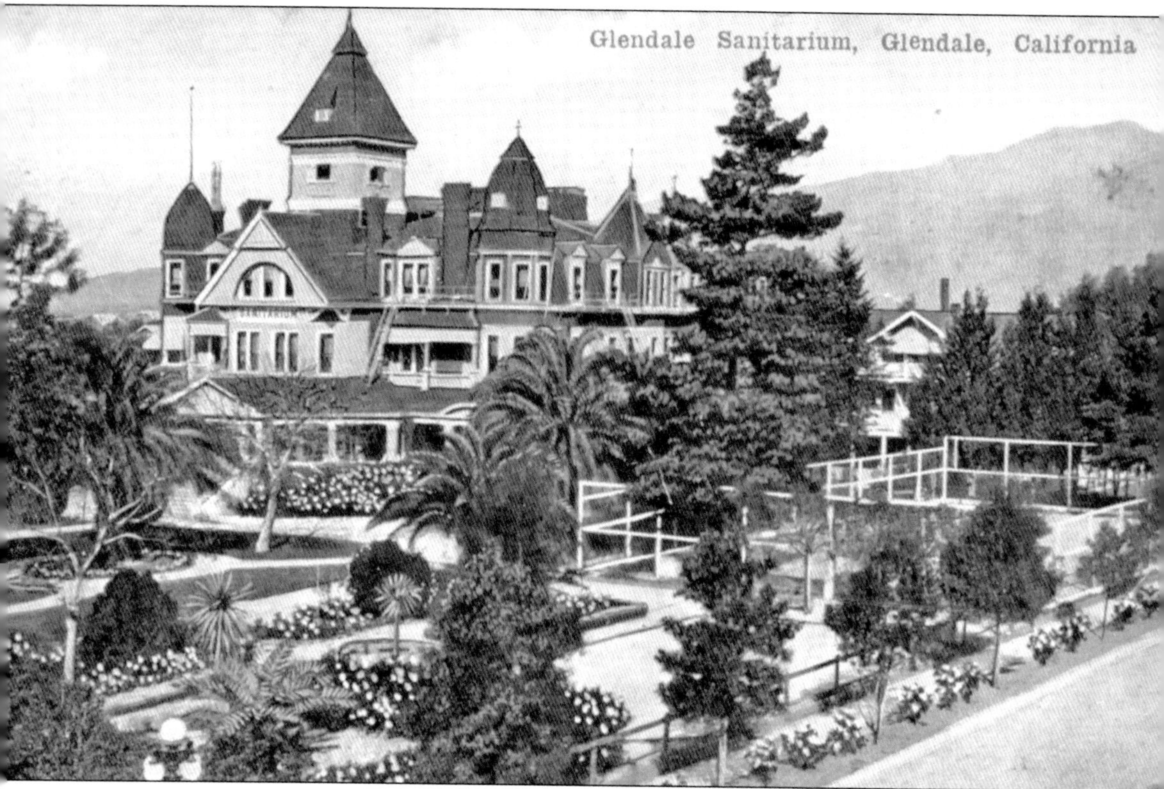

The sanitarium was also home to the Adventist Academy, which opened in the sanitarium basement with 15 pupils in 1907. The school grew rapidly and soon moved into a separate building on the sanitarium grounds. By 1921, the school had expanded to include 12 grades. The grounds surrounding the institution were one of the most attractive and inviting features connected with the health resort. This postcard was published by the Van Ornum Colorprint Company of Los Angeles. (Courtesy of the Special Collections Room, Glendale Public Library.)

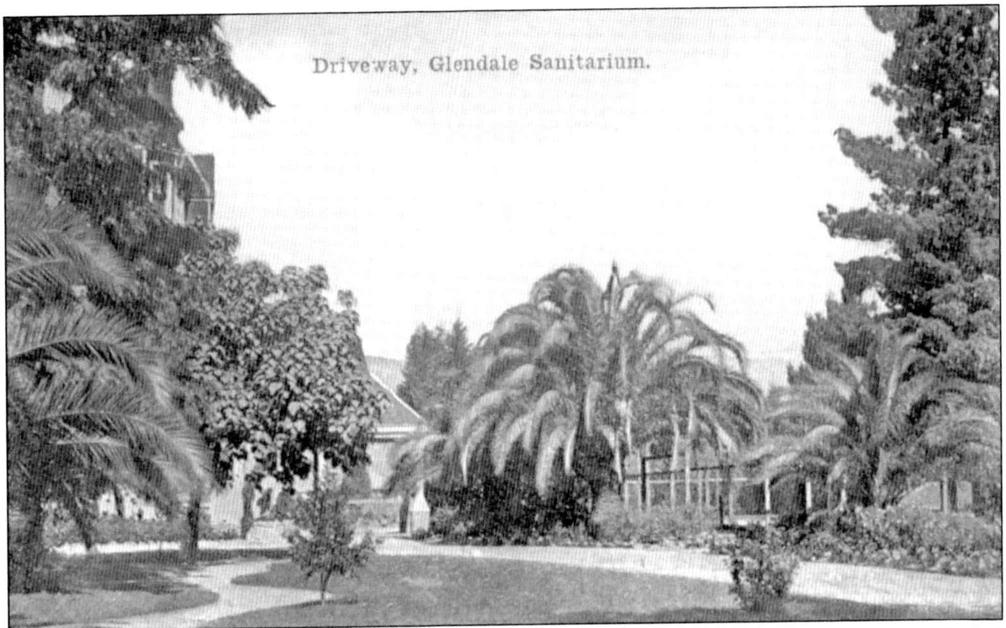

Patients came to the sanitarium for its natural methods of treating people, which included hydrotherapy, massage, gymnastics, and open-air therapy. Their goal was to return to nature, to get away from the unhealthy practices of the time, and to embrace simplicity and a wholesome diet. This postcard was published by the Van Ornum Colorprint Company of Los Angeles. (Courtesy of the Special Collections Room, Glendale Public Library.)

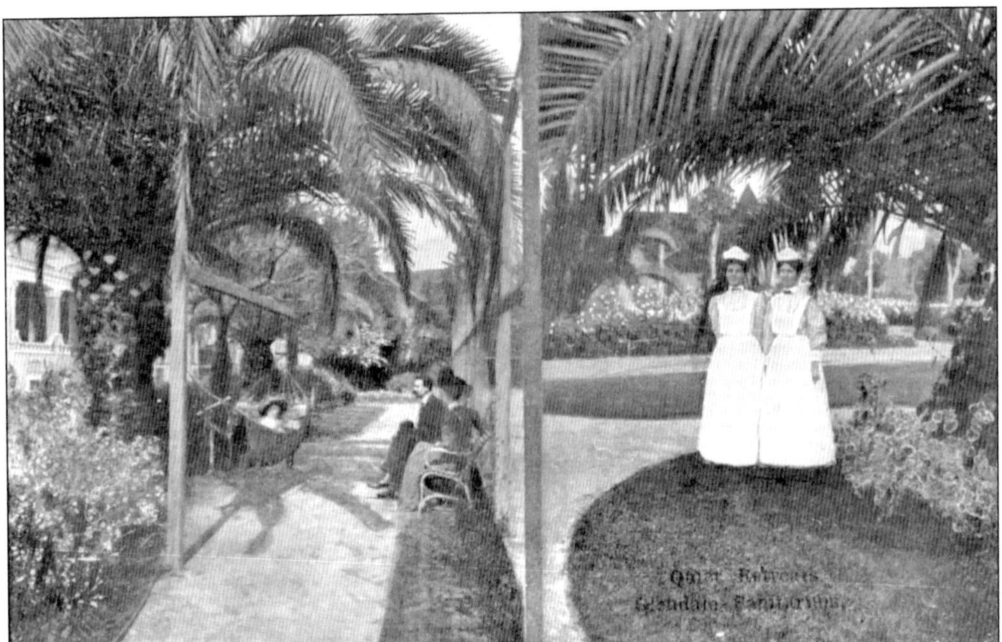

Many patients stayed for a month or more as the waiting list grew steadily. Southern California's moderate climate, with summer-like seasons nearly year-round, was one of the health resort's strongest selling points. (Courtesy of the Special Collections Room, Glendale Public Library.)

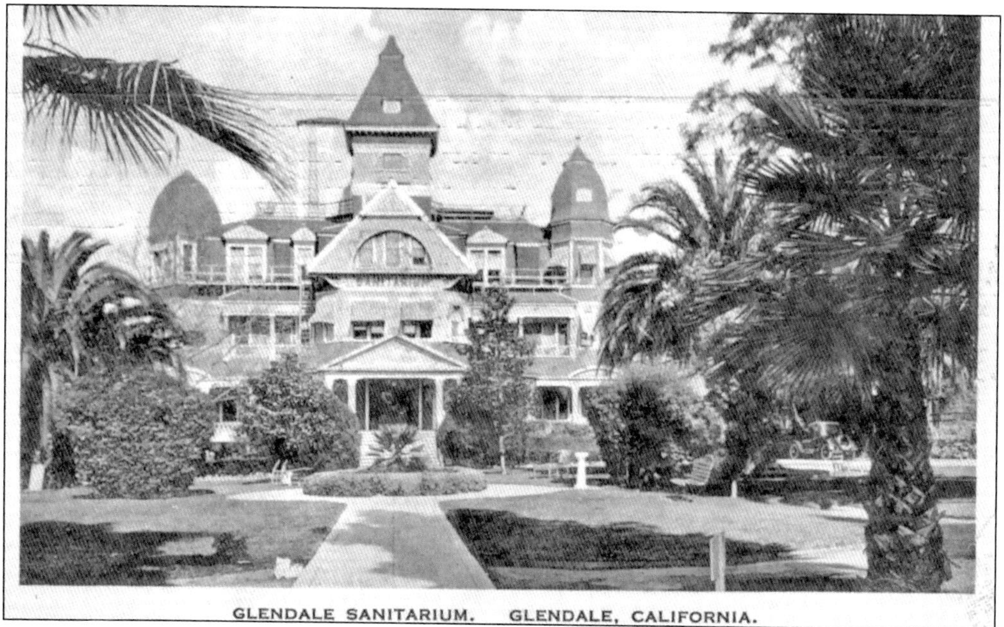

The elegant, Victorian-style building was photographed extensively and the images reproduced on postcards and brochures. It became very well known, as Adventist church members carried the advertising materials with them while they went around the world establishing schools, churches, and missions. This postcard was published by the Western Publishing and Novelty Company of Los Angeles. (Courtesy of the Special Collections Room, Glendale Public Library.)

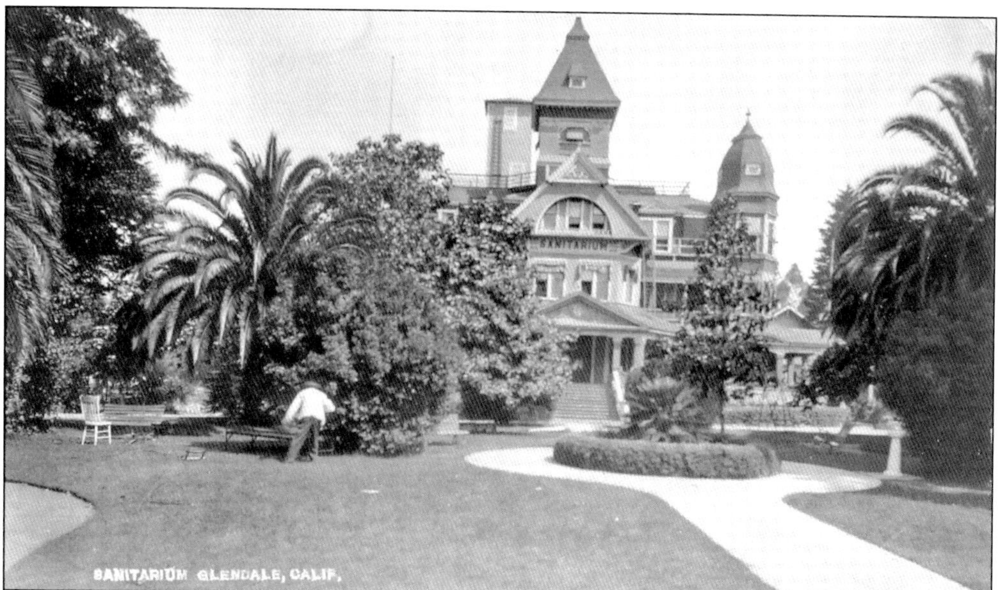

The sanitarium soon outgrew the old hotel. Although another acre of land was purchased and 100 more beds added, the rapidly expanding city no longer provided the quiet and restful atmosphere that the health resort required. The old building was demolished soon after a new sanitarium opened on a hilltop on the outskirts of town. This postcard dates to about 1915. (Courtesy of the Special Collections Room, Glendale Public Library.)

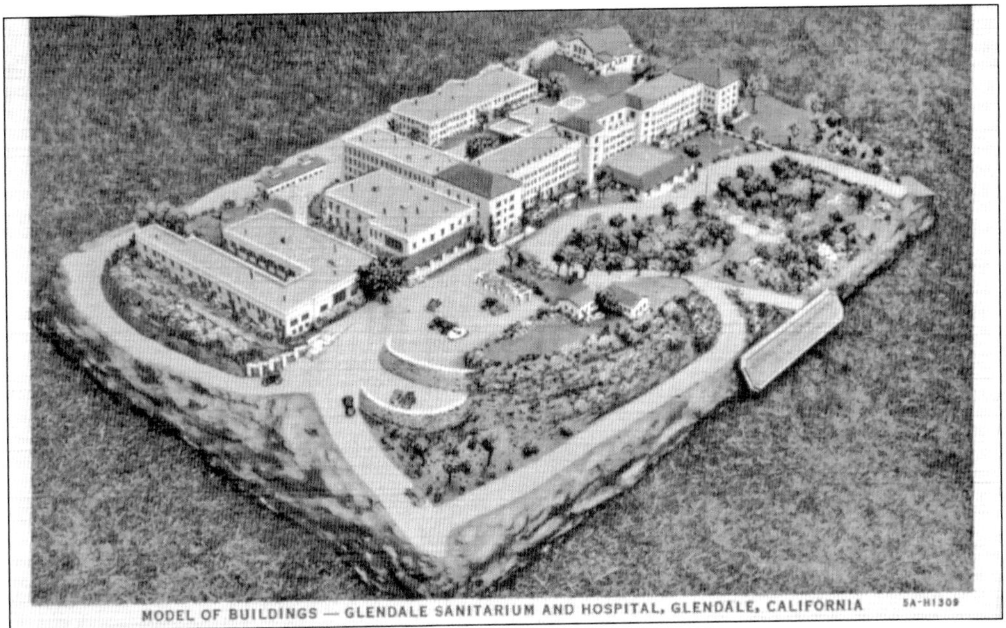

Shown here is a model of the planned sanitarium. In 1924, the facility moved to a multi-story building on nearly 30 acres on East Wilson Terrace. At that time, the property was far out of town, and the sanitarium was advertised as providing a home-like atmosphere for those in need of rest and medical care. This C. T. Photo-colorit was made by Curt Teach and Company of Chicago. (Courtesy of the Special Collections Room, Glendale Public Library.)

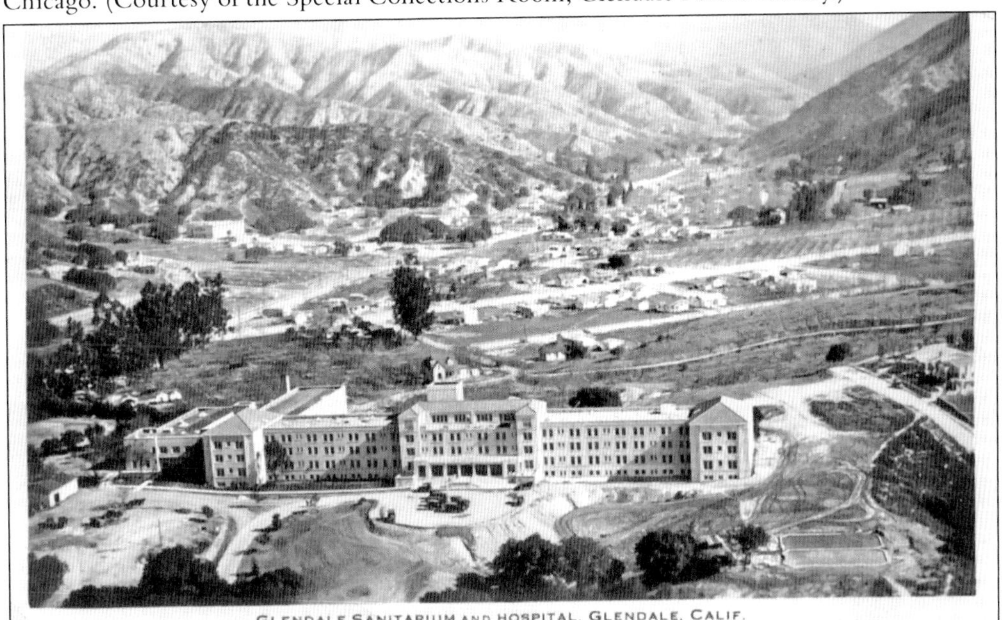

Very few dwellings were in the vicinity when the new sanitarium opened its doors in 1924. Chevy Chase Drive was still a dirt road, and the upper reaches of Chevy Chase Canyon were accessible only by a creek-side horse trail. The academy also moved to new quarters on Kimlin Drive, just off Chevy Chase. This postcard dates to around 1924. (Courtesy of the Special Collections Room, Glendale Public Library.)

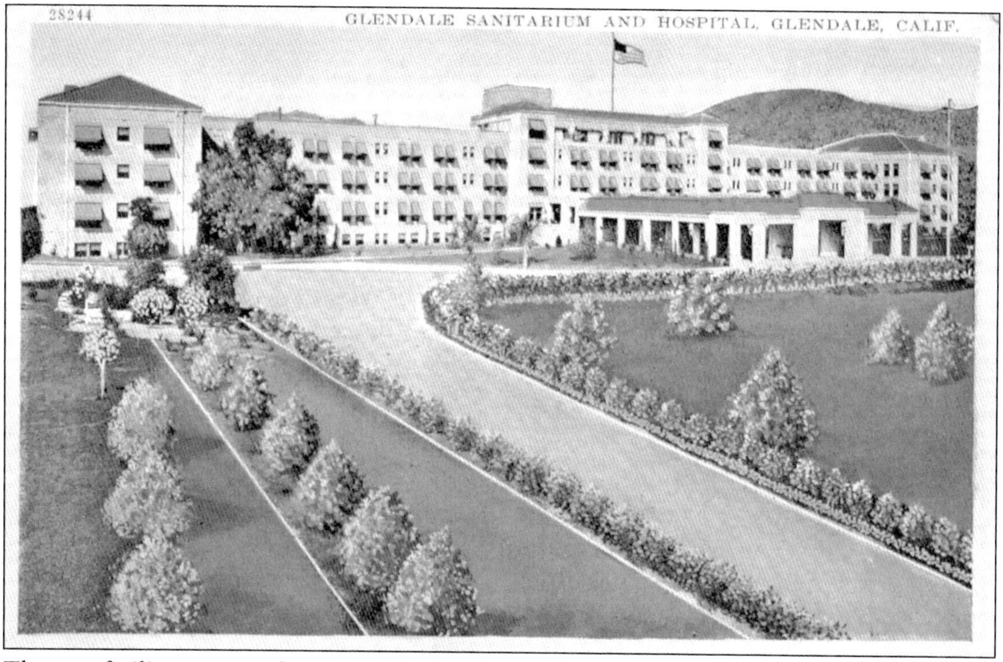

The new facility continued to offer watchful care and highly specialized treatment and diet in a home-like setting. (Courtesy of the Special Collections Room, Glendale Public Library.)

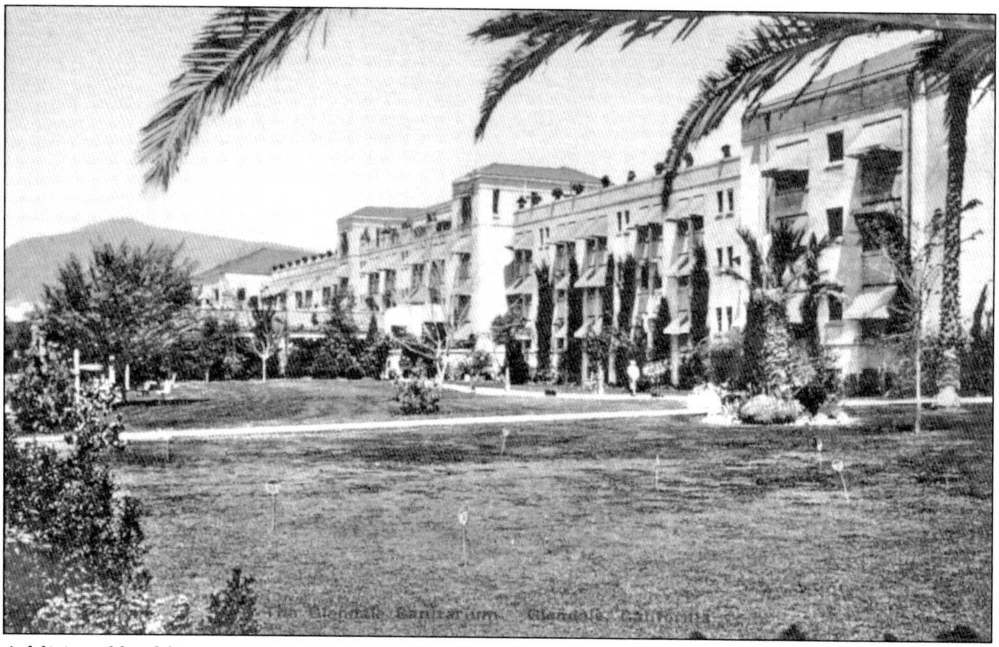

Additional buildings and regular medical updates kept the sanitarium at the forefront of modern medicine. This postcard dates to about 1930. (Courtesy of the Special Collections Room, Glendale Public Library.)

Ten

Transportation

The Southern Pacific Railroad was an enormous factor in starting the infant community that would eventually become Glendale, and the site of the train depot, near the southern tip of the city, could be considered one of the originating points in its history. Southern Pacific began building a line from downtown Los Angeles toward San Fernando in the 1870s. Around the same time, landowner W. C. B. Richardson donated 16 acres of his Santa Eulalia ranch to the railroad for a depot, with the stipulation that the train would stop there for him and his family. A few years later, a wood-frame depot was built on Cerritos Avenue. It was later replaced by the Spanish Colonial Revival–style depot that remains today.

The first airport built in Glendale—and one of the first in all of Southern California—came courtesy of L. C. Brand, who embraced the new form of transportation with great enthusiasm. He constructed an airplane hangar near Grandview Avenue and Mountain Street, just below his home, and by 1912 had hired a pilot to fly his planes. In 1921, Brand gained worldwide attention when he hosted a fly-in party, issuing leaflets that specified guests were to arrive by air. The celebrity invitations included a map marking the spot where planes were to land. Flyers such as Eddie Rickenbacker, Frank Hawks, and Jimmy Doolittle, along with celebrities such as Mary Pickford, Tom Mix, and Cecil B. DeMille, enjoyed L. C. Brand's hospitality that day and rewarded him with air stunts as they flew away.

Following World War I, Glendale became ripe for greatness when pilots, returning from their overseas adventures, sought a place to house their small airplanes. A consortium of businessmen sponsored the construction of a runway in the early 1920s; by 1929, it had matured into a premier airport. That same year, Grand Central Air Terminal became the site of the first airline service from Los Angeles to New York City.

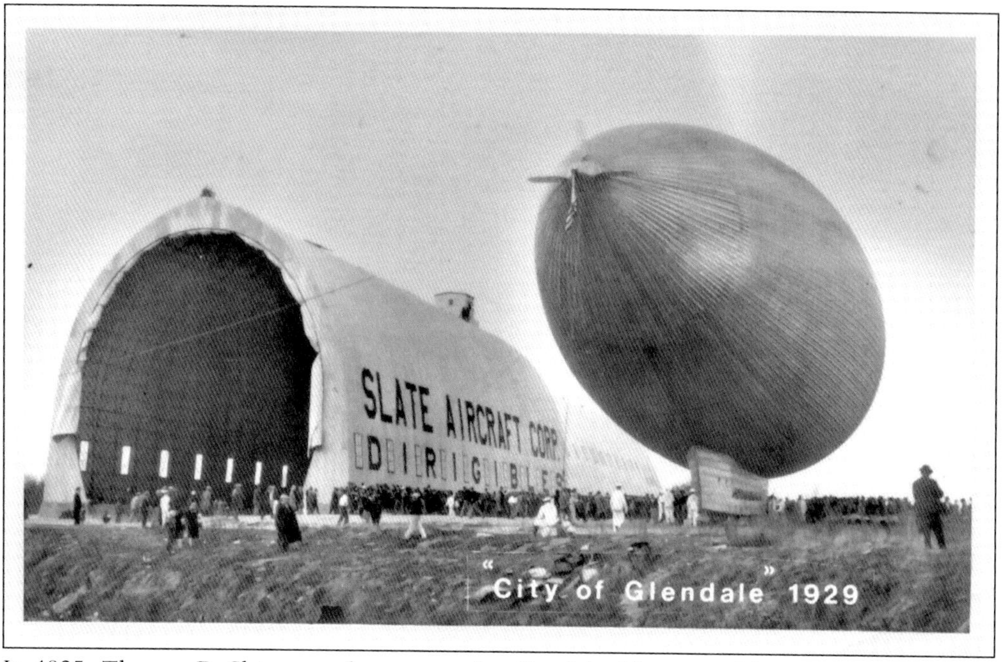

In 1925, Thomas B. Slate rented a spot at the Glendale Airport and began building an all-metal dirigible. He made two attempts to fly but failed due to high winds. He constructed a hangar (the largest in the country at the time) and by 1928 was assembling a new version. The 212-foot-long airship, with cabin room for 35 passengers and 5 crewmembers, was christened the *City of Glendale* and made its first and only flight in 1929. Fuel intake problems damaged the airship and brought it quickly back to earth, where it languished in the hangar. Slate lost his entire fortune in the ill-fated venture, along with thousands of dollars subscribed by his many financial supporters. He never attempted to build another. This postcard was published by Whelan of Long Beach. (Courtesy of the Special Collections Room, Glendale Public Library.)

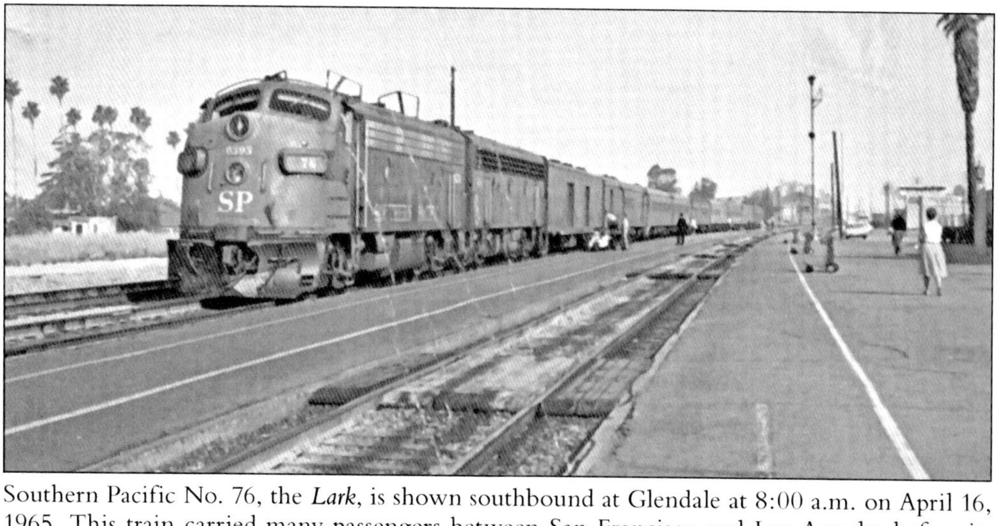

Southern Pacific No. 76, the ***Lark***, is shown southbound at Glendale at 8:00 a.m. on April 16, 1965. This train carried many passengers between San Francisco and Los Angeles before its route was discontinued. This postcard was published by Audio Visual of Earlton, New York. (Courtesy of the Special Collections Room, Glendale Public Library.)

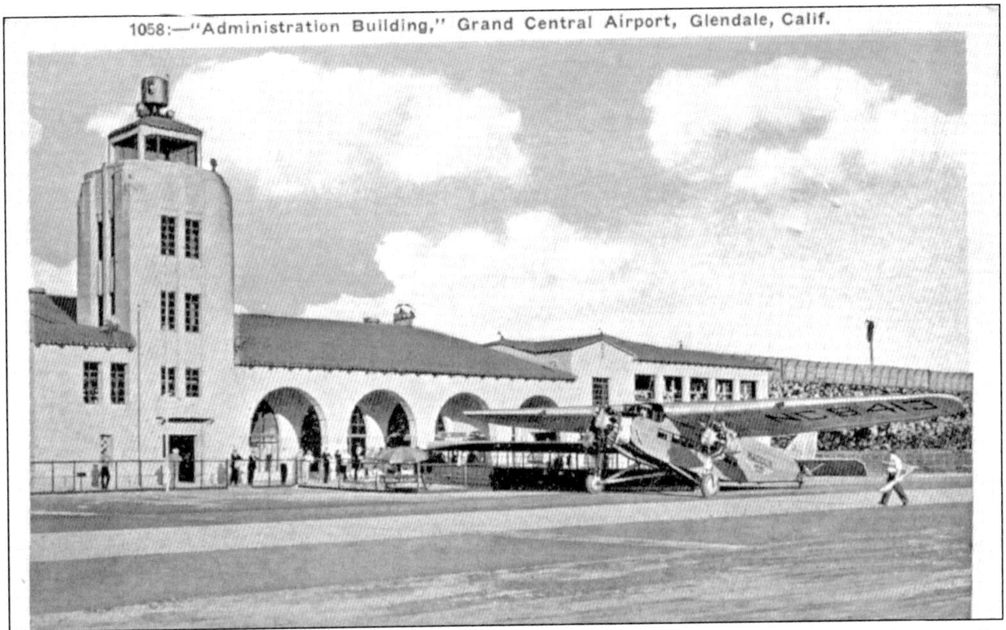

World War I produced a number of young flyers, many with their own biplanes. They sought a landing field where they could build their own hangars and service facilities could be established. Grand Central Air Terminal, dedicated in 1929, provided such a place. (Courtesy of John Underwood.)

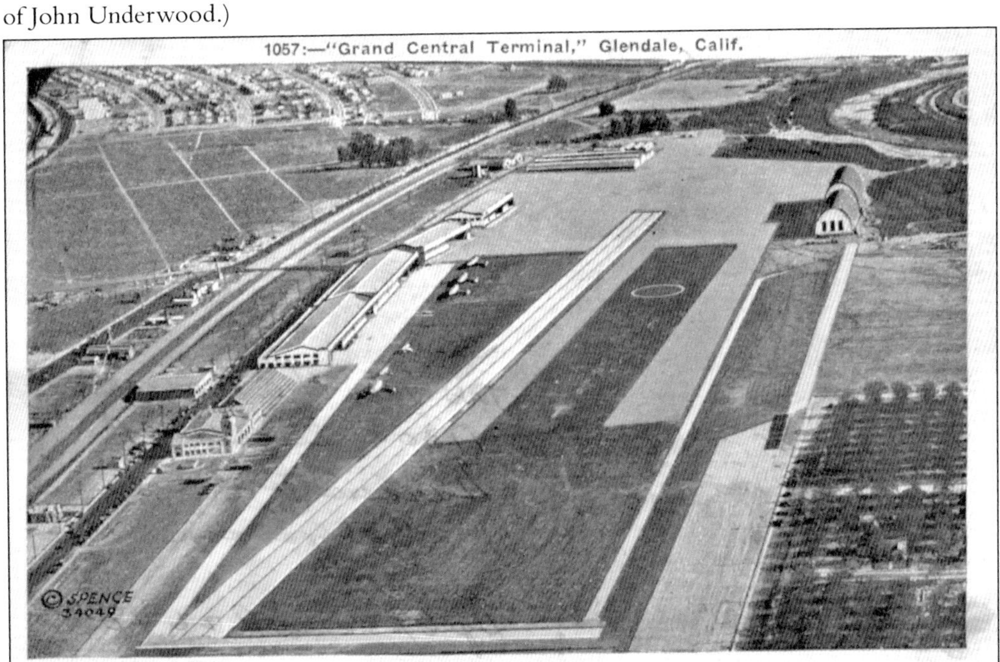

A 32-acre plot at the end of Grandview Avenue, south of the railroad, was purchased by the city. Land was cleared and a runway constructed before a lawsuit was filed declaring the entire project illegal. A consortium of supporters took control, however, and the project continued. Private hangars were built, and the airport became popular with flyers who turned it into a site for air shows. (Courtesy of John Underwood.)

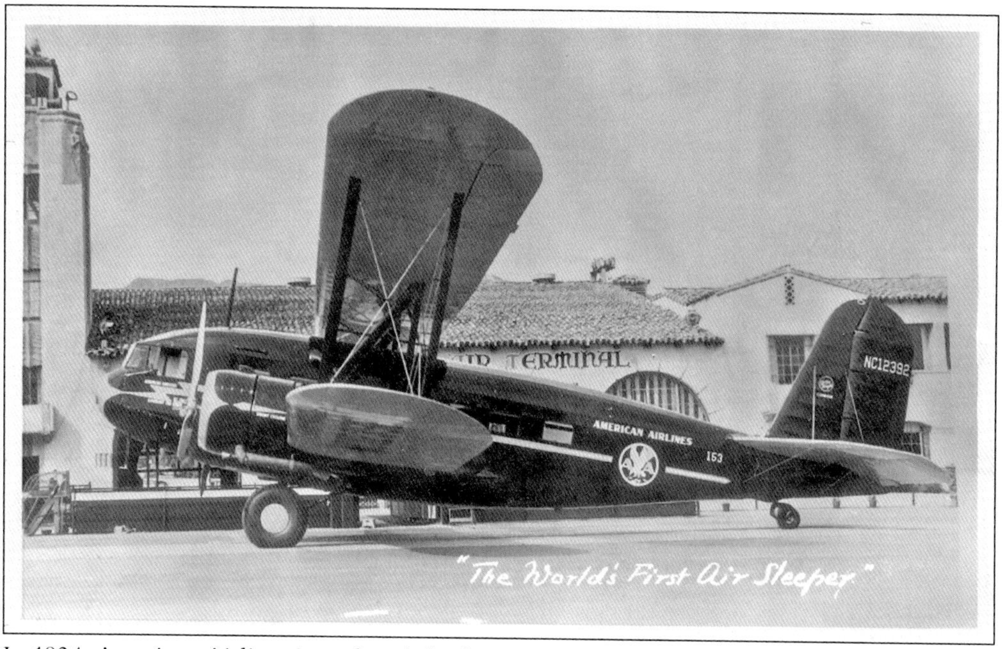

In 1934, American Airlines introduced the first Curtiss-Wright Condor Sleepers, which made the Glendale–El Paso night service more comfortable for air travelers. A dozen travelers could be accommodated on each flight. (Courtesy of John Underwood.)

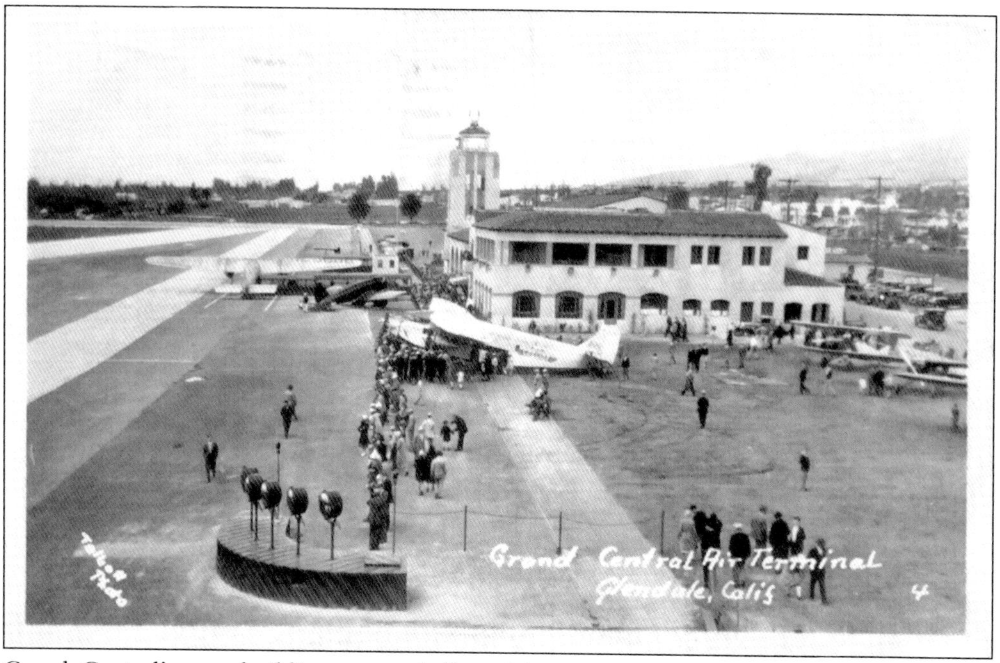

Grand Central's new buildings were dedicated in 1929. The event attracted thousands of celebrants and many celebrities. The first coast-to-coast airline service, from Grand Central to New York, was established that same year. The airplane was piloted by Charles A. Lindbergh, famous for his solo flight across the Atlantic in 1927. Aboard the inaugural flight were movie stars Mary Pickford and Douglas Fairbanks. (Courtesy of John Underwood.)

Bibliography

Art Guide of Forest Lawn. Glendale, CA: Forest Lawn Memorial-Park, 1963.

Forest Lawn Memorial-Parks: A Place for the Living. Glendale, CA: Forest Lawn Memorial-Park Association, 1994.

Gilmer, Maureen. *Redwood and Roses: The Gardening Heritage of California and the Old West*. Dallas, TX: Taylor Publishing Company, 1995.

Lawler, Mike, and Robert Newcombe. Images of America: *La Crescenta*. Charleston, SC: Arcadia Publishing, 2005.

Miller, Bruce W. *The Gabrielino*. Los Osos, CA: Sand River Press, 1991.

Perry, E. Caswell, and Shirley Catherine Berger, Terri E. Jonisch, and Katherine Peters Yamada. *Glendale: A Pictorial History Centennial Edition*. Virginia Beach, VA: Donning Company, 2007.

Perry, E. Caswell, and Carroll W. Parcher. *Glendale Area History*. Glendale, CA: Xanadu Galleries, 1981.

www.tongva.com